AMERICA'S

Flying Book

AMERICA'S Flying Book

BY THE EDITORS OF ***FLYING*** **MAGAZINE**

CHARLES SCRIBNER'S SONS
New York

A–10.72(C)

Printed in the United States of America
Library of Congress Catalog Card Number 72–1213
SBN 684–13003–3 (cloth)

CONTENTS

List of Illustrations

LIST OF ILLUSTRATIONS

LIST OF ILLUSTRATIONS

LIST OF ILLUSTRATIONS

GRATEFUL ACKNOWLEDGMENT IS MADE FOR PICTURES USED FROM THE FOLLOWING SOURCES:

American Airlines, *p. 9*
Leave Bearers, *p. 7 (top right), 129, 131*
Beech Aircraft Corp., *p. 29, 171 (upper left)*
Bell Helicopter Corp., *p. 175, 176 (center)*
Herbert P. Bond, *p. 239*
Carrier Corporation for Army Airfield, Syracuse, N.Y., *p. 7 (center left)*
Cessna Aircraft Corp., *p. 26*
James Gilbert, *p. 6 (lower right), 17, 53, 98, 101, 106, 110–111, 114 (center left), 115 (top), 136, 138 (top), 139, 158–159, 169 (center right), 173 (lower left), 185, 200–201, 205, 206 (top), 207, 209, 210, 211, 256 (lower left and center right), 290–291*
Hans Groenhoff, *p. 5, 18, 30, 125, 132, 157, 232, 242, 244*
Grumman Aircraft Engineering Corp., *p. 171 (lower left and right)*
J. Barry Herron, *p. 253*
Hiller Aircraft Co., *p. 176 (right), 177 (lower right)*
Imperial War Museum, *p. 203 (top)*
Russell Munson, *p. 273, 274, 276, 278, 283, 285, 286, 287, 288*
National Air and Space Museum, Smithsonian Institution, *p. 40, 41, 43, 44*
Port of N.Y. Authority, *p. 7 (lower right)*
A. H. Sanletin, *p. 7 (upper left)*
Sikorsky Aircraft, *p. 177 (upper and lower left)*
Walter Steinhard, *p. 133*
Baron Storey, *p. 70, 73, 74, 75, 77, 85, 89*
Sud Aviation, *p. 241*
Moult Taylor, *p. 261, 265*
Gene Thomas, *p. 218–219, 222–223, 226–227, 228–229*
United Airlines, *p. 7 (lower left)*
U. S. Air Force, *p. 47*

ACKNOWLEDGMENTS

America's Flying Book is the product of the staff of and regular contributors to *Flying* magazine and *Invitation to Flying*, working in conjunction with the staff of Charles Scribner's Sons. While most of this book is new, some of the material has been adapted from articles in those periodicals. In all cases, we have written and revised with special concern for the readers of this book.

Robert Blodget and Peter Garrison have made major contributions, as have James Gilbert, Stephan Wilkinson and Richard Weeghman. Special thanks must also be made to Marianne Garrison and Paul Fillingham for their help in getting it all together.

Robert B. Parke
Editor and Publisher, FLYING magazine

FOREWORD

The country was Ireland at a place called Ballyfree. It was summertime and I was visiting my friend Phillips, whose very large chicken ranch occupied the floor of a lovely valley which was as green as only Irish valleys can be. Here my friend had created his private airport with a grass strip of even more vivid green and he had aimed it so that approaches down the valley were reasonably convenient in bad weather.

At the north end of this bucolic scene he had built a small corrugated metal hangar, added a windsock, and that was all there was in the way of aeronautical improvements. Within the hangar was a Morane-Saulnier Monoplane, vintage 1928, as used by the French Air Force first as a fighter and later a trainer. The Moranes were phased out in the early Thirties and this rare survivor had come into the hands of Hutchinson, an Aer Lingus pilot whose boundless talents included an easy fluency in French. Hutchinson is a spare young man, quietly intent, and utterly dedicated to his profession. He flies Aer Lingus DC-9s for a living and his Morane for love. In a moment of abandon he had offered to let me fly his jewel and I had accepted instantly.

The Morane is a two-place, open cockpit monoplane of most graceful proportions, and is yet another proof that aircraft fly like they look.

Starting the Morane's 250-horsepower Salmson engine involved considerable ceremony, which it pleased us to conduct in French. Somehow it sounded better to shout "*Coupé!*" when the ignition switch was deactivated rather than "Off." The air starting system having disappeared somewhere during the forty-odd years since the Morane's manufacture, we were obliged to use the muscle system, which belonged to Hutchinson. He heaved gingerly on the big metal propeller while I sat in the rear cockpit and pumped fuel until it dribbled out on the cockpit floor. When I announced this development, Hutchinson moved the prop so that the engine was at top dead center and ran for his life. I then cranked furiously on the *magneto de départ* in the hope of sending a formidable spark to the right cylinder—after which, presumably, the Salmson would start. It was something like playing Russian roulette with a nine-chamber revolver and one bullet.

After the passage of nearly an hour and some twenty attempts, the miraculous occurred and the Salmson came alive. The pumping and cranking had not been as easy as I had thought, and after Hutchinson had climbed into the front cockpit we both sat panting during the several minutes' wait while the oil pressure stabilized.

We finally took off into the Irish sky, which was not blue at all, but a misty gray with the lower clouds packed solidly against the surrounding hills. I climbed for the few breaks in the overcast which closed promptly on our arrival. So I was obliged to try what I could within the limits of the valley.

Hutchinson held an exaggerated opinion of my aerobatic abilities and had somehow persuaded himself that I could roll the Morane without losing altitude and loop it without falling out of the top. He claimed he had often botched both maneuvers, which I questioned since he was a very accomplished pilot in every respect. Yet to satisfy us both I tried and, after several embarrassing minutes, I decided he had endured enough disillusionment and thereafter flew the Morane most sedately and found great pleasure in its attributes.

Sometimes, when my rolling had been correct or I had managed a loop which had not the form of the valley's eggs, Hutchinson would turn his head, his goggled eyes would meet my goggled eyes, and he would smile. No words were formed by his lips, but I realized that he was trying to communicate something to me and I vainly supposed that had we been in a cabin protected from the roar of the slipstream he would have passed his approval verbally.

At last, when I had exhausted the limited aerobatic possibilities of the

Morane and was sufficiently at ease to reflect on the odd mixture of an American flying a French airplane over Ireland, I decided that just for the hell of it I would make a long side-slip down to the kind of a landing you can only make on grass. Once we were down I saw Hutchinson turn to favor me with a final smile and suddenly I knew he would not have spoken even if he could have been heard. For his smile was not merely an approving signal of my technique.

This Irish afternoon included my first introduction to Hutchinson, but as we taxied toward the hangar I became certain that I had seen his smile before.

There had been that other luminous afternoon over the State of Washington's Cascade Mountains. Goodell, one of Boeing's top test pilots, had invited me to become acquainted with his latest pride, the 747. When he had completed the routine engine shutdowns and gear cyclings required for the test, Goodell ushered me to the left seat and said, "Now she is yours," in a gentle, solicitous way that I suppose Eskimos might once have offered their wives to dear friends.

The 747 seemed to me much more pleasant to fly than its smaller four-engined sisters so I played around for a while, steep-turning and slow-flying in the manner of a suitor beginning courtship. As each maneuver was completed and then finally after I had eased the great and beautiful craft into a gentle stall, I noticed Goodell would smile. Yet he said nothing, neither of praise nor censure.

When finally we descended and I made three touch-and-go landings at Paine Field, I marveled at the forgiveness of such a tremendous aircraft. Goodell smiled each time and I remembered this in Ireland.

Also on that afternoon with Hutchinson and his Morane I remembered the grinning delight of Cansdale, a pilot for Hughes Air West. He is a vigorous, wonderfully kind man who has devoted almost his entire lifetime to aviation.

Among Cansdale's acquirements is that rarest of birds, a Sopwith Pup. It is not a reconstruction but an original and still wears its Gnome-LeRhone rotary engine. God only knows how much it is worth, but saliva is visible along the lips of all collectors who behold it. Cansdale had given me the ultimate compliment of friendship and confidence. He had offered to let me fly his precious machine.

The locale was Abbotsford on the Canadian frontier and the annual air show had finished for the day. The August air was as still as we had hoped it would be and while the sun descended and turned everything a molten gold, Cansdale gave generously of his wisdom.

". . . You'll find she's heavy on the ailerons . . . and she'll porpoise a bit on you . . . don't worry, it's her nature. . . . Cruise around about eighty and make your approach about forty-five. . . . She'll land about forty and be sure you make it three point . . . do *not* put it on the wheels. . . . You'll be surprised how far one blip will carry you. . . . On take-off it's full stick forward then right away back for climb . . . forget ground run. . . ."

So it went for some minutes while his advice on mixture settings for the temperamental Gnome engine became entangled in a mental horror scene in which I was obliged to face my friend and confess I had scratched his invaluable souvenir of a more dashing era. Here, I knew, was something mere money could not restore and I was acutely aware that Cansdale had never allowed anyone else to fly it.

It went well, fortunately. My desire to fly a World War I combat aircraft was fulfilled and I found among other things that the stories of torque caused by rotary engines were, at least in a Pup, highly colored.

Cansdale had a wooden machine gun in its proper place and while aloft I had several goes at invisible antagonists flying Rumplers, Fokkers, and Albatrosen. Having shot down no less than ten in a few minutes I thought my score not too bad for an aging aviator who happened to have been much too young for that first world war.

When I had done with those juvenile joys I made three very low passes before the astonishing number of people who had suddenly gathered to watch this epilogue to the main show, and at last when I thought Cansdale might become convinced I was afraid to land, I "blipped" the Gnome engine in the best movie tradition and found the total effect the same as using spoilers on a sail-plane. Thus I managed one of the most photographed landings in recent times, three-pointing the Pup exactly where Cansdale had prescribed. When he came running toward me there was that same smile I saw later in Ireland. He took my hand and, beaming, said not a word, as if this sharing of his love was the happy conclusion of a private pact between us.

Yet another day in New Mexico I had witnessed this curious business of the silent smile. The occasion was my flying the controversial F-One Eleven and I had been to school and in the simulator for two days before having at the real thing. My instructor-pilot was Wheeler, a shy and delightful lieutenant-colonel with as much swept-wing experience as any man in the Air Force. He was that kind of airman who knew *everything* about his aircraft and his faith in the One-Elevens, whose reputation had been tarnished by mishaps, was touching.

We lofted into the desert sky after one of the most fascinating take-offs I had ever made; never had I known command of such power and grace. I climbed with wings swept back until we leveled at 20,000 feet and there I played about with the most gentle chandelles, feeling somewhat like a hitchhiker astride an aerial Moby Dick.

I was so encouraged by the ease with which the computerized control allowed me to bend this 80,000 pound aircraft about the sky that I asked Wheeler if I might try a roll.

"Sure. Why not?"

So I tried a roll and once inverted began to dish out until by recovery I had lost 2,000 feet.

"Next time raise her nose a little higher before you start," Wheeler said. And there, as if on signal, was that enigmatic smile again.

The cure was so positive I developed a sudden lust for rolling the F-One Eleven and finally made several passable eight pointers. Then we were on to other things such as terrain following, up, between, and around the wild Sangre de Christo Mountains at 200 feet and 548 knots. Afterward we climbed to 41,000 feet and began a supersonic run that netted us a ground speed of 1270 knots.

FOREWORD

Finally, there was the business of landing, which under Wheeler's quiet advice became almost too easy. I shot three touch-and-goes without trouble and only regretted the ultimate landing because it meant the end of the session.

Taxiing in toward the line, I expressed my admiration for the F-One Eleven and on Wheeler's face there was that same smile I would later discover in Ireland.

It was in Ireland that I began to think about this and recall other aircraft which at one time or another certain brave men had introduced to me. They ranged from P-51s and Corsairs, to B-17s, and Bucker-Jungmans, and from Great Lakes, Stinsons, Ryans, and sailplanes to almost every American transport type of the last forty years. And I decided that those who first took me by the hand and offered their advice were smiling in a way I have never seen elsewhere. Eventually I became convinced the Hutchinsons, Cansdales, Goodells, and Wheelers are an international breed and I found that when introducing another to an aircraft I liked, then I had unconsciously assumed the same mellow expression. This instinctive smile, I thought, was not simply approval of the moment. It created a sense of the mutual. It was the sharing of a profound experience, and that was important.

Too much dubious literature has been written about the ethereal joys of flight. Not enough has been said about the very special camaraderie which is native to those who most appreciate those joys. You will see it here and there, if and when you fly. And in time you may realize how words are unnecessary in the sharing of a fundamental joy. From some men even a hint of a smile can say everything.

The editors of *Flying* are uniquely equipped to lead you into this special experience. This book is a chart of the new world awaiting you. You will find it abundant with opportunities and inhabited by men who still know how to smile with pride.

Ernest K. Gann
San Juan Island, Washington
1972

Introduction

ESSENTIALLY, an airplane is a means of getting from here to there, like a car. It is simply a conveyance, a machine—more or less comfortable, rapid, and costly as the case may be, but nothing more really than a fast bus. You get aboard, fire it up, and sit it out. Nothing more to it.

Or is there? Indeed, there must be something special about airplanes—you can tell by the people who fly them. Not that there is anything special about pilots before they become pilots; they are for the most part quite ordinary people. Airplane manufacturers advertise that anyone can fly a plane. Pilots try to convey the impression, tacitly or explicitly, that *not* everyone can. Again, it's like driving a car; everyone can drive except for a few who for one reason or another can't quite manage it. And yet you've never heard anyone at a cocktail party casually mention having *driven* here or there to an awed and beautiful girl in the confident (and rarely disappointed) expectation of an apotheosis. Everyone drives; no one is impressed, except perhaps by those who race cars. Few fly, and lots of people are impressed—not least of all the flyers themselves.

Flying becomes the hallmark of the people who fly. Whatever else they are, they are pilots, and among other pilots they always find themselves at home, however little they may have in common. Some become incapable of talking about any subject other than flying; they long to bring the conversation round to airplanes, and when they get it there are loath to see it move on. They are in thrall to something—some have let marriages founder and careers pass them by because the spell of an airport was too hard to break and the possibility of getting behind the controls of an airplane again too precious to pass up. The aviator's experience, whatever it may be, is a profound one—one that enters dim and out-of-touch recesses of the soul.

The explanations that pilots usually give seem hollow. "It's just great putt-putting around up there, where never lark nor even eagle flew, just swooping around, dancing with the clouds, great sense of freedom, liberty, helluva feeling." Is that really it? For many people the cockpit of an airplane is the antithesis of freedom; a tiny cell suspended in space, a very metaphor of all that is unsure and terrifying in the human condition. How can you bear it? Some are haunted by the thought of the fall. For others, the boredom of it beggars imagining. How can it be, Joe Pilot, that you are so blissful when others quake or yawn? Or are you blissful? Are there not many pilots who, if they had it out with themselves, would have to admit that they don't particularly *like* flying? I mean, it isn't fun for them in the way playing ball or swimming or even watching television is fun. Are there not some who would have to confess that they have often forgiven the vacuity of one flight with the facile reflection that most of them are different? The next one will be different. Yet they don't have it out with themselves, and despite the cost and the inconvenience and the noise and the crowding and the immobility, they fly and fly, and in the balance—when all their assets and liabilities are spun out in the centrifuge of some last judgment—they have not lost. But not because they wheeled with eagles (an eagle passes a plane looking like a paper bag falling past a ten-story window) and not because they danced with clouds (a cloud is a turbulent pudding as big as a mountain; one cannot dance with it; an airplane cannot dance, but only lunge in slow motion). Because of something else.

What is it?

Flight is a symbol. It is a symbol in a broad, historical sense—a vision to which all men resonate, whatever their age or place or time of birth.

Flight is jailbreak. It is also cunning and indifference.

Flight is mastery, safety, success; also mystery and secession.

There is, too, a special perspective to it, both within and without. In the midst of games, talking, walking on the beach, one looks up and is held spellbound by the silent arrowhead of a jet sliding by far off, almost as it were on the edge of space. It is hypnotic in its separateness, peaceful in its mysteriousness, splendid in its simplicity and sureness, like a lone hawk hanging over a hill. And if the ideal of philosophic thought was once to see in the mind, in a crystal instant, all life and matter rolled into a ball (as spacemen saw it rise over the horizon of the moon), then a pilot's hours are a string of such instants. As he looks down on the immobile earth, all things come at once to his eye, towns and streams and highways and rails, human life encompassed and mapped, ready to be understood. Earth and the flyer regard one another in a kind of mutual perception, in its best moments something like love.

The love colors all your memories. If you have traveled not by car or train but by plane, you have witnessed a tapestry rich in details, myriad in its textures and colorings, vast as the horizons and vaster still, and peaceful as a sleeper's face. You have brooded over the vast abyss, swept across interminable fields which fanned past you like a spinning parasol, and hung in roaring stillness while the arcing line of night, like a monk's cowl, swung down to erase before your eyes the last crescent of the day. You have flown through submarine caverns in which hanging gardens of mist and cloud turned blue-gray in the evening; over rusting deserts where an impeccable sun rose slowly over utter lifelessness; down valleys where shreds of cloud reached toward you from the backs of the windward hills; among thunderclouds whose mile-high cliffs broth-boiling and swirling on both sides of you let no sunbeams enter. In a Texas dawn you saw a grain elevator whose shadow stretched 80 miles to the horizon. If you miss anything when you die, it will be the glow of instrument dials in the darkness; the blissful sunrise; the long, hot, stormy afternoon; the calm and sadness and slowness of evening; the world as carpet, map, model railroad, standing at a remove from you, tinged and enveloped by the delight and melancholy of your own isolation.

Flight is knowledge and power. It is something other people cannot do. That is, in fact, the vile part of it: that suffocating vanity, sometimes unconscious, but often uncomfortably apparent, that suffuses the pilot's motions as

A pilot is a magician, shrinking the earth with his wings. This Stinson was an early post-WW2 design, transport for the family. Function and beauty become one.

he starts the engines under the silent, mystified eyes of his passengers. He is a magician, a fabulous artificer—taking you where you want to go, looking down on mundane concerns with a calm and detached eye, manipulating with nonchalance the instruments and controls which the layman dares not brush with a careless cuff. It's a hard pride to give up, and many pilots find it difficult to teach their wives to fly. It is not to the advantage of heroes for the true nature of courage to become public knowledge.

The modern pilot capitalizes on a myth that has its roots in religion, and whose branches are the Wright Brothers, the Red Baron, Charles Lindbergh, and all the aces of all the wars since a prop first turned in anger. If some pilots find low-wing airplanes more congenial than high-wing ones, it is doubtless because it is easier to daydream a low-wing plane into a P-51 as they climb aboard. One's vanity takes a long time to tire of indulging in small demonstrations of casual competence—supervising the takeoff surge with one hand and eye while the others see to some insignificant dial-twiddling, or conversing casually with the passengers during the landing roundout and touchdown. Never let them think you're worried (not that there would be anything to be worried about if one were as competent as one took pains to convince others one is).

The love of flying is not without its infantile aspects, but there is more to it than that. Flight is quintessentially a symbol of human ambition and daring, of the application of skill and intelligence to problems that seem to defy solution. While it has long since ceased to require either particular skill or particular daring, the art of piloting still glows with some remnants of the heat of its conception. Few pilots—few people, in fact—are insensible of this special aura, and it becomes to those who bask in its warmth a powerful agency, like money, of good or ill. There are many to whom it is only a sop to conceit, an empty snobbery, something to flaunt before strangers. But to the better, it is like the great traditions of old craftsmen; a touchstone for inner growth, a blessing for which one must make oneself worthy, a kind of privilege which should inspire modesty. The remarkable thing about people who fly is not that they are so clever; it's that they are so lucky. The clever ones realize it, and even the least perspicacious catch some spark of a hint of their good fortune. It's what keeps them going despite poverty, divorce, and bad horoscopes. Sometimes it keeps them going despite bad weather as well, and that is the dangerous side of the matter—the sirens' song to which few can stop their ears. The most difficult of the pilot's arts is that of knowing when not to fly. It is also the last test of the real pilot; for if flying is cunning and mastery, it is good sense and self-mastery as well.

Not a WW2 fighter but personal transport for the '70s. A test pilot wears a crash helmet and a parachute as he puts the new machine through its paces.

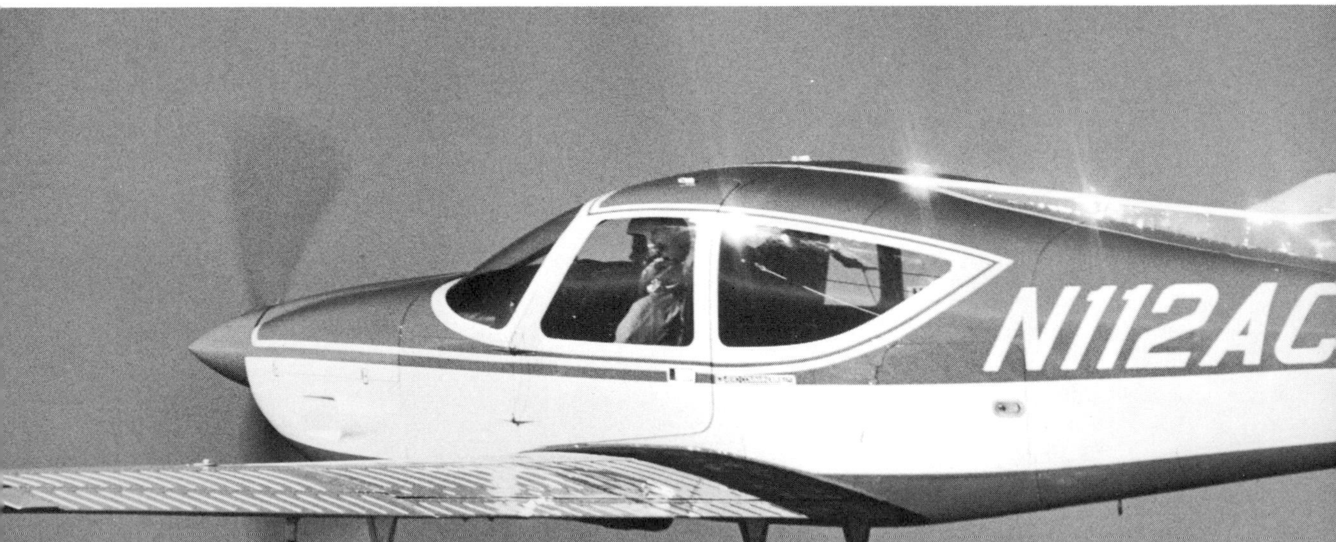

Until a pilot has learned to transcend the faint glory that shines through flight and to subordinate it to his own will, he has not learned the most essential part of imitating birds: that birds fly because it is natural to do so, because they need to do so, not because they admire themselves for doing so. Flying can be a door open to the transformation of life from sheer plod to riding high. It can also be a cul-de-sac, at the end of which a lot of bores sit talking at one another about their nonexperiences. Of all the risks that the joy of flight requires, that of falling prey to the misuse of it is the greatest of all.

If you've always wondered what flying is really like, this book can't tell you. Nothing can but flying itself. If you've vaguely wondered what it would feel like to be gently shepherded into the left seat of an airplane for your first flying lesson, this book can offer some hints. We can describe for you what the instructor will tell you and what he will want you to do as the airplane lifts off for the first time with you at the controls. We can prepare you somewhat for the odd sense of exhilaration and apprehension you will experience, but you will have to fly to know the feeling of entering a new world.

This book is, of course, not a substitute for flying, but it is intended as a way of your getting to know the world of aviation that learning to fly opens for you. It will inform you on such practical matters as how to take up flying, how much lessons will cost, how to choose the right airplane for you, and what price to expect to pay. It will also touch on sports flying—racing, soaring, aerobatics, and the like—as well as discuss aviation in business, pilot careers, and even make a tour of some likely places for air trips and some unlikely planes being flown.

In describing the pleasures and challenges of flying in America, this book may tempt you to go out to a small airport one day to see what you're missing.

AMERICA'S
Flying Book

CHAPTER 1

Getting Acquainted

THE best way to get started in aviation is to spend some lazy afternoons at an airport just watching airplanes fly. It's best to pick an airport where there is mostly general aviation activity. The smaller the airport is, the less formal it is, and the closer you'll be to the airplanes and the people.

If it's a windy day, look for the windsock on the field (usually orange) and notice that the runway (maybe it's turf—if you're lucky enough to have one of the less-busy, bucolic old airports near you) being used by the planes parallels the direction the wind is blowing, with the planes taking off and landing into the wind. At first, just watch the airplanes take off, circle, and land. You'll quickly discover the process involves an orderly beginning, middle, and end. Moreover, if you find something satisfying about observing these maneuvers—almost a hypnotic effect akin to watching waves breaking along the shore—you're on your way!

As you begin to look for detail in the broad picture, you will become conscious of the people in the airplanes. You will observe that pilots, as a class, are both diverse and unremarkable. You will see grandfatherly-looking men and motherly-looking women. You'll no doubt see weekend expatriates from business and professional fields—men and women who somehow manage to look alert and efficient even while wearing jeans and sport shirts. And there will probably be a smattering of enthusiastic, lively-looking teen-agers. What you won't be able to tell—until you learn that instructors sit in the right seat, while future captains-in-command learn from the left seat—is who is teaching whom. For aviation is among those fields of human endeavor in which what you know and how well you perform are paramount. Sometimes this means that the nineteen- or twenty-year-old teaches the grandfather, or the housewife instructs the nuclear physicist.

Looking at airplanes is a satisfying recreation whether from the coolness of the local Fixed Base Operator's office or actually outside.

Making an informal visit to a general aviation airport is the best way, too, of getting a close look at what the "flying world" encompasses. Usually, you are free to walk around and inspect the planes at their tie-down spots. Unless you do something erratic, such as trying to pry open a locked airplane door, nobody will bother you. If you're at one of the more sophisticated fields, you might want—in time, but not too soon—to visit the operations office, where weather information is usually ticking off the Teletype, or the control tower (if you can gain advance permission and can do so without distracting the controllers).

You will, of course, want to turn your attention to the flight office. You'll find that it, too, has a character of its own. Some flight offices (albeit a minority) look as slick as automobile salesrooms. More look like frontier cabins which have been given very little tender loving care, and many are unfancy but functional structures containing a few desks, random displays of flight materials, and unbusinesslike staffs made up of people who like to fly and who have gained varying degrees of proficiency at it and at imparting their information to others.

The variety of planes and activities at an airfield can be breathtaking, as machines of different shapes and sizes taxi, take off, land or just rest under the waiting skies. Sounds of engines range from rasping roars as the planes lift off to virtual silence.

In aviation, form generally follows function, and the forms can be forbidding or beautiful. Some of these control towers are all business, while others move both planes and the spirit.

By careful observation and discreet eavesdropping, you'll be able to find out a lot of what really goes on in flight training. Assuming that you've reached the point where you want to take lessons, you'll be able to gain some insight into the capabilities and personalities of prospective instructors. Anyone with fairly normal judgment of human nature and some understanding of his own personality will probably be able to decide on the right instructor. But it's best to keep a door open should you later discover that a change in instructors would make for a more compatible learning situation.

By now, you have had some close inspections of the airplanes themselves, and it's excusable if your reaction is that they don't look very substantial. True enough, they don't look as strong as tractors, bulldozers, and similar ground machines, but neither do birds look as strong as bears. In truth, of course, both birds and airplanes are enormously strong in the ways that they need to be strong, and light because they must be light. Under these constraints, aeronautical engineers have had to find ways to make use of sometimes unsuspected strengths of light materials.

For example, take a piece of poster paper. Wave it around in the air—decidedly flimsy. But now roll it up tightly, and you could give someone a black eye with it. The same kind of cunning has been applied throughout aircraft structures from the earliest designs.

Most modern structural materials didn't exist at the dawn of powered flight. Aluminum was little more than a laboratory curiosity, since its superb high-strength alloys and heat-treatment methods had not been developed. Modern methods of structural design could not be applied, for the lack of materials to work with. So the first designs used wood and fabric, cleverly braced by struts and wires. Later, much of the wooden main structure was replaced by steel tubing. In time, metal replaced all of the wood pieces. There are still a few all-metal airplanes which use external struts to brace the wings, and there are also a few in which the main cabin structure is welded steel tubing, and some even feature a limited use of wood and fabric.

The great advantage of wood (or steel tubing) and fabric is simplicity. Few tools are required, and design changes are easy to make. An example is Charles Lindbergh's *Spirit of St. Louis,* which was modified from an existing Ryan design, the M-2. Engineering man-hours were 850, with only 3,000 man-hours construction and assembly labor. The project was completed in two months. Such a major modification of a modern all-metal airplane would take much longer.

In spite of this advantage, there were more serious disadvantages. On the practical side, fabric is fragile and subject to damage by both moisture and sun. (There are modern fabrics which have very long life expectancy, but this is not enough to offset the other shortcomings.) Also, there were grave technical problems. The use of a framework for structural strength and a separate covering skin for aerodynamic shape was wasteful. The structure of the planes was heavier than the designers wished, internal space was used up by braces, and there was no way to get rid of outside wires and struts which interfered with speed.

The modern answer is to make the outer skin itself part of the structure; this is called "stressed skin." In most airplanes built in recent years, all of the wing bracing has been put inside; this is called "cantilever" design. The

The DC-2, born in the early '30s and the first of the truly modern airliners, and its successor the DC-3 (shown here), were loved by crews for their rugged dependability and strength. The DC-3 still survives as a cargo and transport plane in the outback areas of the world.

trend to all-metal, stressed-skin, cantilever monoplanes began with the Boeing 247 airliner and reached its early peak with the DC-2 and DC-3. This design has so many advantages that it is expected to be the standard one for many years.

The shape of that outer shell is all-important. The form of the fuselage will be one of the factors that determine the cruising speed and the fuel economy of the airplane. The shape, size, and arrangement of the tail surfaces will determine the stability and control—that is, how solidly the airplane flies hands off (airplanes, like cars, will go along in a straight line for awhile if you take your hands off the controls) and how promptly and accurately it reacts to control signals. Most important of all, the form of the almighty wing will largely determine how fast the plane can fly and how high up and how slowly it can land—and hence how small an airport it can get into and out of.

The elongated teardrop shapes of wing sections are the upshot of much scientific research. What makes them work is what makes the convertible top of a car balloon up in the wind: low pressure resulting from high-speed flow of air above a surface, along with a slower speed of airflow with resulting higher pressure below. In the case of the teardrop-shaped wing, or airfoil, the airfoil is designed to increase the velocity of the airflow above its surface, thereby decreasing pressure above the wing; simultaneously, the airflow velocity below the wing is decreased, thereby increasing pressure below. This combination produces "lift." Because of the shape of the airfoil, each square foot of a lightplane wing can lift 20, 30, 40, or more pounds of airplane into the air. In fact, the air may exert two or three times more force on a wing moving edge-on into the wind than it would if the wing were turned flat side against the wind. But the shape is extremely important; and the "laminar flow" airfoil sections in use on most airplanes today require an accuracy of surface contour within a few thousandths of an inch in order to work at their best efficiency.

The smallest modern metal lightplane is built on the same principles as the largest airliner. Its structure is likely to be "fail safe" in most areas—

which means that if one structural member fails at a momentary extreme load, others will take over from it and maintain the integrity of the aircraft. Lightplanes are, of course, much simpler than airliners, but they are also stronger. Because of the relative fatness of lightplane fuselages and the thickness of their wings by comparison with the longer, more slender ones of airliners, lightplanes are more rigid. You notice in taxiing, for instance, that the wings of a lightplane do not "flap" slightly, as those of an airliner do.

Flexibility alone, of course, does not betoken weakness, nor rigidity strength. But in addition to being rigid, light airplanes are stressed to higher "load factors" than airliners—anywhere from 25 to 100 percent higher. The minimum design load factor permitted in a light airplane by the Federal Aviation Administration is 3.8 G—which means a load 3.8 times as great as that which is continually experienced by the airplane in level flight. Different airplanes are designed to take different amounts of loading, varying between 3.8 G and 6 G or more. The 6 G and above group are called "aerobatic category aircraft" and are cleared for "stunt flying." This group includes several apparently sedate four- and five-seat "family planes" that you would hardly expect to see looping and swooping on a Sunday afternoon.

Beyond the limit load factor of at least 3.8 G (the load past which an airplane may begin to suffer some permanent structural deformation), the FAA requires an additional safety margin of 50 percent, so that an airplane with a limit load of 3.8 G has an "ultimate load" of 5.7 G (the load that, if held for more than three seconds, will cause failure of the structure). Aerobatic airplanes have an ultimate load factor of 9 G. For comparison, the most severe jounce you are ever likely to experience in a car on the roughest road is around 2 G. Yet with all that strength, the average lightplane, though it is much larger overall than an automobile, weighs less than half as much.

The uncomplicated-looking metal bird you may call a "little plane"—or, if you're terribly behind the times, a "Piper Cub"—is really very complicated. It is the product of thousands of engineering hours and years of testing and progressive refinement, and it has been through an exhaustive series of federal tests to ensure that it at least meets, and preferably, sur-

Nestling behind a Vermont oak sits an aerobatic two-place Citabria. Its surface is made of fabric; yet the aircraft is designed to an ultimate load factor of 9G—far higher than any airliner.

passes, the requirements of a fat book called Federal Aviation Regulations (FAR), Part 23.

FAR 23 tells how strong aircraft must be, and how they may and may not achieve that strength. It lays down rules about the materials to be used, the methods by which flight loads will be calculated, the tests that new aircraft must undergo, and how the controls must look and behave. Defective television sets may be returned or repaired, and defective cars towed back to the dealer. But there can be no defect in an airplane, and the Federal Aviation Administration and the manufacturers cooperate to assure that there will be none. If a defect turns up on one aircraft that could appear on others, a notice—an "airworthiness directive"—is promulgated to dealers, maintenance facilities, and owners. If the defect is serious, all aircraft of the type are grounded until it is analyzed and corrected.

Defects are magnificently few. Unlike automobiles, airplanes are not hastily assembled and then pried into shape; they are scrupulously built and as scrupulously inspected. Rivets that are improperly formed are drilled out and replaced; nuts and bolts are wired down so that they cannot work loose; fuel tanks are pressure-tested, and control systems flight-checked for smoothness and accuracy of response. Each airplane is individually flight-adjusted for rigging and trim, and its radio and navigational equipment tested and calibrated.

The care is not confined to the conclusion of the manufacturing process. From the very beginning, the metal panels and extrusions are kept free of even slight dents and scratches. Critical parts are X-rayed, magnafluxed, or dye-tested for cracks or flaws. Absolute uniformity is maintained to close tolerances. There are no nicks, no rough edges, no rattles in a light airplane. Only the best goes in, and only the best comes out.

All this, of course, costs money. Because an airplane is a precision instrument of extreme reliability, as refined and complex as a watch and infinitely more robust, it costs three or four times as much as an automobile of the same class. The airframe itself—the actual "airplane"—despite the requisite accuracy of its contour and the lightness and complexity of its construction, as well as the specialized high-strength alloys of which it is made—is surprisingly cheap, sometimes half or less than half the cost of the finished aircraft. But to this shell is mated hardware: instruments, controls, power plant. Automobile engines cost about $2 per horsepower; aero engines about $20. Designed to run for long periods at near maximum power output, scarcely ever allowed to loaf or idle, air-cooled, compact, and astonishingly reliable, modern engines run 1,500 to 2,000 hours between overhauls, covering perhaps 300,000 miles with no more serious maintenance than changes of spark plugs, oil, and filters. An aircraft radio the size of a common table radio may cost $1,000 or more. But, again, it will be designed for the utmost in accuracy and reliability, and required to pass stringent tests before being put on the market. Even noncritical accessories such as cabin appointments are chosen for light weight, and may be more costly than heavier, commoner materials. It's all part of making a ton-and-a-half of metal and men climb into the air at 1,000 feet a minute, cruise along at three miles a minute, and last for 50 years without falling apart. It's worth what you have to pay for it. In many respects it may be worth quite a bit more.

Most of the airplanes found at a small airport have only one engine, and you may have wondered whether or not they are safe. Isn't it true that more engines make for more safety? Or that any number less than two is unsafe? The answer to the first part is "sometimes"; to the second part, "no." The safety in numbers of more than one engine is offset to some extent by increased demands on the skill of the pilot.

It is certainly true that early airplanes, like early automobile engines, were fragile and uncertain, in addition to being weak. The airplane engines looked worse because they had to work harder; but since the problems of flight environment have been solved, they look very much better. There are now several makes and models of aircraft engines which are certified to operate for 2,000 hours between overhauls. That is the equivalent of 200,000 to 400,000 miles of travel, and aircraft engines can be overhauled several times before it becomes uneconomic to do so. Looking at the time between overhauls from another angle, it's about seven years of flying, at 300 hours a year, which is roughly what the average pilot flies.

In spite of the early engine reliability troubles, the purpose of designing airplanes with more than one engine was not to enhance safety. It was simply the only way to install enough power to get the bigger machines to fly at all. The famous Fort Tri-Motor is a good example. In spite of its three engines, it could not sustain flight when fully loaded if even one of them failed.

As engine reliability improved, and as new designs succeeded in realizing more power from a single engine, the emphasis changed. Air transport category airplanes are now required to prove their ability to continue flight after an engine is deliberately failed at the most critical time of takeoff. This demand is not made on light airplanes, for several reasons. On the philosophical side, the reasoning is that people who fly as passengers in light airplanes do so with friends or associates, and are free to choose whether or not to go, while common carrier passengers must assume that their safety is assured. On the practical side, general aviation airplanes are smaller, lighter, and more maneuverable; and their pilots can defer any operation which seems chancy, whereas the air carrier must obey schedules, unless something really severe occurs.

But whether a pilot captains a single-engine or a twin-engine lightplane, to fly efficiently and safely obviously demands a full understanding and complete mastery of the art. Of the many areas in which the pilot is expected to be proficient, none—excepting weather—is more crucial than an intimate understanding of his airplane's control and engine. These topics are touched on here not in the form or detail presented to aspiring pilots, but as background information for those whose curiosity about planes has at one time prompted the question, "How does it fly?"

AIRCRAFT CONTROLS

Because an airplane moves in three dimensions, you would expect that it would have more controls than a car, which moves in only two. You would be right, of course, but you may not be prepared for how many more there are. Even something that looks familiar—the wheel—acts very differently from the steering wheel of a car. Let's begin with the flight controls.

Airplanes move on three axes, called pitch, yaw, and roll. In pitch, the nose moves up or down; in yaw, it moves from side to side; and in roll, one wing goes down and the other goes up.

Movable control surfaces on the tail and wings do the work. The horizontal tail surfaces, called elevators (a misleading term), control pitch; the vertical surface is called the rudder, and controls yaw; the surfaces at the trailing outside edges of the wings are called ailerons, and control roll. These are connected, by rods and cables or a combination of the two, to the cockpit controls. These consist of a stick, or wheel, and a pair of rudder pedals. Although most airplanes have wheels, it's easier to see what happens by looking at the stick first.

The stick can move forward, backward, to either side, and any position in between. When it is moved backward and forward, the elevators move up and down. When it is moved from side to side, the ailerons move. If it is moved back and to the left, the elevators move up and the ailerons move in the direction of a left bank. The unrestricted movement (within its limit stops) of the stick allows blending of any amount of control in pitch or roll or both. The ailerons move differentially: when the stick is moved to the left, the right aileron moves down and the left aileron moves up. The result of the aerodynamic forces on the ailerons in flight is that the left wing goes down, and the right goes up.

The wheel does the same things with the elevators: pulling back on it moves the elevators up; pushing forward moves them down. Turning it to the left moves the ailerons the way the stick does when it is pushed to the left, and so on.

The wheel in the airplane gives the new student trouble at first because of his prior experience with automobile steering wheels. The airplane control wheel does no steering on the ground. The confusion passes quickly—partly, perhaps, because the student is so busy getting used to something really new and strange: the rudder pedals.

The function of the rudder was seriously misunderstood by most of the early airplane designers, including the great Professor Langley. Unlike the rudder on a boat, the airplane rudder is not the primary turning control. It was the Wright Brothers who proved that an airplane turns by banking its wings, this being their most important contribution to the science of powered flight. Langley's unsuccessful airplane, the Aerodrome, was rebuilt by Glenn Curtiss, who made extensive modifications (including installation of ailerons), based on the Wrights' work, and it flew. (In a series of misstatements by a later secretary of the Smithsonian Institution which lasted

Like the rudder of a boat, a plane's rudder operates in an axis perpendicular to the main surfaces.

for many years, the Aerodrome was credited as being the first successful powered, man-carrying airplane, and this led to the original Wright machine being sent to the British Science Museum in London. Fortunately, a later Smithsonian secretary, Dr. C. G. Abbot, publicly corrected the error in time for Orville Wright to agree to return of the airplane before he died in 1948. It is now on display at the Smithsonian.)

The first Wright machine banked by having its wings twisted, or "warped." This was awkward, leading to the development of the separate aileron surfaces. Unfortunately, not even ailerons are perfect. When an aileron goes down (and the other goes up), it increases the lift of that wing, but it also increases the drag. The result is that as the airplane begins to roll into the bank, the nose moves in the opposite way. This is called "adverse aileron yaw."

Ailerons are movable surfaces at the trailing edge of the outer wing, as shown here.

This is where the rudder comes in. As the pilot applies aileron pressure to start the bank, he adds rudder pressure on the same side. This produces a yawing movement in the direction of the turn, and the pilot applies just enough rudder to overcome the adverse yaw produced by the ailerons. It is sometimes said that the main purpose of the rudder, in flight, is to correct the mistakes made by the ailerons. (There is one general aviation airplane which does not have aileron yaw. This is the Japanese Mitsubishi MU-2, in which the wings are banked by spoilers. Although the design is covered by patents, it is probable that it will eventually be adopted by others.)

In a normal turn, rudder and aileron are applied together on the same side. This goes against normal motor coordination in walking, when, as the left leg moves forward, the right arm moves back. These difficulties disappear with practice. Beginning with that first Wright airplane, attempts have been made to connect ailerons and rudder together. The problem is that it is hard to develop a system which gives perfect coordination at all speeds.

In all but a handful of airplanes, the rudder pedals are also connected to the third landing gear wheel, whether at the tail or the nose. Thus the rudder *is* the primary steering control on the ground. Finally, each main landing gear has a brake, and each brake is operated by pressing on the top of the rudder pedal on the same side: left pedal, left brake. To stop the airplane, both brakes are used together. To make a sharp turn, braking on only one side does the trick.

Since both feet are occupied with the rudder pedals, and since there is no need for frequent power changes, as in a car, there is no accelerator pedal. The power controls, throttle, mixture, and propeller pitch (on airplanes with controllable or constant pitch propellers), are operated by hand.

With very few exceptions, notably the Beech Bonanza, United States airplanes are equipped with two sets of primary flight controls. The advantages are important and well worth the extra charge, if any. The airplane can then be used for instruction; also, either pilot can fly the plane to give the other a rest or time to do flight planning, and if one pilot becomes unable to fly, the other can take control.

The final elements of the normal flight control system are the wing flaps, sometimes inaccurately called "air brakes." Flaps are movable surfaces attached at the trailing edge of each wing. In cruising flight, they are

Flaps are movable surfaces at the trailing edge of the inner wing. When extended they increase the surface area of the wing, providing increased lift so that the plane can be flown more slowly. Not all planes are equipped with flaps.

retracted; when they are extended, they increase the surface area of the wings, thereby increasing lift. When lift is increased, the airplane can be flown at a lower speed. The ability to fly at a lower speed increases safety and reduces the length of runway required. Low speeds are desirable for landings, and in many airplanes, flaps are also used for takeoffs. Most modern airplanes have electrically-operated flaps, while older models have their flaps extended and retracted by a hand lever in the cockpit.

The last two controls of prime interest, mixture and carburetor heat, are engine controls. (The throttle is relatively familiar.) The purpose of the mixture control is to allow adjustment of the fuel-air ratio at different altitudes. Air is thinner at altitude than it is at sea level, so less gasoline is needed to maintain the best mixture. Carburetor heat is required to prevent carburetor ice, or to remove it if it has formed. As the gasoline is vaporized in the carburetor, it gets cold enough, under certain conditions, to freeze water vapor out of the air and deposit it in the carburetor intake. Unless the ice is removed, the engine will stop. In normal operations, the heat control is in the "cold" position because the engine develops full power on cold intake air. If ice forms, the heater knob directs heated air into the carburetor, which melts the ice. Engines with fuel injectors instead of carburetors are immune to this kind of internal ice formation, eliminating the need for carburetor heat controls.

These are the controls which are basic to flight and which are found in all airplanes, except as noted. As you proceed, you will be exposed to other kinds of controls—fuel system, electrical, and radio—to keep the list short. It is no secret that what a pilot is required to do, and the way he has to do it, appears infinitely complicated. Nevertheless, the systems can be learned and mastered, even by people who are not mechanically inclined.

There are two types of aircraft engines: piston (often called "reciprocating") and turbine. Piston engines range in horsepower from 60 to 400, and turbines from 575 up. There are two kinds of turbine engines: the pure jets and the turbines which drive propellers, called turboprops. Piston engines are of two kinds, also: "normally aspirated" and supercharger. One is direct or gear driven, the other driven by the engine exhaust gases, known as "turbocharged." The turbines hold all the high ground in the horsepower range, although they have been working down in recent years toward piston territory. So far there is no turbine engine which produces less than 575 hp in use in fixed-wing airplanes. It seems likely that matters will remain about where they are now for the foreseeable future. There are some new developments in piston engines soon to go into production, which will reduce the differences in smoothness and life between pistons and turbines while retaining the piston engine's edge in fuel consumption.

Engines represent a large part of the cost of an airplane. Piston engines in power ranges comparable to those found in automobiles cost several times as much, while turbine engines are sold at prices which simply take one's breath away. The most obvious difference is that automobile engines are built in the millions every year, while aircraft engine production is in the low tens of thousands. This means that the automatic machining operations which have been standard in the automotive field for forty or more years are simply out of reach for the aircraft engine manufacturer. One of the major aircraft engine companies, Continental, has invested several million dollars in automatic equipment, but for at least the next several years the result will be better engine quality and performance rather than lower prices.

Modern aircraft engines represent the acme of internal combustion engine design. They have to produce full power over long periods and are expected not to break down. Generally they are light in weight and air-cooled.

Full power for takeoff.

But volume of production, important as it is, isn't the entire answer. The real difference is that aircraft engines live a much harder life than do automobile engines. If proof is needed, aviation history is full of cases in which people tried to adapt automobile engines to aircraft, with every one a failure.

An airplane engine must run at full power for fairly long periods, and at three quarters of its rated power for most of its life. Its power rating is determined in what is called "ready to fly" condition, with all of its accessories attached and operating. Automobile engines are never asked to deliver full power; they spend most of their lives loafing along at 15 to 20 percent of the book figure. Even that is misleading because car engines are measured on a test stand with no exhaust system and no power-absorbing accessories connected. So a 200-hp automobile engine could not possibly produce 200 hp in an airplane, even for short periods. People who race "stock" automobiles spend as much as $25,000 modifying a standard engine, and even then many of the engines break down before the end of a 200-mile race. It may be useful to assign an arbitrary value to the differences in work load and environment between the two types—say a factor of four. This makes the aircraft engine look like a much better buy. The fact that car engines are under no severe weight penalty and aircraft engines are is another cost factor of importance.

GETTING ACQUAINTED

Aviation engines cannot run on automobile gasoline, no matter what the gasoline octane rating may be. There are two reasons: power and cooling, with cooling the most important. Aircraft engines are said to be air-cooled, but the air-cooling fins are only one of three cooling elements. Oil is another important one, since oil can absorb a lot of heat and carry it away from the hot parts of the engine. This is why most aircraft engines are equipped with oil coolers and why they hold more oil in their crankcases than comparable automobile engines.

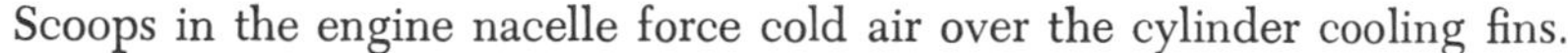

Scoops in the engine nacelle force cold air over the cylinder cooling fins.

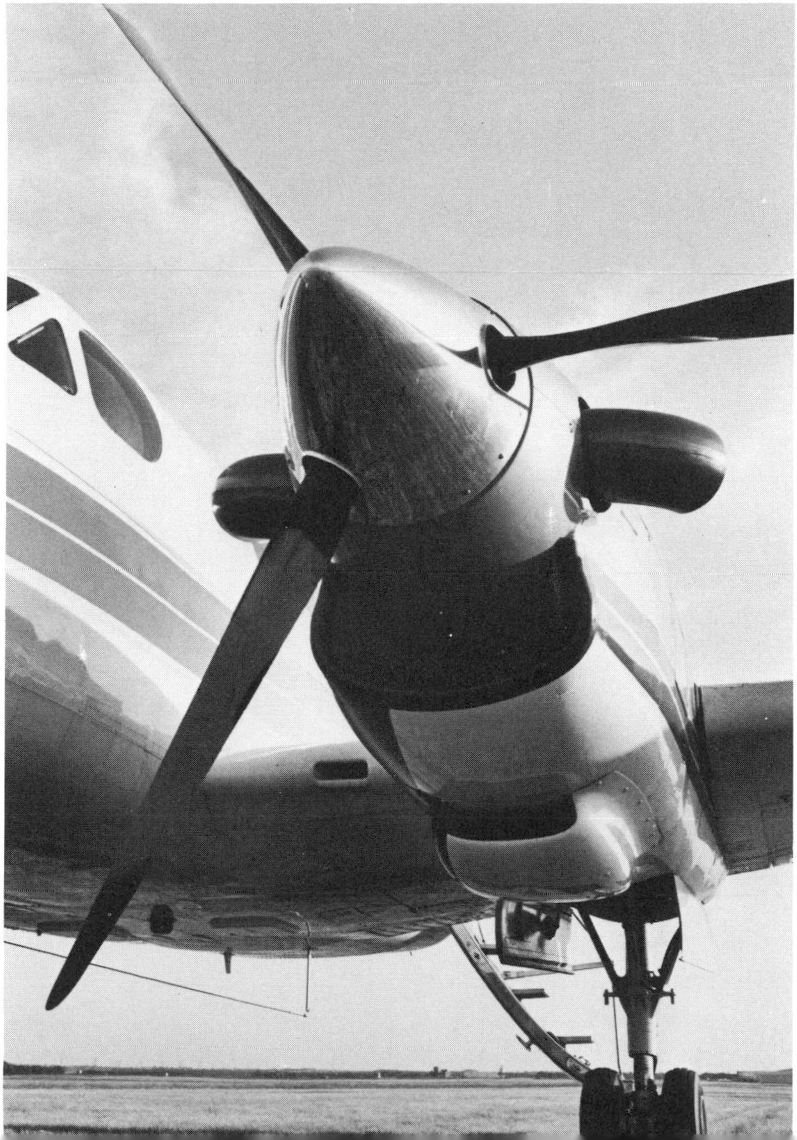

The final element is cooling by evaporation of the gasoline, and this actually does a higher percentage of the cooling than either of the others. Aviation gasoline is much more volatile than automobile gasoline. As it vaporizes, it cools the air-fuel mixture entering the cylinders and provides the critical cooling. It also sometimes causes carburetor ice to form, as we have seen. An aircraft engine designed to run on 100 octane aviation gasoline will suffer serious damage in less than half an hour if it is asked to develop full power while being fed automobile gasoline of the same octane number. In fact, it won't last much longer if it is run on 87 octane aviation fuel.

These are the main reasons for the high cost of aircraft engines. If you will remember that they run as much as 400,000 miles between overhauls and that they can be overhauled three or more times before they are worn out, they turn out to be good bargains.

For a plane a straight line is always the shortest distance between two points, a constant advantage over surface transportation.

THE INSTRUMENTS

It has been happening for years. The newcomer asks: "What are all those instruments for?" The insider misses the depth of the question. He points around the panel and the cockpit: oil pressure, oil temperature, cylinder head temperature, outside air temperature, fuel quantity, fuel pressure, fuel flow, tachometer, manifold pressure, artificial horizon, directional gyro, magnetic compass, turn and bank, airspeed, altimeter. Radios, radio indicators, fuel selectors, handfuls of switches, fuses, circuit breakers. Almost always, the pilot forgets one. The newcomer wants to know what that one is. It turns out to be the panel clock—in fact, it even says CLOCK on its face.

Airplanes are designed to fly and move in three directions, and man is not. Man's steering and balance systems have evolved in the stable, two-dimensional, conventional gravity conditions of earth-supported movement. They are insufficient for flight. Hence part of the challenge of flying is learning to understand what these instruments—these voiceless friends—can tell us of man's situation in this new environment.

On earth, gravity always pulls the same way, straight down. In flight, we find a different sort of gravity, which the airplane carries along with it. Inside the cabin, in normal flight and normal turns, dropped objects fall straight to the floor. But it is only in level flight that this gravity pulls in the same direction as earth's gravity. If the airplane's wings are banked 20 degrees, the gravity pull inside the plane will be pointing twenty degrees to the right or left of true gravity, depending on which way the airplane is turning. This is a blessing in some ways; otherwise the plane's occupants would be thrown from side to side in turns as they are in ground vehicles. Unfortunately, this same advantage sours when the airplane enters cloud and the ground cannot be seen. Because our balance and directional senses cannot detect any difference between turns and straight flight, we find ourselves in serious trouble. This was a great puzzle to pioneer pilots. They could fly very well as long as they could see the ground, but once they flew into cloud, even the best of them lost control. They found that their compasses seemed somehow to share the plague: relatively calm and accurate

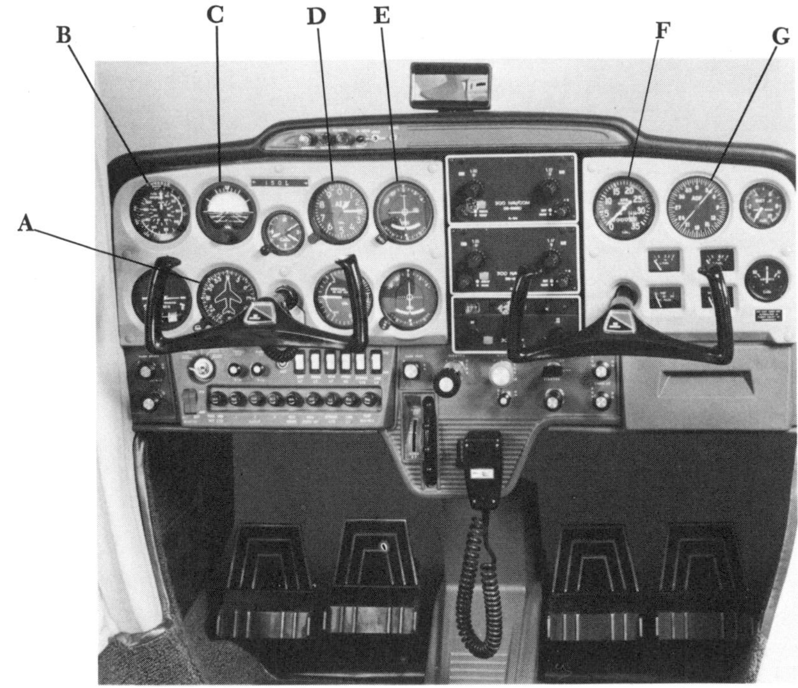

FROM LEFT TO RIGHT.

A. Directional gyro, which is set to the magnetic compass, tells the pilot in which direction he's going.

B. Airspeed indicator lets him know how fast he's getting there.

C. Artificial horizon provides the pilot with pitch information either for instrument flight or for when there's no horizon. It also tells him about bank information.

D. The altimeter tells the pilot how high he is, and can also tell him whether he's going up or down.

E. This indicator provides course information through the VHF radio navigation unit mounted at right. It can also tell the pilot when he's lined up for an instrument landing and give him descent information.

F. The engine rev counter or tachometer.

G. ADF indicator—the needle points to the radio beacon.

in sunshine, they lost all restraint and spun wildly soon after the ground was lost to view.

The first auxiliary instrument was a clever gyroscopic device called a turn and bank indicator. It had no direction ability and it couldn't tell when a wing went down, but it could indicate if the airplane was turning, in which direction, and at what rate. Next came another gyroscopic device, the directional gyro. It can measure the heading of the airplane fairly accurately, once it has been set against the magnetic compass. It cannot give direct information on rate of turn. Finally, there is the gyroscopic artificial horizon. It has no directional, heading, or turn-indicating abilities, but it can determine whether the airplane has its wings level or not, and if not, by how much.

Here, therefore, is a capsule explanation of the functions of some of those instruments. To make up for the pilot's inability to sense turns when he can't see the ground, he has the magnetic compass, which indicates where north is but, like the pilot himself, becomes confused in turns. The pilot can then consult the turn and bank indicator, which can tell him if the airplane is turning—and in which direction. The directional gyro is good for turns to headings once it is set to agree with the compass. And the artificial horizon reports the attitude of the airplane compared to the horizon. In similar fashion, others of the seeming maze of instruments and gauges offer varying degrees of information which the pilot uses in order to fly efficiently and safely. The attempt to master his air environment through the help of these instruments begins with the pilot's first flight, and does not cease until his last.

STALLING

When an automobile engine stalls or stops, the automobile usually stops moving. Annoying as this can be, the consequences are seldom serious. This same thinking is usually transferred to a "stalled" airplane, so that it is a common belief that if the engine stops, the airplane will also stop moving and fall out of the sky.

That isn't what happens. In the first place, aircraft engines are never said to stall. They simply stop, which is today a rare event unless they have been allowed to run out of gasoline. More to the point, the airplane continues to fly, although it will not be able to fly upwards, and it cannot even fly level. Though it can only fly down toward the ground, it is still a fully controllable flying machine.

The word *stall* applied to airplanes has quite a different meaning. It means that the wing no longer has any "lift," and has stopped flying. This happens when the airflow over the surface of the airfoil is disturbed in such a way that it interferes with the smooth flow of air, creating "burbles" over the top of the wing. The burbles destroy the balance between the low pressure over the airfoil and the higher pressure under the wing—the necessary conditions for creating lift—and the plane stops flying. Even this is not anything like the end of the world: the wing can be made to fly again in a matter of seconds, and the pilot is trained in how to do this. He is also trained in recognizing the approach of a stall and how to avoid it.

Moreover, it will come on quite a gentle slope. The distance an airplane will go over the ground for each foot it goes downhill is different for different planes, but a comfortable average is about ten to one. Thus, if the airplane is a mile above the ground when the engine loses power, the pilot has an area with a ten-mile radius beneath him within which to choose a place to land. This will not demand a split-second decision, either: it will take at least five minutes to glide down from a mile up in the air, and five minutes is a long time if the pilot keeps his wits about him.

The chances are that he will, too, because he is given practice in simulated emergency landings from early in his training. He is shown how to plan his flight path so as to keep within reach of suitable landing areas. It doesn't take much of this to develop quite a cool head. One of the most serious situations has also been well covered: engine failure on takeoff, when there is little altitude.

Finally, a word about spins, which everybody has heard about and which have a bad reputation. The reassuring fact is that an airplane will not spin—cannot spin—unless its wings have first been stalled. Modern airplanes are constructed to be stall- and spin-resistant. Pilots are trained in stall recognition and recovery, and instruments to warn of approaching stalls are now required on all new planes.

COSTS

Money, like love, is supposed to be one of the universal languages. It is common, whenever we become interested in anything new, to start the process of education at what seems likely to be the beginning. We ask: "What does it cost?" In most affairs, this serves us quite well, since we can compare the answer with what we already know about money, particularly with respect to how much of it we can command. Most of the time, we have previous experience to draw on.

Unfortunately, aviation is a field in which money's universal tongue fails. The most likely response to the question of cost is "It all depends." It does, indeed, and the trouble is that it depends on so many different

The fabled V-tail Bonanza.

things, each of which is unfamiliar, that there is no clear way through the thicket. Take that pretty single-engine airplane with the distinctive V-shaped tail, for example. That's a Beechcraft Bonanza, probably the best-known light airplane ever built, and the one you're asking about has a price tag just a bit over $50,000. It's brand new, and it's equipped with all the instruments, radios, and navigation aids to qualify it for flight under instrument conditions. Its engine has an exhaust-driven supercharger, which allows flight at high altitudes and produces very satisfying speed. Fifty thousand dollars! Even today, this is a princely sum, and will buy a reasonably princely house. Moreover, that house can be paid for over a period of 30 years. How long did you say you can finance an airplane? *Five years?* Too much. Before you go away, take a look at the other V-tailed Bonanza just

Another V-tail Bonanza, but an early one. Compare side windows.

across from the $50,000 one. Hard to tell them apart, isn't it? The prices are different, though. You can buy the second one for less than $8,000.

What's the catch? None. The high-priced one is brand-new; the other has been flying happily for some 20 years. The new one can fly very fast at altitudes the old one cannot reach, but at lower altitudes, there isn't much difference between the two. The new one has much more extensive avionics equipment, including an autopilot, and that gear alone costs well over twice the $8,000 cost of the older Bonanza. For a person or a company already versed in the use of an airplane, the price of the new one is justified. For a newcomer, it is not: the older one will serve him very well for some years.

It's important to remember that airplanes are quite unlike cars. Not only are they designed and built for infinite life, they are also *required* to be maintained in airworthy condition. This is not to say that there are not some very old dogs for sale—only that they are rare. They can be found out easily and at little expense simply by having an authorized repair station run a complete annual inspection.

The same cost comparisons between old and new models of other makes follow the same pattern. Although there is depreciation in aircraft values, as in everything else, airplanes more closely resemble real estate than most consumer goods—particularly automobiles. It is a steady financial fact that one can buy a modern, all-metal airplane, ten years old, fly it for three or four years, and sell it at the same price paid; sometimes even higher.

So in the matter of buying an airplane, the initial investment can be very much less than buying new, and the risk is low. If for any reason the aircraft must be disposed of, the investment will be fully recovered in all probability. On the other side, if the owner wants a better airplane after five years, he gets full value for the one he may have just finished paying for. This is in fact what usually happens when a new, high-priced airplane is sold. The owner has had two or three previous machines and has kept adding to his aircraft equity. This is really quite straightforward, though it does take some getting used to.

What is really baffling is explaining the fact that airplanes only fly

Annual premium for a plane like this is around $1,200, covering liability and "hull" damage—the aeronautical equivalent of collision insurance.

hours, not miles. A simple bit of arithmetic will show that the measuring stick has to be hours flown. There are always two fixed charges which apply to any airplane: storage and insurance. Storage charges vary, but $50 a month is quite common. At airports with a large aircraft population, this will be simply a place to park outside. At small country airports, it will be inside storage. The annual cost is $600. Insurance rates are variable, too, but a typical annual premium for an airplane in the $15,000 class is $1,200, covering both liability and "hull" damage, which is equivalent to collision insurance in cars.

These two fixed charges add up to $1,800 a year. If the airplane flies one hour (possible but unlikely) during a year, the assessment against flying time from storage and insurance is $1,800 an hour. If the airplane flies 100 hours a year, the cost per hour is $18—much lower, of course, but still unacceptable. If the annual flight time is 300 hours, which is about average for a small airplane flown only by the owner, the figure drops to a reasonable $6 per hour. And if the flight time reaches 1,800 hours a year, which is possible for the same airplane in commercial service, the cost per hour for storage and insurance is a very satisfactory $1.

Depreciation is another fixed annual charge which follows the same route of reduction in cost per hour as annual flying time increases, and carries an even higher degree of penalty for low time.

Other costs are directly associated with flight time. If the airplane doesn't fly at all, it needs no fuel, no oil, no reserve for overhaul, and no provision for routine maintenance. It will have to have an annual inspection to keep its Airworthiness Certificate, but this is not likely to be over $200 in cost.

Furthermore, because the airplane flies in the air, which can be in motion against the machine, there is no such ground-bound measurement as miles per gallon of fuel. Instead, the pilot figures cost per hour.

The insidious effect of the hourly basis of measurement reaches its peak when the newcomer asks: "How much does it cost to learn to fly?" The answer, usually again qualified in advance by "It all depends," seems simple. "For a private pilot license, you'll need at least 40 hours, about 15 solo, and 25 with an instructor. Our rates are $20 an hour dual, for instruction flights, $15 solo. So it will cost about $750. Then you have your ground school, and that will run about $50, maybe $75. You'd better figure on about $800, give or take a little."

This is probably the point at which our mental gears clash most grindingly. Forty hours is a standard work week: are you saying that I'm going to have to shell out *eight hundred bucks in one week?* Well, not exactly . . . you can spread it out. Of course, you can. Indeed, you must. Given the doctrine that anything is possible, it is most unlikely that anyone can begin flight training on Monday and pass his private pilot flight test near sundown on Friday, meanwhile having taken and passed (and been informed of his success in) the required written examination. Three months is more likely—

which makes the cost of training look more manageable—although that's really the wrong way to look at it.

The right way is to consider the cost of training as a lifetime investment, and on that basis, it matters very little as to the exact cost. That's the most important reason why shopping for price in flight training is wrong. You ought to shop, but it should be for quality.

Finally it becomes clear that there are ways for people of average income to enter aviation. The commitment can be—in fact, should be—limited in the beginning, so that it does not become a burden. The first ten hours, as a general rule, will see the student through to about the point where he is ready to fly alone for the first time. This is an especially important time to keep the commitment limited. After a few solo flights is a good time to reassess one's enthusiasm and accomplishments and compare them with one's pocketbook and idea of a lifetime investment. Then a decision can be made on the scope of commitment.

Airplanes do cost more than automobiles. Flight training is more expensive than driver training. The strange idea of cost per hour takes some time to become familiar. But aviation costs are manageable and affordable down to very modest income levels. The real issue is what it's worth to each individual. It's quite likely that the contents of a trout fisherman's creel, over a year's time, might have cost him $50 a pound. Even if he knew that, it wouldn't stop him from fishing, because he finds satisfaction in it. And flying provides stronger personal satisfaction than most other things a man can do.

OPPOSITE. The sun is sinking fast, but for the pilot there's still time to put in a couple more "touch and go's"—practice takeoffs and landings.

CHAPTER 2

Humble Beginnings

THERE are few more fascinating true stories to be told than that of the evolution of human flight. Fittingly, the story has been related again and again (the Bibliography of this book will direct you to some histories), and need not be repeated here—except to mention the most dramatic part of it: those now far-off years when the "impossible" was done for the first time, the years when powered flight began.

In retrospect, it was inevitable that during the decades just before and after the turn of the century man would build and fly successful flying machines. It was probably not apparent then, but the rare and curious elements that often come together to make possible a breakthrough were present. Engines that were powerful enough to lift an airframe and just light enough themselves to be lifted were being built. Years of experimentation with gliders and man-powered machines had revealed, fleetingly, a few of the necessary aerodynamic fundamentals. Most important, a scattered few men in the United States and Europe were practicing the blind and illogical determination to find answers that seemed nonexistent to the accepted experts.

For those fanatics to climb into those machines and set out to discover for themselves how to lift from the ground, stay aloft, and return to the earth safely demanded perhaps more courage than it took for the astronauts to commit themselves to a landing on the moon. Those earliest planes had no "backup systems," no manuals or records of unmanned flights. The first time a powered plane went up, a man was aboard, taking his chances. And each of those earliest planes was an entirely new flying challenge, containing its own peculiar dangers. It was a brave and magnificent time—with the modest but explosive first leap from the ground nearly going unnoticed.

When, in December 1903, the Wright Brothers contrived to fly a powered airplane, they took much of the scientific world by surprise. Many authorities of the day continued to doubt the accuracy of the reports of powered and controlled flight for years. It seemed vastly improbable that two men, as short of formal engineering experience as were the Wrights, should hit upon the delicate combination of shapes and forces that permit an airplane to fly.

"I have not the smallest molecule of faith in aerial navigation other than ballooning." (Lord Kelvin, the famous scientist.)

"If such sensational and tremendously important experiments are being conducted . . . is it possible to believe that the enterprising American reporter . . . would not have ascertained all about them and published them long ago?" (*Scientific American*, January 1906, in an article titled "The Wright Aeroplane and Its Fabled Performances." The Wrights had then been flying for two years.)

". . . [We are] of the opinion, indeed, that all attempts at artificial aviation . . . are not only dangerous to human life, but foredoomed to failure from the engineering standpoint." (The editor of the Engineering Supplement to the London *Times*, January 1906.)

Against this kind of climate of opinion—and not just opinion, but informed, educated opinion—it is perhaps small wonder that five long years passed before the world really began to believe that the Wright Brothers could fly.

The Wrights' relationship with the press was never a happy one. On the December day in 1903 when they first brought off this marvelous trick of powered flight, they had ended their proud telegram home: "Inform Press Home Christmas," only to find that the press either didn't believe it or didn't much care. Such coverage as the event did generate was a completely garbled account in a local newspaper that had been tipped off by one of the telegraph operators who had handled the cable. Even when the story was offered to 21 other papers up and down the land, only five cared to run it.

Pioneering days: before a suitable engine was found, birdmen soared at the mercy of the wind. Note the structure of this early glider with its foreplane (originally intended to stop stalls) instead of the rear stabilizer of today. Note, too, the machine's strength and quaint beauty.

Then there was the little matter of the press demonstration of this newfangled "flying," in Dayton, the following spring. A dozen journalists had shown up, by invitation, only to learn that the wind was too fierce and they must wait till it died down. Which it did, all of a sudden, to nothing. Which was no good either, the Wrights told them, for they were only using a short length of launch rail, and must have some breeze to become airborne. Would the gentlemen of the press wait in case the wind got up again? Toward evening, as the calm persisted, the Wrights announced at least a demonstration of their launch procedure, but then they couldn't get their Flyer's engine running. Would the journalists care to come back the next day? A few did, and saw the Flyer rise six feet, and cover perhaps 75 feet

Wilbur Wright

Orville Wright

across the meadow before slithering to an untidy standstill. They were unimpressed, though they wrote kindly accounts, making the most of the little they had seen. None returned later. Did the Wrights appreciate the pressures the reporters were under? the angry editors back in the office hungry for copy? the work piling up on untidy desks, while the reporters stood and shivered, cursing the wasted day? Every crank and crazy in the land was building a flying machine, and a press man soon gets too experienced to be easily fooled.

The Wrights were perhaps shy men, with feelings easily hurt. If the reporters couldn't spare the time, neither could they. But the field the Wrights used was alongside the railway tracks, and it puzzled Dayton commuters, who would often see the experiments, that they never read about them in the papers. They would call at newspaper offices and ask why, and years later the city editor of the Dayton *Daily News* recalled that so many inquirers came they got to be a real nuisance. Why wasn't there ever anything in the paper? "We just didn't believe it," he said. "Of course you must remember that the Wrights were terribly secretive." *Secretive*, flying right there in an open field? "I guess," he allowed, with a rueful grin, "the truth is we were just plain dumb."

Nor were the Wrights natural PR men, adept at setting dumb journalists straight. The managing editor of the Dayton *Journal* knew them well, having chatted with them as they rode together on the train. He felt "sort of sorry for them neglecting their business, wasting their time day after day on that ridiculous flying machine." He sensed the Wrights were reluctant to talk of their experiments. "Done anything of special interest lately?" he asked Orville one evening.

"Oh, nothing much," Orville replied. "Today one of us flew for nearly five minutes."

"Where did you go?" he was asked.

"Around the field."

"Oh, just around the field. Nothing much. Well, we'll keep in touch with you, then."

The earliest planes were little more than gliders with engines at the back. If the engines had been placed at the front as they are today the machines would not have flown. This is the Wright brothers' 1903 airplane.

It well suited the Wrights to be left alone, and they used their time well, improving the design of their Flyers, and—perhaps even more important—really learning how to fly them. In truth their first, the Kitty Hawk machine, had not been much of an airplane. The front elevator and the rear rudders had been mounted far too close to the big wing to have any reasonable moment arm, and the bird was barely under control. It would only fly at all in a series of terrifying oscillating swoops, and the capricious gust of wind that overturned and wrecked it after its one good flight—852 feet in 59 seconds—perhaps did the Wrights a favor. It had only barely enough power, for the output of its heavy homebuilt motor quickly declined from 16 to more like 12 horsepower as it warmed up. Also, the Wrights made insufficient allowance for scale and endplate effect in their wind tunnel

By 1909 the Wright brothers had placed the pilot in the accepted seated position. The reason for the change was that when prone both brothers suffered cricks in their necks from constantly making turns around the field. This is Orville Wright at the controls of a 1912 model plane.

measurements, and didn't achieve the lift over drag they had hoped for from that first powered Flyer.

The two brothers had some embarrassingly narrow squeaks in that little Dayton meadow. They got the center of gravity so far behind the center of pressure on one machine that 70 pounds of iron bars were needed on the front boom to make it fly at all. They used white pine instead of spruce for the spars, but then had to rebuild the wings in spruce when the pine spars snapped on landing. One day Orville dived vertically into the ground. The upper main spar came down across his back, but a two-foot section snapped out of it—just wide enough for it to miss him. After rebuilding, they again got the center of gravity too far aft, and after the first launch the Flyer pitched up so sharply that when it crunched down again it was actually flying *backward*. They were much bothered by incipient loss of control—happily they were at altitudes so low a spin never got a chance to develop—and fitted what they called "blinkers," fixed vertical vanes on the front elevators, to give the movable rudders something to work against. Before they did this, Wilbur one day snapped into a thorn tree, where a happy glancing blow against a bough arrested the Flyer's rotation so that he was able to recover, bounce off the meadow's rough surface, and fly back to the hangar with a small tree branch still embedded in the structure.

By 1906 they were devoting their energies to building a better engine. As they worked, the full import of just what they had achieved began to sink in. Though still not to others; at least not to the farmer cutting corn in the next field. "Well, the boys are at it again," he would remark to his hired hand, as the great white mechanical moth floated round and round. The farmer and his lad kept right on shucking corn, keeping a wary eye on the thing whenever it, or they, got near the fence. The "durned thing" was up for half an hour that time, and the farmer "thought it would never stop."

The Wrights had begun their experiments with no thought of commercial gain, but once success was achieved, it dawned on them that at the very least their invention had enormous potential for military scouting. It was to this end that they offered it to the U.S. Army Ordnance Board for $100,000. However, the Ordnance Board in those distant days of peace and isolationism didn't have that kind of money to spend and was little disposed to waste its energies and maybe embarrass itself investigating the claims of two bicycle mechanics to have invented a flying machine—something that must have seemed about as likely as a perpetual motion machine. Had not the great Hiram Maxim, inventor of the Maxim gun (something the Board could more easily appreciate), dissipated the bulk of his fortune experimenting with flying machines, reaching the conclusion that it could not be done?

And the Wrights, in their turn, would make no real open public demonstration of their machine without a signed contract guaranteeing their reward if their invention did all they claimed it could do. They were fearful of revealing their secrets to all, and then being told "no deal." Thus a fine Mexican stand-off developed. Interested emissaries of the British and French military also came to observe. From them the Wrights demanded an even more extravagant $200,000.

The stalemate and the haggling endured for two and a half years, during which period, incredibly, the Wrights, believing themselves five years ahead of all other experimenters, virtually gave up flying.

In the end everybody suddenly saw reason at the same time. The Army, deciding it had nothing but face to lose, made a firm offer of $25,000 (a quarter of the Wrights' original demand) if the Flyer would do all that was claimed for it. The Wrights virtually wrote their own contract, but regulations required that the offer be made open to all, and there were 40 entrants besides the Wrights: 39 cranks and one con man who simply hoped to underbid the Wrights, get the contract, then sell it back to them. And the American press fell on the U.S. Army with savage glee. At the same time the Wrights closed a licensed-manufacture deal with a group of French industrialists.

Thus the spring of 1908 found the two brothers preparing, finally and at last, to give the world the public demonstrations that would end all doubts and disbelief of what they had wrought. First they had to put in a few hours of practice. Then they would set off—Wilbur for France and Orville for Washington.

Wilbur was ready first, but even so, he took his time uncarting his bird and setting up its rigging and engine.

"*Le bluff continue* . . ." sagely opined a French newspaper, as the days went by. The suspense was real, and captivating. Unlike America, France was a hotbed of would-be aviators trying to fly, and they were all there to a man, waiting to see if Wilbur was really bluffing, if the Wrights were, as the press questioned, "flyers or liars."

Only one other group in the U.S. was experimenting with flying machines. Its sponsor was the Scotsman Alexander Graham Bell, inventor of the telephone, and its principal luminary was Glenn Curtiss. But in France whole bunches of experimenters were hard at it, with generally little success, despite the publication in French both of the Wrights' patents and of explicit descriptions of their Flyers. The best the French had achieved was a very wobbly twenty-minute flutter.

Wilbur didn't bother with any private test flights once he was ready, but simply announced when and where he would fly, so that a large audience was assembled. His first flight lasted less than two minutes of banks and circles, before a smooth landing, but it was enough to stun his audience with amazement. The degree of *control* Wilbur had over his Flyer astonished the French aeronautical experimenters—the way it banked and swooped and climbed at his lightest command. Said one of the audience, at last: "We are beaten! We just don't exist!" Said another: "It is a revelation . . . we are as children compared with the Wrights." Said Louis Blériot: "A new era in mechanical flight has commenced . . . it is marvelous."

Wright Type-A with Orville Wright at the controls. There was considerable competition for the prizes that would go to the first successful plane. In France, Wilbur was competing for contracts with European armies. Less than a year after this picture Orville completed his most successful demonstration flight, observed by President Taft, and was awarded $30,000 plus a $5,000 bonus for his plane by the Army.

Wilbur flew often, and all Paris came to watch. Going to watch him fly became absolutely *the thing* to do. But after that first hop, he seldom announced his demonstrations in advance, and one had to take a chance that he'd be flying the day one went to watch. One American lady of position in society arrived only to be told that Wilbur was taking a nap and would not fly that afternoon. "The *idea,*" she said, petulantly stamping her foot, "of his being asleep when *I* came all the way down here to see him in the air!"

The French were enchanted by Wilbur's modest, unaffected character. He simply wouldn't play the hero. He wouldn't even speak at a dinner where he was guest of honor. "I know of only one bird, the parrot, that talks," he explained, "and it can't fly very high."

Meanwhile, back home, near the nation's capital, brother Orville had a brief, equal success. Then one day one of the two propeller blades on his Flyer cracked along its length leaving its fellow still generating full thrust, and the resulting imbalance broke the prop shaft so the propeller thrashed about and cut the rudder boom stays, whereupon the Flyer crashed and Orville's passenger, Lieutenant Selfridge, became the first man to die in a powered airplane. Orville was in poor shape for a while, but he made a good recovery, and along with his sister Katherine went to join Wilbur in France, where the triumph continued.

The French resumed experimenting with a vigor close to frenzy. Hitherto their approach to flying had been diametrically opposite to the Wrights'. The French had sought stability above all, with big tail planes mounted out on long rear booms, and enormous dihedral angles. The Wrights had grasped as no one else the importance of three-axis control, and particularly control in roll and the need for rudder coordination. The Wrights proceeded ponderously, scientifically, with a deal of measuring in their wind tunnel, testing, and evening argument and discussion. The French proceeded by more frenzied methods: they would have an idea, build a machine incorporating it, then with a hop, a skip, and a crunch *wreck* the machine, then start on the next idea. Blériot, for example, was at one point involved with three completely different airplanes at the same time. The French saw the airplane as cousin to the boat or automobile—something that should maintain its own equilibrium, wherein you only put the tiller to go about. But the Wrights saw the airplane as more of a flying bicycle—a machine to be ridden, with its balance coming from the rider's skill at the controls. To this end they made their Flyers positively *un*stable in pitch and roll, a front elevator (the French called such an airplane a "canard" from their word for duck) and no fixed stabilizer surfaces at all. Why not? A bicycle is divergent in roll, while a tricycle isn't, but who prefers a tricycle?

The French did immediately start incorporating roll controls into their own machines. Soon huge makeshift ailerons drooped from the wing tips of every ponderous French boxkite aeroplane. Warping they were less certain about, though the monoplanists such as Blériot, Santos-Dumont, and Levavasseur tended to prefer it.

Once the essential Wright principle of three-axis control had been firmly grasped, practically any structure could be made to fly, and some bizarre designs appeared amid the general flood of new flying machines. One American experimenter resident in England produced a structure so intricately architected it was known as "The Cathedral"; Santos-Dumont evolved a monoplane so small and so noisy it was nicknamed "The Infuriated Grasshopper."

Strangely, many of the Wrights' concepts were quickly discarded as impractical. They themselves had already abandoned the idea of the pilot lying prone. ("I used to think," Orville once said, "the back of my neck would break if I endured one more turn around the field.") And they had replaced the rocking body cradle that warped the wings by a lever. Even the two brothers could not agree on what control arrangement was best, but Wilbur's Flyer, the one the French saw, had a big lever on each side of the pilot: the left one moved the elevator, forward/back for down/up in the modern sense, while the right-hand lever warped the wings if moved left/right and turned the rudders if moved forward/back. It was Blériot who pioneered the modern control system, with a bell-shaped structure mounted on the bottom of his single-control stick to which the elevator and warp wires were attached. And a foot-operated rudder.

The French could see no sense in the Wrights' ponderous launching rail and catapult, for they had smooth greensward meadows instead of the sands of Kitty Hawk and the tussocks of Huffman Prairie. Even French-built Wrights quickly gained bicycle wheels. The fuselage, like the aileron, was a French concept, which is why we still use French words for them (also *longeron, hangar, nacelle,* and *pitot*). The French soon found that instability was quite unnecessary for effective control, and moved their elevators to the back of the plane, where they have stayed ever since. The Wrights' motive for front elevators had been "to prevent nose dives." Their wind tunnel experiments had shown how the center of lifting pressures moves forward as the wing climbs, till when the wing is climbing too steeply its travel suddenly reverses and the airplane "nose-dives." The Wrights imagined that the lift of their front elevator would be reaching a peak at this moment—enough to hold the nose of the Flyer up and prevent it from diving at all. The textbook explanation of what happens with a foreplane is that it loses its ability to lift before the main wing. As to what really happened aeronautically to a Wright Flyer when it stopped flying, who knows? It cannot have been too pleasant, for even the earliest purchasers of license-built Wrights began mounting a horizontal stabilizer on the rear rudder booms; a poor solution, for the Wrights had carefully stressed their structures, and the rudder booms were not up to accepting heavy vertical stresses. The Honorable C. S. Rolls, the "Rolls" in Rolls-Royce, died thus.

Nor did the Wrights' elegant geared and counterrotating pusher propellers long persist, despite their efficiency. Slapping a propeller straight onto the end of the crankshaft and putting it out front was an easier way, and the easier way is with us still.

So rapid was development that Blériot's cross-Channel Type Eleven monoplane, a *modern* airplane in every respect, was flying very much less than a year after Louis Blériot caught his first glimpse of Wilbur Wright's

Blériot, a French pilot in a French machine, snatched the prize money for the first pilot to cross the English channel.

flying birdcage. Once the Wrights had shown their secrets, the Europeans took charge of aviation progress and kept it till Lindbergh and the *Spirit of St. Louis* came along twenty years later.

Though the Wrights met their contracts, and were duly paid, and made others too, in a sense the very thing they had feared did happen. The world came and watched them fly, and looked at their machines, and saw how it was done, and went away and did it themselves, slightly differently. Perhaps something so momentous cannot effectively be patented. Perhaps in truth there was little that was entirely original in their Flyers, beyond the constructors' profound persistence and patience. Had they never been, the birth of the airplane might have been but little delayed, for a circular mile had been flown in France even before Wilbur had made his celebrated demonstration. And both the French and Glenn Curtiss had already stumbled on the idea of the aileron. Orville promptly fired off a letter to Curtiss charging rather speciously that Curtiss's ailerons infringed the Wrights' warping patent. The truth is, just about anyone who built a workable airplane of any kind was bound to infringe the Wright patent, whether they knew it or not. Curtiss and the Wrights got into a patent battle that was particularly venomous and protracted, and did no one a wit of good except the lawyers.

How did they fly, those early aeroplanes? Only just, and not too well. And astonishingly slowly, usually in the range of from 21 to 35 mph. A good sprinter can hit 21 mph, which means that in any breeze (and many of the pioneers, notably the Wrights, were not afraid of winds), their groundspeed was about that of a pedal cyclist. Early aeroplanes were slow even for their time; Glenn Curtiss, for instance, had set a motorcycle speed record of 136.3 mph in 1907, before he ever took up aviation. And no mere flying machine went faster until 1917.

As for those original unstable Wright biplanes—there may be some old gentlemen still about who flew a front-elevator Wright, but it's doubtful. Lord Brabazon was an English pioneer who bought one of the first French boxkite-type aeroplanes, and he said it was "like sitting on a jelly in a strong

OPPOSITE, TOP. Another Blériot—in the process of restoration, in case you didn't spot that E-type Jaguar behind the fence.

OPPOSITE, CENTER. Glen Curtis was the other American front runner in early plane design. He got involved in a serious law suit with the Wright brothers over who was the inventor of the aileron. He was the first builder to use a nosewheel and his earlier designs also featured a foreplane as did the Wright brothers' aircraft. This is a 1912 Curtis.

OPPOSITE, BOTTOM. A 1910 Blackburn. The trellis of wirework used to provide rigidity also created considerable drag in early planes. Note the skids mounted inside the wheels.

A.V.ROE & Co
7

SWEETHEART
1912 CURTISS BIPLANE

The Bristol Boxkite of 1910.

breeze." The other thing he always remembered with passion was the appalling unreliability of engines in those days. The thirty-seven minutes that Blériot's three-cylinder Anzani held together while he crossed the English Channel was just about the longest running time for one of those Anzani engines. The Wright engines were better than most in this respect, and the French built them under license. The first really reasonable engine was the Gnome rotary, which might run for eight or twelve hours before requiring overhaul.

A boxkite—a Bristol Boxkite, front elevator and all, was one of the types built in replica for the movie *Those Magnificent Men in Their Flying Machines. Exact* replica, except that even the brave men that built it blanched at the thought of including an original engine. It got a modern Rolls-Continental 90 hp engine, which promptly began duplicating the antics of its forebears, showing cylinder temperatures that made strong men shudder and quitting cold (or rather, hot) for no obvious mechanical reason. Overheating of the air-cooled engine due to the pusher installation was the cause, just as it often was in 1910, and it was cured by an equally ancient fix: enlarging the fuel intake to make the engine run constantly too rich.

With the Bristol Boxkite, the movie men discovered another of the snares that faced the would-be 1910 aviator: the cruel dishonesty of 1910 brochures. "The control system of the Bristol biplane is simplicity itself," ran the deceiving puff. "It can be mastered in a few minutes, and it requires so little physical effort that a child can maneuver one of these machines in flight. There is, indeed, only one movement that calls for the slightest physical exertion, and that is the movement of the control lever away from the body to the right; but this is felt only when there is a strong gust of wind exerting its force to tilt the machine up on one side."

Here's Neil Williams, test pilot and aerobatics champion, on how the boxkite really is: "That thing is a *devil* to fly. It is unstable in pitch due to the perverse effects of the foreplane. If you deflect it too far it tends to go all the way and it takes tremendous force to get it back. At any other speed than exactly 31 mph you lose altitude. And the lateral forces are *very* heavy."

So much for these early aeroplanes, "on the ragged edge" at all times so that all those early superstitions about "air pockets" and days when there was "no lift in the air" become quite understandable. Says Williams: "You can't really decide beforehand where you're going to go. You just have to accept that you'll change your direction to suit the vagaries of the wind. You have to 'play it off the cuff' all the time.

"Those stories in the old days of 'being forced down' are absolutely true. Almost any control movement or change of incidence will create enough extra drag to bring you down. At all times you have absolutely nothing to spare."

One of the things about Wilbur Wright's public flight that so astonished the French aviators was that he *banked* to make a turn. They didn't; for one thing, the loss of lift would have brought them down. And at speeds that low, you hardly *need* to bank to make a shallow turn. They sought at all times to keep the wings level; for if a wing did go down, their primitive ailerons or warping might not be up to getting it up again.

And the almost inevitable engine failure was almost inevitably followed by a crunch. As Neil Williams explains: "When the engine stops, the aeroplane stops very soon afterwards." The machinery is very light, you see, and the drag is really enormous. "The angle of glide in the Boxkite is an incredibly steep *35 degrees!* And it's very difficult to do a glide landing in any of these things, because if you misjudge it, your speed is gone, clonk."

This problem persisted into the First World War, as witness this verse from one of those songs they sang in the Royal Flying Corps:

> He died in an hour and a quarter,
> And this is the reason he died:
> He'd forgotten the fact that "iota"
> Is the minimum angle of glide.

Shutting off the engine and gliding down was called "volplaning" in the early days, and it was an airshow trick, attempted only by the most brave and reckless pilots. Of which there were plenty, spurred on not only by an ordinary human spirit of adventure, but also the large sums of cash offered by airshow promoters and newspaper proprietors and other plutocrats in that age of great personal wealth. Blériot got $5,000 from the London *Daily Mail* for crossing the Channel; while Louis Paulhan got ten times that for the first overland flight from London to Manchester, a far less hazardous undertaking. Gate receipts at a popular aerodrome could easily exceed

An Avro Triplane. Despite its three wings this Avro prefers rather shallow banks. Its rudder is its best control.

$100,000 in a year. So rabid was the public's appetite for aviation that they might tear the place apart if an aviator did not fly when promised.

The finest collection today of these early aeroplanes is the Shuttleworth Trust's, kept at Old Warden in Bedfordshire in the English Midlands. Once a year, on the last Sunday in September, they have a flying display (called "Edwardian" after the English king of those times) devoted to these very early machines. Here the Boxkite is slowly coaxed in gentle circles up to its ceiling of maybe 300 feet. Here the only remaining Anzani-Blériot still flies if "flying" is the right word for those feeble hops.

The Shuttleworth's Blériot is an original, as is their 1912 Blackburn, a kind of Blériot derivative, but powered by a Gnome rotary (as were all the later Blériots). The Gnome, for all its virtues, brings its own problems, as Neil Williams explains: "You have five engine controls: throttle, fuel control, and air levers, magneto switch, and an off/on cutout or 'blip' switch. The throttle is not used, except to get the engine set up and running before takeoff. Once running smoothly, it is left at full throttle at all times. Power is controlled by the off/on switch.

"The trick," says Neil, "is to err on the side of lean mixtures at all times, so if the engine does cut, you can enrich the fuel mixture to get it running again. If the engine quits from too rich a mixture, the plugs are fouled and that's it."

Blackburn, the builder of this monoplane, went on to found his own manufacturing company, now part of the Hawker Siddeley combine. A. V. Roe was another English pioneer who did the same, and the Shuttleworth has a replica of one of his triplanes, which flies quite strongly. "To fly the Avro properly," says Neil, "you have to yaw the aeroplane gently from side to side until you feel warm air from the engine on your body. And some days it just won't fly at all, however hard you try. No life in the air—or something." Although a triplane, this Avro does not like being banked: anything over 20 degrees gives the pilot a profound feeling that it is going to run away from him.

The rudder was perhaps the best control on these early aeroplanes, and even it seems peculiar to modern pilots, being very light, with almost no feel, and yet not terribly effective. This kind of rudder persisted for years: most First World War fighters were like this.

Perhaps the predominant feeling these early aeroplanes instilled in their pilots was insecurity. There you were, perched naked in the airflow, with no wind-screen and often no shelter at all, no safety harness, not much control, and not enough power, and such thrust as you did have likely to vanish at any moment. It is no wonder most early flying was done below 50 feet. Those pioneers were brave men above all, for crashes were frequent. After Lieutenant Selfridge's death in a powered airplane in 1908, four more died in 1909 and 33 in 1910.

Courage, first; then, second, money. A new Wright would cost $5,000. And remember, as for learning to fly, there were no instructors. Lord Brabazon's repair bills for his Voisin Boxkite averaged $1,500 a month!

Thus, the early aeroplane: clumsy, expensive, and dangerous, but it flew. Perhaps the real surprise is that it took so long, for as the Wrights themselves once wrote: "The claim . . . often made . . . that the lack of sufficiently light motors alone prohibited man from the empire of the air was quite unfounded. At the speeds which birds usually employ, a well-designed flyer can in actual practice sustain a gross weight of 30 kilograms for each horsepower of the motor, which gives ample margin for such motors as might easily have been built 50 years (earlier)."

Maybe the scientists, the Lord Kelvins, with their prognostications of manned flight's impossibility, are to blame. Perhaps we should pay more attention to the poets, for Lord Byron had written in 1822: "I suppose that we shall soon travel by air-vessels: make air- instead of sea-voyages; and at length find our way to the moon, in spite of the want of atmosphere."

What are the Byrons of today prophesying?

CHAPTER 3

Learning to Fly

NOT the least of the hazards faced by the pioneer pilots was teaching themselves to fly. It was not uncommon for the neophyte to have to make major repairs on his machine and himself after each flight. Today pilot training, if not an exact science, is nonetheless infinitely safer. It involves a series of carefully planned flights with an instructor during which time the fundamentals of maneuvering the aircraft are explained and demonstrated by the instructor and then practiced by the student. Gradually what seemed awkward and discomfiting becomes smooth and familiar. What appeared at first to be casual and imprecise turns into a demanding and exacting program. Before you know it, simple challenges are simply being met and small rewards are becoming major satisfactions.

Perhaps you've wondered what it would be like to take flying lessons. Let us say you want to take a few lessons to see whether or not flying really is for you. If so, the next step is to check into the flight schools in your area.

At first, this may seem a bewildering task. Flying schools exist in great variety, ranging from full-time residence schools to one-airplane operations with a part-time instructor. They defy classification as to excellence. Some part-time instructors with only one airplane are every bit as good as the biggest residence schools. Most schools hold certificates from the Federal Aviation Administration and call themselves "FAA Approved"; but the certificate is not the aeronautical equivalent of the Good Housekeeping Seal, and there is still a wide range of quality.

There is a curious philosophy characteristic of flying schools: it is nearly impossible to find one where students fail. The basic doctrine is that anybody can fly who can drive a car; therefore, the only difference among students is that some learn faster than others. Neither military nor airline flying schools subscribe to this idea, of course. If they did, and if the facts supported them, there would be an even greater portion of taxpayers' money spent on teaching an inept student to fly the F-4 and little need to pay airline captains up to $60,000 a year.

Flying schools are businesses and must be profitable to survive. This being the case, it follows that what you already know about businesses in general can be applied to flight schools. By and large, the clean, well-managed school with a cheerful, competent staff will succeed, where a sloppy one with careless employees will fail. In much the same way, you know what good equipment looks like, even if this is the first time you have ever seen an airplane up close. The plane should be well-maintained on the outside, and the engine compartment should look clean enough to dine in. (An excellent mechanic is seldom found in a sloppy shop.) And, just as piano teachers worth their salt don't work with untuned pianos, the best flight instructors are not found working with badly maintained airplanes.

The age of the airplane is less important. There is nothing wrong with an older model, if it shines—but there is some question about a new airplane with a streak of oil down its belly. You can do a lot of preliminary screening of this kind just by looking and without letting anybody know that you are a prospective flight student.

Once the preliminary selection is out of the way, it's time to talk to the owner, manager, or head of the flight department, and ask some questions. Are the school's instructors full- or part-time, or a mixture? (There are some excellent flight instructors who work only part-time, but problems arise if you want to fly on days when they are not available.) What is the school's policy about assignment of flight instructors? Can a student count on starting and finishing with the same one? If not, why not? Be suspicious of attempts to explain the so-called advantages for a student to fly with several instructors.

Also, what happens if the student feels that he is not working well with his assigned instructor? Will a graceful change be made at the student's request? How about schedules? Are they well-managed and carefully kept? Is the student charged for a missed appointment? And what if the student shows up and the instructor does not? Is the student allowed any credit for his expense and disappointment?

Ask about ground school and look over the classroom. Is the schedule convenient? Is there a ground school instructor on the staff? He need not be a specialist, as flight instructors can also hold ground instructor certificates. A few schools insist that students have passed their FAA written exams by the time they have logged 20 or 25 hours of flight time. This is a very sound idea, since you cannot take your flight test without proof of having passed the written exam. Many schools are vague on this. Watch out for them.

The FAA private pilot written examination consists of about 75 multiple-choice questions. They are fairly technical, covering principles of flight, rules of safety, navigation and radio procedures, federal air regulations, and emergencies. The information necessary to pass the test is available in a number of books and home-study courses which may be bought at most flight schools. Most good flight schools also offer ground school classes designed to cover the same material.

A ground instructor explains some of the uses of the computer to a class—a circular slide rule pilots use to solve math problems the easy way, in and out of the cockpit.

This is a good point to begin thinking about costs. Rates for similar airplanes, without instructor, tend to be much the same in any area. These are set by a combination of operations costs and competition, both of which are relatively independent of the age of the airplanes. But there is often a sharp difference when an instructor is added because of the different rates the instructors are paid. Many young pilots are willing to accept low rates of flight pay in order to build up their experience, which will make them more attractive to the airlines. There is nothing wrong with this, except perhaps from the student's viewpoint. It is a good general rule that you will be better off with the higher-paid, or salaried, instructors—both as to the quality of instruction and the total cost to qualify for a license. If this seems curious at first, consider the fact that the instructors at the lowest rates are usually not paid at all when a student is flying solo. It is a rare instructor who can avoid the resulting problem completely, and it is generally true that you will get more dual instruction under these conditions than you would were you receiving training from a salaried instructor.

When you have picked a school and been assigned to an instructor, ask to see his FAA license and medical certificate. If he is the kind of man you want to be flying with, he'll produce them with no hesitation. If he refuses and says that he is not required to show them to anybody but an FAA inspector, he's right. So are you, if you decide not to fly with him.

The next thing you should talk about in detail is the method of payment. Some schools would like you to pay for the entire course in advance. Don't! If for any reason you do not complete the training, you may find it difficult to get a full refund. In the beginning, up to first solo, it is best to pay as you go, one lesson at a time. After solo, if you decide to continue, purchase of "block time" is best. Most schools allow a discount for prepayment of $100 or $200 worth of flight time. You fly at the discounted rate until your deposit is used up, then make another payment.

Some schools advertise that flight training can be bought on time, but few actually carry their own accounts. The student is usually sent to a bank, where a personal loan is negotiated. In general, if you prefer to spread the cost over a year, you are better off making your own loan arrangements. All of this may sound grim—an unattractive descent from the sublime dream of learning to fly to the depths of grubby bargaining. But it can save you trouble, and quite likely money, too. If you approach it as part of the game, your anticipation will survive, if not increase. Moreover, you'll become a better pilot—and that's really what you want most. The difference between the best instruction and the poorest will not exceed a couple of hundred dollars. Spread over a lifetime, that's not much.

The following is an outline of what you can expect during the first several lessons.

LESSON 1

YOUR FIRST FLIGHT should be a pleasant introduction to the airplane and the local flying area. You'll experience the sensations of flight and learn how to use the controls and some of the instruments. Your instructor may take you on a short cross-country hop to a nearby airport and back as part of your get-acquainted ride. The specific areas you'll cover will include:

- Getting to know the airplane
- Outside walk-around
- Inside the cockpit—instruments and controls
- Starting the engine
- Using the radio
- Taxiing
- Pretakeoff check
- Takeoff and climbout
- Using the controls, and their effects
- Straight-and-level flight
- Turns
- Flight area familiarization
- Landing and parking

Postflight discussion
Preview of next lesson

Getting to Know the Airplane

Before you climb in for that first ride, the instructor will take you on a walk around the airplane, pointing out the control surfaces and how they work. He'll demonstrate how the ailerons move up and down, how they "disturb" the airflow to simultaneously lift one wing and lower the other. He'll show you how the elevators (or stabilator) at the tail move up and down against the airflow to raise or lower the nose in flight, and how the rudder swings left and right to move the tail from side to side.

The walk around. Preflight inspection is a must, your last chance to check the exterior of the plane before you get airborne. An instructor shows a student pilot how to check flaps, the under-surface of the wing, the landing gear and brake lines for indications of damage. Telltale oil leaks from the left engine would lead to fuller inspection before flight was attempted. Note that the aircraft is still tied down.

When you are seated in the airplane and your seat belt is fastened, your instructor will explain at least some of the instruments and controls in the cockpit. For the first flight, four instruments are most important: the airspeed indicator, which tells how fast you're flying; the altimeter, which tells how high you are; the compass (or directional gyro), which indicates the direction you're heading; and the tachometer, which measures engine speed in rpm (revolutions per minute).

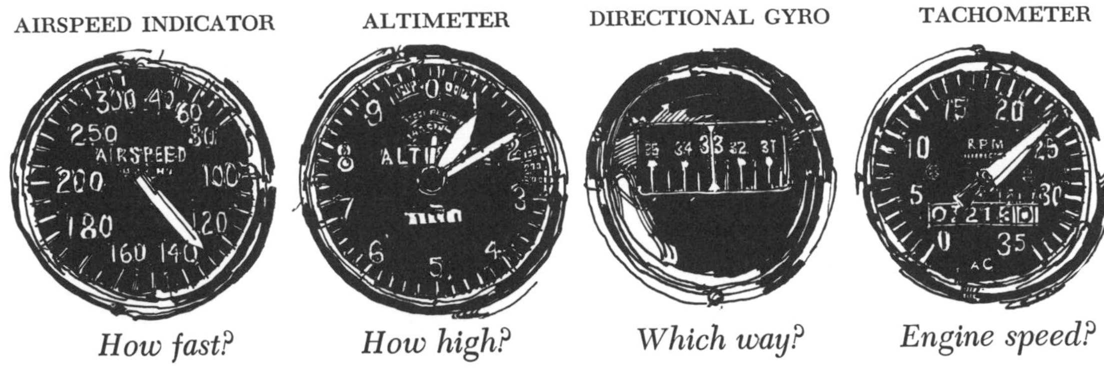

How fast? *How high?* *Which way?* *Engine speed?*

In addition, you'll be concerned with three main controls on the first flight: the control wheel (or stick, on some airplanes), the rudder pedals, and the throttle. The wheel operates both the elevators and ailerons. Move it forward and back, and notice how the elevators move up and down at the tail of the aircraft. Pull the wheel back in flight and the nose will rise, or appear to move toward you. Push it forward and the nose will drop away from you. By turning the wheel to the left and right like the steering wheel of a car, you operate the ailerons. Turn it left in flight and the left wing will drop; turn it right and the right wing will drop.

Remember that in flight, control movements produce the same effect in relation to the pilot no matter what the position or attitude of the airplane with relation to the ground.

Push the left rudder pedal with your left foot. When you're in flight, this will swing the nose of the airplane to the left. Push the right rudder pedal and the nose will swing to the right. Although the flight controls will feel slack and lifeless while the airplane is sitting on the ground, in flight they will assume a "live pressure" or resistance (from the movement of the air past them) and will tend to remain in a neutral, "centered" position. The airplane is controlled by putting light pressure on the wheel and rudders, so think of *exerting a force* on the controls rather than *moving* them.

The throttle is like the accelerator on a car, but you operate it by hand. It works like a push-pull rod, and projects from the instrument panel so you can reach it with your right hand. Push it in, and you open the throttle and move the airplane forward. Pull it out, and you reduce throttle and slow the airplane down.

Starting the Engine

Most aircraft engines have a self-starter like an automobile, but there are a few extra things to fuss with in a plane. Before you turn the key in the "ignition" or magneto to engage the starter, you must (1) turn the fuel tank selector knob "on," (2) push the fuel mixture knob in, and (3) turn on a master switch that opens the airplane's electrical circuits. Then push the throttle in about a quarter of an inch, open the window, and shout "Clear" in a loud voice to warn bystanders away from the propeller.

To work the starter, either turn the key all the way to the right or (in some airplanes) push a separate starter button, and this will crank the engine. When the engine has "caught," adjust the throttle to a comfortable idling speed (usually about 1,000 rpm on the tachometer). Also, check immediately to see that the oil pressure needle is rising. If it hasn't risen within 30 seconds, you should shut down the engine to prevent damage.

Using the Radio

The instructor will set the two-way aircraft radio to the correct frequency to talk with ground control, a man in the control tower who guides traffic on the airport ramps and taxiways. Either you or the instructor will call to ask for permission to taxi to the runway for takeoff.

All the pilot has to say is *who* he is, *where* he is, and *what* he wants to do. Identify yourself by the aircraft call numbers (printed on the side of the plane and also on the instrument panel), give your location in the airport, and say you want to taxi to the runway in use. The important thing to remember about aircraft radio communication is that it be clear and brief. Though you will pick up certain common terms, don't be afraid in the meantime to get the message across in your own words. Your instructor's first demonstration call to ground control will probably sound something like this: "Bridgeport Ground, Cessna 1153 X-ray at Hangar D, taxi, takeoff." However, in *your* first attempt, you can just as well say: "Hello, Ground Control, I'm Cessna number 1153 X and I'm in front of Hangar D. May I please taxi for takeoff?"

Ground control will reply in what will probably sound like a torrent of unintelligible information. But broken down, it should tell you several important things: the number of the runway in use, how to taxi there, the direction and strength of the surface winds, and the altimeter setting. He might say something like: "Cessna 1153 X-ray cleared to runway three-five, wind north at 12 (knots), altimeter 29.96, taxi via the north-south taxiway."

You can acknowledge by just repeating an abbreviated version of your call numbers: "53 X-ray."

Taxiing

On the ground you steer the airplane with the rudder pedals. At first you'll probably have a tendency to try to steer with the control wheel, as you would a car, but you'll soon discover this has no effect. Push left rudder to steer left, right rudder to steer right. Simply *rest* your feet on the rudder pedals. You'll find it comfortable to rest your heels on the floor and place the balls of your feet on the rudder pedals. When you push one pedal in, the other will move out, toward you. Don't push both pedals together because the pedal you want won't move in unless the other is allowed to move out.

To operate the brakes, press down with your toes on the top portion of the rudder pedals. Each pedal operates the wheel brake only on its side of the airplane (left pedal, left wheel brake), so press both down simultaneously for an even stop without swerving.

To get the aircraft away from its parking spot, slowly push in the throttle until the plane begins moving, then ease back the throttle to about 1,000 rpm on the tachometer so the propeller won't be pulling the airplane too rapidly. Before leaving the parking area, gently try the brakes. Then continue taxiing, but no more rapidly than a fast walk.

Don't use so much throttle that you must constantly "ride" the brakes. Taxi around corners slowly to avoid wear on the tires. Unless there are strong surface winds, you can hold the control wheel in a neutral position while taxiing. (Later your instructor will explain how to position ailerons and elevators when taxiing in high winds.) As you taxi, listen for further instructions from ground control, which will keep you posted on other taxiing aircraft that may cross your path.

Pretakeoff Check

The instructor will demonstrate this important procedure. The purpose of the pretakeoff check is to make sure the airplane is functioning perfectly: to see that the engine and its controls are operating correctly, that the flight controls are free and moving correctly, that the elevator trim is properly set, that a well-filled fuel tank has been switched on to feed the engine, and that all the instruments are working. You should always use a written checklist to avoid forgetting anything.

When ready for takeoff, the instructor will switch the radio frequency, call the control tower, and announce: "Bridgeport Tower, Cessna 53 X-ray ready for takeoff." The tower will reply by saying you are clear to take off or he may ask you to hold your position while another aircraft lands or he may tell you to taxi out into the center of the runway but await his permission to start rolling for takeoff.

Takeoff and Climbout

Either your instructor will make the first takeoff or he'll "talk you through" it. After getting permission from the tower, taxi to the center of the runway and push in the throttle smoothly, but fairly rapidly—all the way. Steer straight down the runway with the rudder pedals, just as you did while taxiing. Take care to keep your toes off the brakes. Hold the control wheel firmly but gently in a level, neutral position until you feel the air pressure exerting a mild effect. Then slowly pull back on the wheel until the nose of the aircraft has risen slightly, so it looks as though it's climbing up a gentle hill. (Your instructor will indicate how much.) Then, when the aircraft has built up enough speed to fly, it will lift off the runway of its own accord.

Cleared for takeoff, the trainer accelerates down the runway. In a moment the pilot will ease in back pressure on the wheel and she'll be flying.

Don't force the airplane into the air by pulling back too hard on the wheel at this point. If you do this before the craft has sufficient flying speed, it may settle back to the runway again or the nose may rise at too steep an angle after leaving the ground. You should have to hold a slight amount of back pressure, however, to keep the right climb attitude, and you should not relax this force before the airplane is off and flying, or once again the airplane may settle back to the runway. In most lightplanes, you will keep full power throughout the climb and will try to hold a specific airspeed that gives the best rate of climb for your type of aircraft. *Remember:* Always hold the controls lightly with the fingers. Don't grab or squeeze them. Light finger pressure is enough to perform practically all flight maneuvers. If the controls are in the right position, the plane will respond easily.

Using the Controls

The instructor will probably introduce the controls to you one at a time once you are leveled out from the climb, and no doubt he'll let you experiment with them to get the feel of the airplane. In teaching you to handle the controls, he'll use several basic terms: *attitude, pitch, bank* or *roll,* and *yaw:*

Turn and bank indicator during level flight.

During properly coordinated turn to left (ball centered).

During uncoordinated left turn (ball uncentered due to right yaw). To remedy "step on the ball."

Attitude describes the position of the airplane's nose and wings in relation to the horizon.

Pitch is the angle of the nose of the airplane with relation to the horizon.

Bank or *roll* (they are synonymous) describes the angle or tilt of the wings against the horizon.

Yaw is the left or right movement of the tail or nose.

First of all, it helps to know that the airplane can fly quite well all by itself in smooth air, hands off, and the instructor may demonstrate this. But how can you tell if you're actually flying straight and level (holding a given heading and altitude)? The most obvious way is by looking outside to check the relation of the wings and nose against the horizon. The wings are level (and therefore you aren't turning) if both tips have the same position with respect to the horizon. In level flight at a particular airspeed, the horizon will cross the windshield at a certain point. Make a mental note of this position with respect to the windshield. Then if the nose drops below that position and the horizon seems to rise, the aircraft probably is descending.

Straight-and-level flight even in smooth air is a series of gentle recoveries from slight turns, dives, and climbs. To make a turn, roll the airplane into a bank by turning the wheel (which operates the ailerons). Turn it left (or counterclockwise) to roll left, and right (or clockwise) to roll right. At the same time you must do two other things: (1) pull back gently on the wheel and (2) squeeze in some rudder in the direction of the turn (left turn, left rudder). When you have the desired amount of bank (your instructor will indicate this), you may relax both aileron and rudder pressure and return the control wheel to a neutral position. The airplane now will remain in the turn by itself. However, you must continue to hold a little back pressure on the wheel (and elevators) to keep from losing altitude.

Attitude—the word used to describe the relation of the horizon to the airplane's nose and wings—is important for level flight. At a particular air speed the horizon apparently crosses the windshield at a certain point in level flight, as shown here. Recognizing this point quickly becomes second nature with practice.

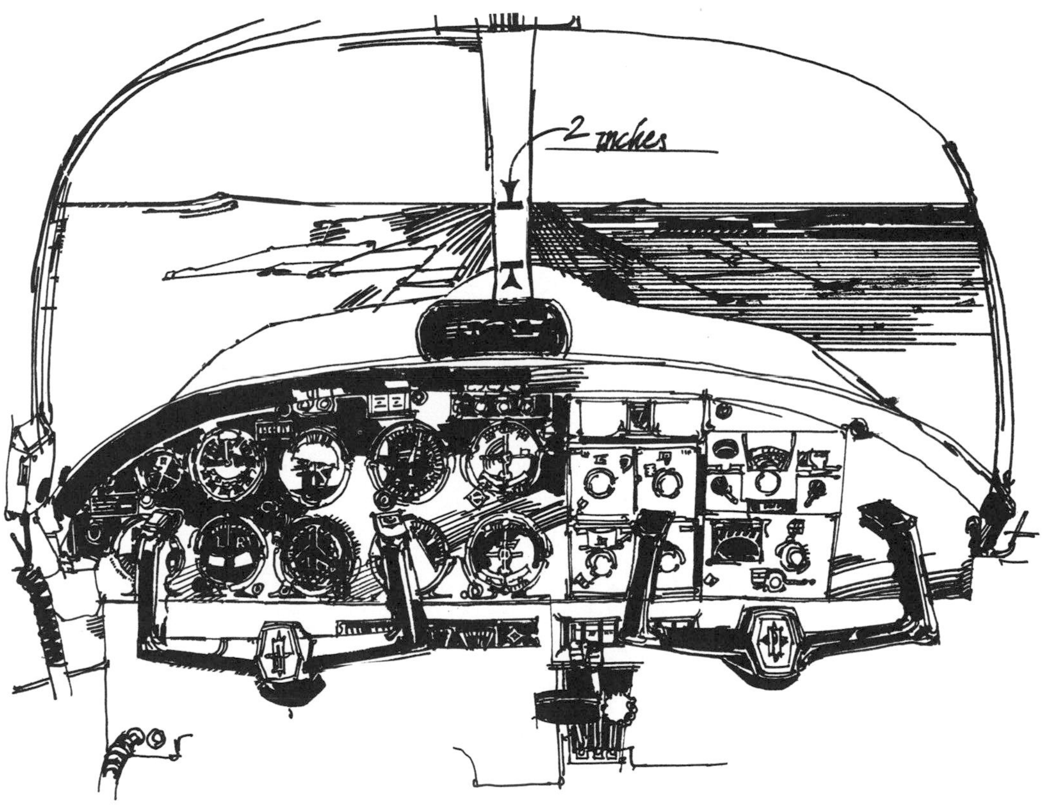

Rudder in a turn is used to compensate for the extra drag caused by the "down" aileron on the rising wing. This lopsided drag causes the airplane to yaw away from the turn. Using rudder pressure in the same direction as the turn (left bank, left rudder) counteracts this. Therefore, as soon as you've stopped using aileron pressure, you stop using rudder pressure.

Understand that turns are not made with the rudder. Turns are made by tipping or canting the direction of the lift of the wings from the vertical to one side or the other, causing this "lift" to pull the airplane in that direction. It is because of the resulting decrease in vertical lift (counteracting gravity) that you must pull back on the wheel or stick during the turn to keep from losing altitude. When you return the wings to level flight, you ease off on the back pressure because the vertical lift is fully restored.

While learning turns, you will probably have an inclination to lean your body away from the direction of a turn in an attempt to keep upright with respect to the ground. Don't—ride with the airplane because you are perfectly balanced by centrifugal force.

Flight Area Familiarization

On your first flight the instructor will point out terrain features and landmarks that will help you orient yourself with respect to the airport.

Landing and Parking

To keep an orderly flow of traffic around each airport, a standard pattern over the ground is flown by all aircraft, using the landing runway as a reference. This standard "traffic pattern" is rectangular, and is flown at a fixed altitude above the ground.

On your return to the airport, the instructor will demonstrate how to enter the pattern by means of a 45-degree path onto the "downwind leg," then onto "base" and "final aproach" for landing.

At the end of the ride, he will give you a postflight critique and tell you which maneuvers you can expect to practice on your next flight.

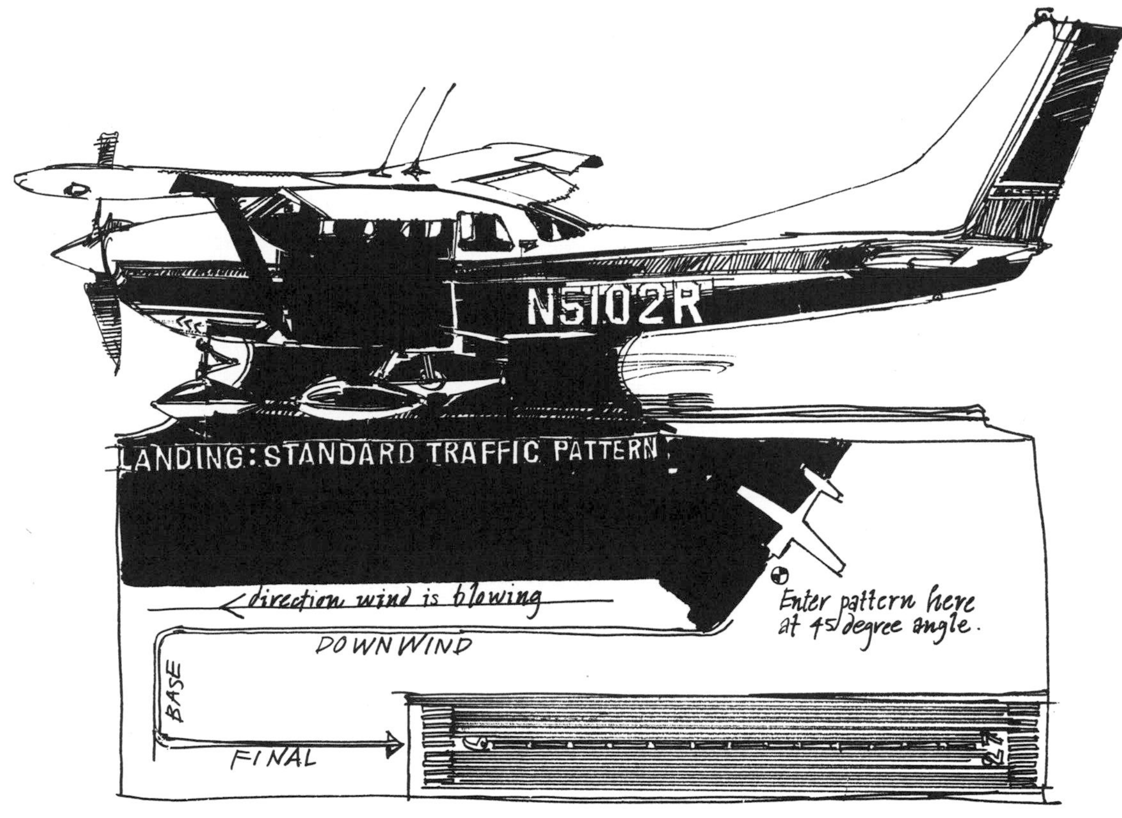

LESSON 2

DURING THE SECOND lesson, the student pilot will begin to become familiar with the four basic flight maneuvers: straight-and-level flight, turns, climbs, and descents. He should learn to perform these by himself with only verbal help from the instructor. He'll also start taking responsibility for doing a thorough preflight inspection—an act he'll be carrying out in one form or another every single time that he flies.

Preflight Inspection

Before each flight, there is one elemental question you'll want answered: "Is the airplane in perfect flying condition?" The only way to be sure is by carefully looking it over yourself, maintaining a healthy distrust for the assumption that "somebody else has already done it." Use a checklist, so you won't forget anything. You can find one in the airplane flight manual provided by the manufacturer. Next, lower the flaps on high-wing aircraft for a better look at the flap mechanism on your walk-around. Then turn the master switch off and make sure the magneto switch is also off, so the engine won't accidentally start if you move the propeller. (It's a good idea to take out the key and put it on the seat.)

The walk-around inspection should include at least the following basic checks:

- *Propeller*—see that it has no nicks. (They lead to stresses, cracks, and possible breaks. A mechanic can quickly file them smooth.)
- *Carburetor air filter*—clean, not jammed with bugs or weeds.
- *Engine cowling air intake*—no bird's nests.
- *Nose gear*—tire in good condition. Strut extended two or three finger-widths.
- *Engine compartment*—open the inspection panel and look for excess oil, loose wires, fuel leaks. Check oil quantity with the dipstick (like an automobile's).
- *Fuel strainer*—drain for at least five seconds. The purpose is to eliminate sediment and water that may have accumulated in the strainer.
- *Landing gear*—tires in good condition, no leaking hydraulic fluid (dark red) from the brake lines. Wheel chocks removed for taxiing.
- *Wing tank drains*—drain for at least five seconds from the fuel tank drains under the wings. If a plastic cup with a metal probe is available (look in the glove compartment), drain at least three cups to check for sediment or water. Water from condensation inside the fuel tank will form a separate, obvious layer at the bottom.
- *Wings*—no dents on the leading (front) edge, ailerons securely hinged and moving freely, flap mechanism okay, inspection plates properly fastened. Tiedown ropes released.

- *Fuselage*—no damage.
- *Tail*—rudder and elevator moving freely, securely hinged, rudder cables in good condition. Tiedown rope untied.
- *Pitot tube*—make sure it's not obstructed. This is the air intake probe that provides air pressure to the speed indicator.
- *Static air source*—this is a little hole in the fuselage that supplies air to the altimeter and vertical speed indicator. Make sure it's not obstructed.
- *Fuel tank vent*—usually a tube behind the wing strut, under the wing, or a small bleed hole in the gas cap. Make sure it's not obstructed, or the fuel tanks won't feed properly to the engine.
- *Fuel caps*—check the amount of fuel in the tanks as a double check of the fuel gauge in the cockpit, and make sure the caps are secure. (Line boys occasionally forget to replace them, and fuel could siphon out during flight.) On high-wing aircraft, you may have to get a small ladder to make the check. Do it. It's worth the trouble.

Starting the Engine

Now that you know *how* to start the engine, use care *where* you start it. First, make sure the prop blast isn't aimed at nearby aircraft, spectators, or the open door of the flight shack. Second, make sure the surface under the prop is firm enough so that pebbles or cinders won't be hurled back into the tail or fuselage of the aircraft or damage the prop itself. Remember to use a checklist for the start procedure, just as you did for the walk-around inspection.

Using the Radio

Same as lesson 1.

Taxiing

Same as lesson 1.

Pretakeoff

Same as lesson 1. Be sure to use a checklist.

Takeoff and Climbout

You'll notice on the takeoff roll that the airplane may tend to veer slightly to the left. Correct this by squeezing the right rudder. Try to keep the aircraft right on the centerline all the way down the runway. The tendency to yaw to the left will increase as you lift off the runway and climb out, so hold a bit of right rudder pressure throughout the climb. This corrects for what is called "torque" or "P factor."

How can you tell if you're holding the correct amount of rudder after takeoff? First of all, look straight out the windshield. If you are *not* squeezing in enough right rudder pressure, the nose of the airplane will slowly turn to the left. (Later on you'll develop a seat-of-the-pants feel for this veering, or yawing.)

Besides holding the wings level and the nose straight during climbout, try to keep a constant airspeed. (Your instructor will tell you what this speed should be.) *Reason:* There is just one airspeed that will give the *best rate of climb* for a particular type of aircraft. Rate of climb is the speed at which the aircraft is gaining altitude, measured in feet per minute.

How can you hold a constant airspeed? By gently using forward or back pressure on the control wheel when the airspeed varies from the desired figure. Pull back on the wheel, and the airplane will want to climb more steeply. At the same time it will slow down, just as a car going up a grade will. Naturally, the reverse happens when you push forward on the wheel: the aircraft starts moving "downhill" and begins to speed up.

Remember, use forward or back pressure gently, a little at a time. Push or pull too abruptly and you will find yourself chasing the airspeed up and down. Later on your airspeed corrections will become automatic.

If you find that you have to hold an uncomfortable amount of forward or back pressure on the control wheel to keep a constant airspeed, the airplane is "out of trim." This is corrected by means of a "trim wheel," which allows you to position the elevators to compensate for fore and aft pressures. The trim wheel is usually located on a pedestal under the instrument panel, by your right hand. Rotate it forward, and the elevators will force the nose down; turn it backward, and the nose will rise. Get in the habit of always "trimming out" control pressures; it'll take a lot of the work out of flying. And remember, every time you change airspeed, the elevator pressures will change correspondingly, calling for a change in trim.

In the climb, as in all maneuvers, you will learn to depend (sometimes unconsciously) on a variety of cues to tell you when the aircraft's attitude or airspeed are changing. You may rely on all of your senses—your eyes, ears, sense of touch, and kinesthesia (body feel)—to help you fly. For example, when you begin a climb, your airspeed will decrease. The horizon will drop lower in the windshield "frame of reference," perhaps even falling below the engine cowling. As the airspeed drops, the sound of the air moving by the aircraft will diminish, and the tone of the engine will change as the power plant slows down and begins to "labor." Furthermore, the nose will feel heavier because of the drop in airspeed, requiring more back pressure, or back trim, on the wheel.

The aircraft instruments will provide another set of cues. There are many who believe a student should learn to use these right from the start, correlating each instrument with the maneuver it defines. But other instructors prefer to introduce the instruments gradually, teaching the student to rely first on the more obvious sensory cues mentioned above.

This reluctance is due in part to the beginning pilot's tendency to develop a fixation about instruments. He will stare constantly at one while trying to correct a flight condition such as airspeed or rate of climb or angle of bank. But all the while, he will remain oblivious to the other changes about him. For example, the student learning to climb at a constant airspeed will tend to stare at the airspeed indicator, forgetting about his bank angle and other air traffic.

He must learn to use the airspeed indicator as part of his ever-moving cross-check—meanwhile glancing both in and out of the cockpit, looking outside at the position of the horizon with respect to the nose and the wing tips, searching for other air traffic, and keeping a watch on his position over the ground, so he will not become disoriented and lost.

Climbing Turns

As you roll into a turn, use rudder with ailerons to prevent adverse yaw. A good turn is called a "coordinated turn" because you are coordinating rudder with ailerons in just the right amount. During climbing turns, however, since you are already holding some right rudder pressure to counteract torque, you may find that in a left turn all you have to do is ease off on the right rudder, rather than add left rudder.

Remember, once you have rolled into a bank, you can tell if you are maintaining the correct bank angle by observing the angle of the horizon across the windshield.

The instructor will have you fly a certain path or pattern over the ground immediately after you take off. The pattern usually is as follows: At 500 feet above the ground (though at some airports the instructor may prefer another altitude), make a 90-degree left turn, level the wings, and then make a 45-degree turn to the right. This heads you away from the airport and gives you a chance to look out for other aircraft entering the landing pattern.

Notice that in your new world of flight, left and right turns are described in terms of arcs of a circle: 45 degrees, 90 degrees, 180 degrees, 360 degrees. So your instructor may say: "Make a 180-degree turn to the left" or "Make a 180 to the left" or "Make a 90 to the right." As a rule, you can gauge when to roll out of the turn simply by spotting some point of reference on the ground. So for a 90-degree left turn, first glance off the left wing for some landmark such as a road, river, mountain, tower, or section line (the prevailing rural grid pattern of roads east and west, north and south). Then turn until your nose is *almost* pointed at it (to allow for a lead) and roll out to level-flight position. Later on, you can learn to make more precise turns by using the instruments.

Straight-and-Level Flight

Same as lesson 1.

Medium Turns

For instruction purposes, turns are divided into three classes: gentle, medium, and steep. Medium (or medium-bank) turns are taught first because they are the easiest to do. Gentle turns are performed with so shallow a bank that most airplanes tend to level themselves because of their natural stability. Conversely, in steep turns, the airplane tends to "overbank," or bank even more steeply than the pilot wishes. In a medium turn, however, most airplanes will tend to hold a constant bank angle without force on the ailerons.

Your instructor will show you how a medium turn looks and feels, so that you can duplicate it. Remember, as you bank into a turn, *coordinate rudder with aileron* (left aileron, left rudder; right aileron, right rudder), and at the same time ease in enough back pressure to compensate for the loss in vertical lift. When you have the correct amount of bank, smoothly release aileron and rudder pressure simultaneously, but retain back pressure.

How can you tell if you're using enough rudder to counteract adverse yaw (the drag of the down aileron in a bank)? At first this will be difficult to sense; later you'll be able to gauge it by "body feel" and by referring to the turn-and-bank indicator. The instructor can best show you what happens by demonstrating adverse yaw in the most extreme condition: a rapid bank with no rudder. He will have you bank sharply into a turn without using the rudder, and you will be able to see that the nose of the airplane tends to pause for a moment straight ahead instead of veering in the direction of the turn. On some airplanes the nose may even momentarily swerve or yaw opposite to the direction of the bank when no rudder is used. But if you apply rudder along with aileron pressure in the right amount, the nose of the airplane will turn smoothly in the direction of the bank.

Slow Flight

Part of learning to fly is probing the extreme ranges of the aircraft's flying qualities. Slow flight will show you how slowly the aircraft can fly without losing too much lift and "stalling." The knowledge will enhance your ability to have full command of the aircraft at all times. Slow flight simulates, in slightly exaggerated fashion, normal flying conditions you will encounter on each flight. For example, you are in a form of slow flight when you take off and first begin to build up airspeed. You also approach slow flight when you enter the airport traffic pattern for landing.

To put the aircraft into slow flight, pull back the throttle smoothly and reduce power. With the power reduced, the airspeed will steadily decrease, and the nose will feel heavier, requiring back pressure on the control wheel to hold altitude. Remember, you'll want to hold a *constant altitude* during slow flight.

When the airspeed has dropped to the desired level, smoothly push in the throttle to keep from "setting" or losing altitude. You'll find that to hold a given altitude at low airspeed, you must use a surprisingly large amount of power, and you'll be flying along with the nose quite high in the air. This will call for some nose-up trim for comfortable control wheel pressures.

At these low airspeeds torque will reassert itself, requiring you to hold quite a bit of right rudder to keep the nose of the aircraft straight. You'll also notice that at these low airspeeds the controls feel "sloppy" and have lost some of their bite and effectiveness because of the reduced wind pressures on them. So greater control movements are required to change pitch or bank angle. This sloppiness of controls is an important cue telling you that the aircraft is not far from its stalling speed.

Power-off Stalls

A stall occurs when the wing no longer provides enough lift to support the weight of the airplane in the air. This happens when the wing is forced to hold a high "angle of attack" (the angle of the cross section or chord line of the wing to the flow of the wind). This in turn causes the smooth flow of air over the wing to break away and become turbulent, sharply reducing lift.

To demonstrate, the instructor will pull back the throttle to idle after first pulling out the carburetor heat knob. As the airspeed drops, he will keep easing back on the control wheel to hold altitude. When the airspeed has dropped to about 35 to 45 mph, the controls will become sloppy, and the aircraft will begin to buffet. If the wheel is held farther back as the buffeting continues, a stall will occur, with the nose dropping rather abruptly.

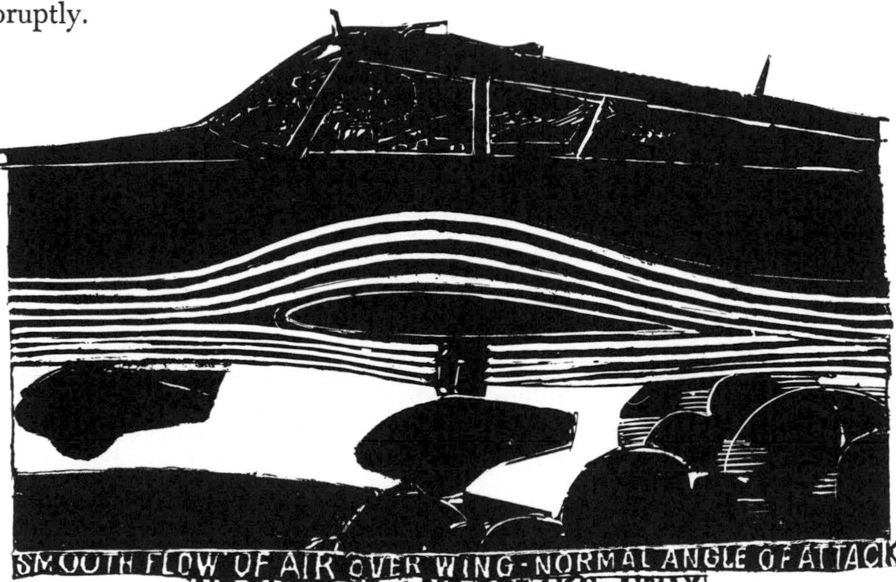

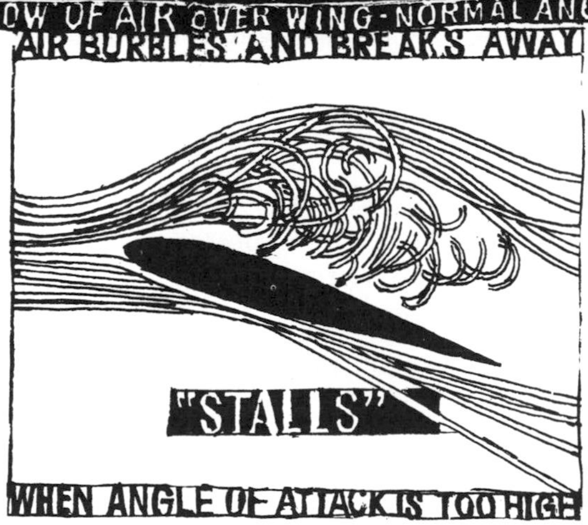

Simply releasing back pressure on the wheel will enable the aircraft to recover from the stall by reducing the angle of attack and restoring lift to the wing.

To further speed the stall recovery and prevent unnecessary loss of altitude, the throttle should be pushed in smoothly, all the way, giving an added blast of wind over the wing, increasing lift and airspeed. At this point, the carburetor heat knob is pushed back in and, as the airspeed picks up, power may be reduced to a cruise setting. As you practice stalls, you will learn to release back pressure on the control wheel and add power simultaneously for the quickest possible stall recovery, all the while keeping the wings level by means of the ailerons.

Why practice stalls? To learn to recognize when the aircraft is approaching a stall during normal flight and to build a habit of making quick and effective recovery almost automatically. This is especially important when the aircraft is flying at low altitude during landing or takeoff.

Steep Turns

On this ride the instructor will merely demonstrate to give you the feel and look of a steep turn, this being your first mild introduction to G force. The G force is simply centrifugal force in a turn, tending to press you down into your seat. Centrifugal force keeps you perfectly balanced inside the airplane, even though both you and the aircraft are at an odd angle to the horizon. It will feel strange at first simply because you are unused to it. Also, the exaggerated angle of your body to the ground in a steep turn will present a new sensation.

Gliding Turns

To practice gliding turns, pull back the throttle all the way to an idle position. As in the climb, the key to a controlled descent is to maintain a constant airspeed. Holding 60 to 70 mph in the glide will allow you to experience the sensation of maneuvering for a landing.

With power off in the glide, the nose will tend to yaw a bit to the right—just the opposite of a climb. So add a bit of left rudder as needed to keep the nose straight. *Remember:* In a climb, you'll need right rudder; in a glide, left rudder.

Your instructor will ask you to make medium turns left and right as you descend. Notice how in the glide you will have to make larger control movements to achieve the same effects you did at higher airspeeds.

Once again, remember not to stare at the airspeed indicator while trying to hold a constant airspeed. Use all the other cues you've learned to sense: the sound of the wind, the feel of the controls (whether taut or sloppy), the position of the horizon in the windshield, and the position of the wings above or below the horizon.

Approach, Pattern, and Landing

Same as lesson 1.

Taxiing and Parking

Same as lesson 1.

LESSON 3

DURING THE THIRD lesson, the student should become fairly proficient in the four basic flight maneuvers: straight-and-level flight, turns, climbs, and descents. He must also learn to perform by himself slow flight, power-off stalls, and simple coordination exercises. With this lesson too, the student should assume responsibility for the preflight inspection, as well as starting the engine, using the radio, taxiing, and parking—all without direction from the instructor.

Preflight Inspection

Now that you can tell whether an airplane *appears* in safe flying condition before you hop in and fly away, it's a good idea to know whether it is *legally* okay to fly and *mechanically* well cared-for. So begin to include the aircraft's "bookwork" in your preflight thinking.

Ordinarily, the first step in the inspection of any "strange" aircraft is to check to see that certain papers required by law are in the aircraft—just as the registration must be in your car and a license plate on the bumper before you can legally drive it. These documents are actually your first tentative "endorsement" of aircraft safety and reliability. They are the airframe and engine logbooks, the certificate of airworthiness, the registration, and the weight and balance papers. A flight manual must also be in the aircraft, and a pilot's operating manual (a separate booklet from the flight manual) should be along for the pilot's reference. When you take your flight exam for your private pilot's license, you must be able to explain the function of all this "paperwork."

Granted the logbooks probably won't be in the airplane when you're learning to fly since most flight schools prefer to keep them in their maintenance shops. But your instructor can get them for you. They are extremely important because they record malfunctions and corrections, provide the pilot with background on the airplane's mechanical idiosyncrasies, if any, and tell him if faults have actually been corrected. In addition they record regular maintenance inspections required by law. (The average lightplane is required to have at least one thorough inspection a year—a "periodic inspection." Aircraft used for flight instruction must, in addition, receive a thorough inspection each 100 hours of flying time.)

Takeoff

Same as lessons 1 and 2.

Traffic Pattern and Departure

Same as lessons 1 and 2.

Climbs and Climbing Turns

Same as lessons 1 and 2.

Level Off from Climbs and Glides

To level off from a climb or glide at a selected altitude—say 3,000 feet—the main point to remember is that it's necessary to begin arresting your

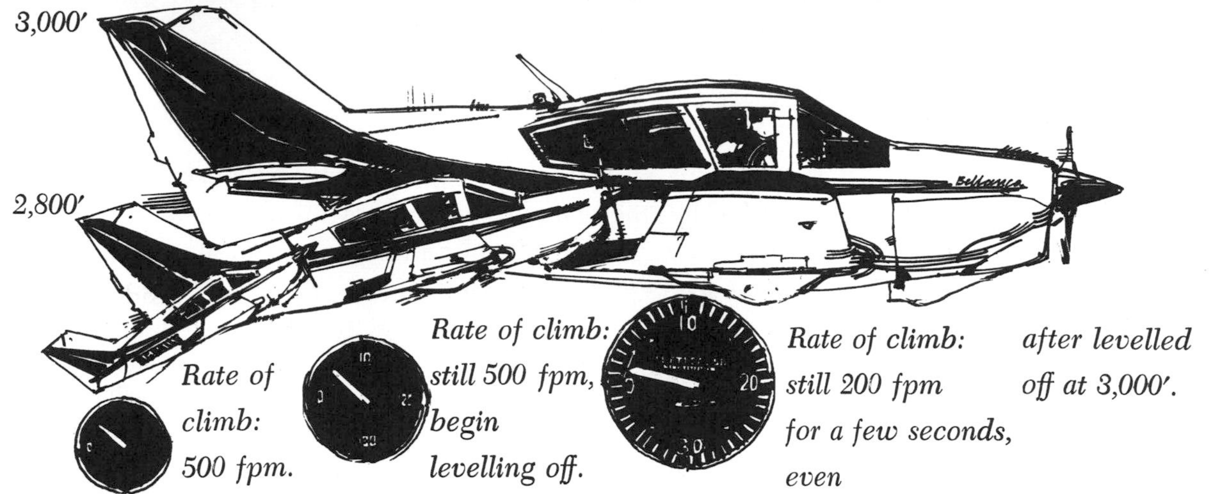

climb or descent a bit early, to prevent overshooting the selected altitude. Naturally, the greater the *rate* of climb or descent, the more lead should be allowed. Another factor to consider is the tendency of the altimeter and vertical speed indicator to lag in their readings. So if you were climbing to 3,000 feet at about 700 feet per minute (on the vertical speed indicator), you would start easing in forward pressure on the control wheel at about 2,800 feet, trimming off pitch pressures to a comfortable level. Hold full throttle until the airspeed has risen to a cruise level. Then smoothly reduce power to a cruise rpm that will hold the desired airspeed.

Leveling off from a glide, again start early, and slowly add power to hold airspeed.

Straight-and-Level, Medium Turns

Same as lessons 1 and 2.

Coordination Exercises

At this point, the student probably needs to practice his turns to develop his skill at coordinating wheel and rudder. Therefore, he may try a series of medium-bank turns, left and right, to help him develop his touch.

Learning how to use the turn-and-bank indicator (or "turn coordinator," as some are called) will help in these exercises. The "ball" will show whether a turn is properly coordinated. If the turn is a good one, the ball will be centered. If not, it will slide off to one side or the other.

The ball tends to move with the rudders, but in the reverse way. So if you squeeze in left rudder, the ball will tend to move to the right; if you push right rudder, the ball will move left. In a turn you can think of "stepping on the ball" to keep it centered. In a left turn, while using aileron to bank, you must squeeze in a certain amount of left rudder (to counteract adverse yaw). If, for example, you do not use enough left rudder in left bank, the ball will sag to the left of center, toward the bottom or inside of the turn. Conversely, if you use too much left rudder, the ball will move to the right of center, toward the top or outside of the turn.

Once, again, remember that the ball should be used as a cue, not a constant reference. Use it to develop your "seat-of-the-pants" feel—your kinesthetic sense. Also, don't be timid about squeezing in rudder when you bank. In the beginning the instructor will prefer to see you using a bit too much rudder rather than not enough.

Speed Changes in Level Flight

When you add power in level flight to increase the airspeed, the airplane will immediately want to climb. To prevent this and stay at a *constant* altitude, you must add forward pressure on the wheel as you increase throttle. Conversely, when you reduce power, the airplane will want to descend.

Power controls climb and descent, and *pitch* controls airspeed. Actually, this is something of an overgeneralization, but the idea is that a pilot can control his rate of climb or descent more effectively in most situations by his use of power than by using the control wheel. Except for aerobatics, the pilot always shoots for the steady state—a constant rate of climb, constant rate of descent, constant airspeed, constant altitude, constant pitch and bank attitude. This power/pitch relationship really begins to make sense during the landing approach, and we'll return to this farther on.

Slow Flight and Stalls

Same as lesson 2.

Glides and Gliding Turns

Same as lesson 2.

Approach, Pattern, and Landing

On the way back to the airport, tune in the tower frequency on the VHF radio and listen. Often you can hear the tower give other aircraft the information you'll need to land, and you won't have to ask him to repeat it for you. But if the tower is not talking—traffic is light—call him. Tell him who you are (give your full aircraft identification number), where you are in relation to the field, and say that you want to land.

He will reply by telling you the runway in use for landings, the altimeter setting (which allows you to adjust your altimeter to local atmospheric pressure), plus the direction and strength of the surface winds at the airport.

Your call would sound something like this: "Bridgeport Tower, Cessna 1875 X-ray, five miles west, landing."

His reply might be: "Cessna 1875 X-ray, landing runway three-two, altimeter 29.94, wind northwest at nine, report downwind." (If you had already noted this information by listening in on the tower's conversation with other aircraft, you would have made the same call, but added that you "have the numbers.")

The next step is to descend smoothly and gradually to traffic pattern altitude. While descending, your instructor will help you visualize in which direction the runway is pointing so you can enter the traffic pattern at a 45-degree angle to the runway. This doesn't have to be perfectly precise; you may judge it roughly.

Once on the downwind leg (flying parallel to the runway, opposite to the direction you will land), get in the habit of going through a prelanding checklist. Check that your mixture is full rich. (You may have leaned it at higher altitudes; then when you advance throttle at low altitude, the engine might cough and sputter from lack of fuel.) Pull out carburetor heat, and then reduce power so the airspeed drops to about 70 mph. The instructor will suggest a power setting (in engine rpm) that will give the desired airspeed.

You will learn where to locate your downwind leg by reference to the landing runway. This is usually a matter of judgment based on "the way things look," though some instructors will suggest a point of reference on the ground, such as a road or house, to help you set your pattern spacing. Others may note how the runway, when seen through the cockpit, appears to intersect the wing or wing strut at a certain point with proper spacing. At any rate you should try to hold a constant altitude above the ground until you are opposite the intended point of touchdown.

Opposite the "approach end" of the runway—the end at which you'll touch down—reduce throttle a bit more and allow the aircraft to descend slowly. Again, remember to hold a constant airspeed. Then make a 90-degree left turn onto base leg, using a medium bank. Then turn onto final approach, still descending.

Now you are in that phase of flight that demands the most finesse and judgment of the student pilot—the landing. A good landing requires three things: a good final approach, a good flareout, and an exact touchdown.

The key to a good final approach (the glide path down to the runway) is to hold a *constant* airspeed and constant glide angle. The airplane's path of descent should be as straight as a ruler, at a constant angle to the ground. The airspeed should remain the same all the way down final approach.

The idea is to level the airplane out just above the runway and hold it there until it simply will not fly any more and settles down.

The skilled pilot will peg the main wheels of the airplane (tricycle-geared type) not more than an inch or two above the runway at this final, gentle settling, and the airplane will ease softly down with scarcely a bump.

Naturally, this will take a good deal of practice to perfect, and it may seem like eons before you're able to judge your height above the runway in inches. But all of a sudden, it will come. And then you're on your way—to that first solo, those first tentative cross-country forays away from home base, and through the blue door marked "pilots only" to a sky full of challenge, fun, and adventure.

NAVIGATING

In the earliest days, of course, knowing one's position wasn't much of a problem. Airplanes didn't fly high, and they didn't fly far. In fact, they didn't even fly often. For the most part pilots began their flying careers from familiar ground, and by the time their machines were capable of carrying them out of sight of the point of takeoff, they had learned to read the ground from the air.

Fairly well, that is. Pilots did get lost, and amusing stories, generally with happy endings, were told of the primitive methods the early pilots resorted to in finding their way about the country. One such tale (which was carried in *The New York Times* in 1930) had the lost pilot—who had been circling a golf course in a state of indecision—drop a note in a bottle asking directions from a wary golfer. After gesturing frantically but unsuccessfully for some minutes, the frustrated golfer finally lay on the turf with his head pointing in the proper direction. Shortly after, as the story goes, pilot and 11 passengers landed safely at their destination, a nearby airport.

Pilots still get lost; but a pilot who gets lost nowadays has simply not been paying attention. The wonderful truth is that today we have a system of air navigation which allows the newest private pilot to do a better job of navigation than all but a handful of the master aviators of the 1920's.

In the beginning there was literally no system of air navigation. There weren't even automobile road maps, since cars and planes are contemporary inventions. There were several kinds of ground maps, none of which helped the airman much. One of the most useful navigation aids was the nationwide system of railroads, and following railroad tracks became very popular. But it was soon obvious that following roads or railroad tracks violated the principle of flight, which allows freedom to move in any direction, restrained only by terrain and weather.

The first air navigation methods drew heavily on the experiences of seafaring men, which may explain why aviation uses the word "chart" instead of "map." Progress was slow: in fact, there were no charts developed expressly for aviation until late in the 1920's.

Things are different now. We have charts for use in clear weather under Visual Flight Rules (VFR) and charts for use under Instrument Flight Rules (IFR). The most common VFR charts, called Sectionals, are beautifully prepared and printed in colors. Next are World Aeronautical Charts (WAC's), also primarily for VFR, a bit larger than Sectionals, but covering a much larger area and, of course, corresponding in less detail. There is also a series known as Operational Navigation Charts, using the same scale as the WAC's, but showing four times the area covered and therefore four times as big, making them too unwieldy in the confines of a small airplane's cockpit. All of these are published by the United States Coast and Geodetic Survey and widely distributed for sale through aeronautical chart dealers throughout the United States, most of them at airports. They are masterpieces of cartography and marvelously low in cost.

Several states have issued their own state charts. These cover the entire state, which few Sectionals do (two-and-a-half Sectionals, for example, are needed to cover California) and therefore are unable to show as much detail on the same size sheet of paper. Most of them are published by Jeppesen Company, and they use an entirely different cartographic method of illustrating elevation. Unfortunately, charts are not available for all states. The scales are of necessity widely different and revisions are at the whim of the state budgets.

For instrument flight (IFR) there is an entirely different series of charts. Whereas the VFR charts are essentially intended for cross-country flight, and show only minimum detail about airports and terminal areas, the IFR charts must deal precisely with all three. So there are en route (or airways) charts, area charts, and individual charts, called "approach plates," which display in a highly stylized shorthand notation exactly how to maneuver so as to keep clear of obstacles and find the airport after letting down through the clouds.

There are two sources from which to obtain instrument flight charts, both of which sell primarily by subscription. One is Jeppesen Company, whose founder, United Air Lines Captain E. B. Jeppeson, invented the whole system. The other is the United States Coast and Geodetic Survey. There are differences between them in style and format, and it's easy to find pilots who strongly prefer one over the other. Coast and Geodetic is slightly less expensive for the initial subscription, slightly higher on renewals. In most "coverages," meaning the specific areas selected by individual pilots, Jeppesen is less expensive after the first year.

The second difference is more important: though both services issue revisions whenever made, Jeppesen gets the revisions out weekly, Coast and Geodetic only every four weeks. A minor, but very important bonus of the Jeppesen service is that each revised chart, whether airways, area, or approach plate, carries a notation showing what changes were made.

The modern air navigation system, the offspring of the marriage of electronics to aviation, is a truly remarkable achievement. Its concepts and technical execution are the result of more than a generation of hard work by brilliant people, yet its operation is so simple that by the time a new student is ready for his flight test he has mastered the essential uses of it. He has proved his understanding in a written examination, and he will be further examined for practical competence in the flight test. He cannot get his license if he does not do an acceptable job, but very few candidates fail on this count.

Travelers on the surface of the earth have been asking directions of friendly strangers for as long as mankind has been traveling. Unlike the ground travelers' friendly strangers, the electronic friendly strangers who serve the airman are always competent, day in and day out, nights, Sundays and holidays, fair weather and foul. In addition, today's and tomorrow's aviators do not even have to do the asking: they have cockpit helpers, which are part of the airborne electronics gear, who do the asking and report the information to the captain. The process is continuous.

A system of ground stations covers the United States, transmitting signals in all directions which are picked up by navigation receivers in airplanes. This is called a "Rho-Theta" system. The principle is simple: Rho stands for distance, Theta for direction.

Direction information comes from the VOR (meaning Very high frequency Omni Range) ground station, detected and displayed by the airborne VOR receiver. Distance is determined by a piece of airborne equipment called DME (Distance Measuring Equipment), which gets its information from another element of the ground station. This can be tuned to any ground station within reception range, but it is usually set to the same station as the VOR receiver. DME can do more than just tell distance: it can figure and show ground speed, or it can tell the captain, as he requests, how far in minutes he is from the station.

The "Rho-Theta" system has proved really remarkable and has allowed the development of a nationwide network of airways with a very high degree of accuracy and reliability. Unfortunately, it isn't possible to have airways which go from everywhere to anywhere. The electronics art has recently been called upon to solve this problem, too. The solution is called Area Navigation, abbreviated R Nav. The heart of the R Nav equipment is an electronic computer, which works with the standard direction and distance information from the ground navigation stations, and the existing airborne receivers. The computer allows the pilot to tune in any navigation station within range and electronically "move" it from where it is to some other place where the pilot would like to have a ground station. This might be at the airport of destination, so that he could fly direct to it, as well as making it easier to find if he has never been there before. Or he might "move" several stations to create his own "airway" direct from starting point to journey's end. So R Nav saves time by shortening distances. And because it makes following the published airways unnecessary, it will help to reduce traffic congestion on those airways. It can be used either VFR or IFR.

At present, the cost of R Nav equipment ranges between $2,500 and $30,000. The highest-priced equipment is for airlines. As always, prices can be expected to come down as volume increases.

What if the aircraft navigation receivers fail? If the communication transmitter and receiver are working, ground stations can guide an airplane in two different ways. Flight Service Stations can use a special piece of equipment to find the direction the plane would have to fly to reach their station, and the Air Traffic Control people can use their surveillance radars to locate a given airplane.

Most instrument approaches are based on the primary distance and direction system. There are two other ways to get down out of the clouds in position to land. One is called ILS, for Instrument Landing System. It provides both directional and vertical (glide path) guidance and brings an airplane right to the touchdown spot on the runway it serves. Advanced versions of this will eventually permit landings in true zero-zero weather.

The other instrument approach method uses one of the earliest electronic airborne navigation devices: the automatic radio direction finder, or ADF. This was once the primary navigation instrument, but the newer national system is so much better that ADF's and ADF approaches are now secondary.

The inventors and designers of navigation equipment haven't stopped. Their final goal is a self-contained navigation system, which doesn't require any ground stations. Two systems are already in use: Doppler and inertial guidance. These will be too expensive for general aviation for a while yet. But it should be remembered that everything we now have at affordable prices was once too expensive for anything but the airlines and the military.

THE SUDDEN STORM

In our lives apart from aviation, unless we are farmers or follow some other calling which requires us to keep daily track of the weather, the weather does seem to change suddenly and capriciously. A sunny day is forecast and so the family goes on a picnic. Right in the middle of the outing, there is a thunderstorm. A day is planned on the beach, and an ocean fog rolls in. These are distressing enough on the ground. What, the newcomer wants to know, can a pilot do about them when he is in flight? Weather puzzles pilots, too, though not in quite the same way.

Weather and gravity are the two great antagonists of aviation. Both are enormously powerful and have managed to keep some of their secrets hidden from our prying eyes. There are differences of great importance. For

The student pilot learns to become his own weather prophet, several stages beyond the homey "red sky at night" variety. These gentle banks of evening cloud have a bearing on tomorrow's flying weather.

example, every airplane must overcome the pull of gravity on every flight, while a great majority of all flights have little if any involvement with bad weather. Powerful as it is, gravity is at least consistent.

The weather is almost exactly the opposite. We know a lot about what it consists of, where it comes from, where it goes to, and what causes changes in it. But it is not consistent. With all our knowledge, we cannot foretell the weather very accurately, and the farther ahead we would like to predict it, the less accurate the prediction will be. In this sense, compared to an astronomer's prediction of a solar eclipse, the weather is not predictable at all. Fortunately, prediction gets better the shorter the interval, and at the time span of an average flight (which seldom exceeds five hours between origin and destination, or between origin and fuel stop), the accuracy is pretty good, and the pilot's problem is manageable.

If the weather becomes worse than forecast, it won't become so instantaneously. If the weather has been good at the point of departure, the chances are that it will remain good for at least a couple of hours. And if the weather ahead isn't promising, the pilot can escape by going back to where he came from. Also, the pilot is trained to think about the weather and to plan an alternate course of flight and an alternate airport in case the weather turns bad. One vital factor in this is that all but the very slowest airplanes move through the air considerably faster than all but the very fastest weather systems. This is in stark contrast with the conditions faced by the men of the sea, where the fastest ships cannot escape the slowest storms.

As a pilot progresses, even in his training for the basic private pilot license, he is required to master the rudiments of flight by instrument reference alone, without being able to see outside the cockpit. This is simulated training. Instead of actually finding a cloud and entering it, the pilot puts a hood on his head which allows him to see the panel instruments, but not the outside world. Although this brief exposure is far from being complete instrument flight training, it does give the pilot a sense of confidence in his ability to keep the airplane flying if, by misadventure (usually caused by himself), he should lose ground reference.

Until recent years there were not many pilots who continued their training up to the level of an instrument rating, which fully qualified them to fly in cloud. That is now changing and quite rapidly, as aircraft performance, instruments, and radios have been improving. Instrument flying ability gives such benefits in aircraft utility and safety that every pilot should obtain an instrument rating. However, even under instrument conditions, the weather continues to interfere with airplanes. But the same conditions of slow rate of change still hold true, and the instrument pilot and his airplane are better able to cope with any adverse weather conditions.

The actual amount of weather information and service available is almost beyond belief. Weather observations are taken at hundreds of stations throughout the United States every hour, and transmitted by Teletype throughout the system. To these are added forecasts of winds aloft, conditions in terminal and other selected areas, and severe weather. Reports of winds aloft, derived from several kinds of sources, including pilots in flight, are made every six hours. There are surface weather maps, weather depiction charts, constant pressure charts, radar summary maps, pilot weather report summaries, hurricane advisories, and simplified surface analyses and prognoses. The whole list is even longer than that.

The pilot can obtain this information by visiting a weather station at an airport, a Flight Service Station, or one of the growing number of "one-stop" stations, where Flight Service and Weather Bureau are adjacent. He can get it by telephone, either from a weather briefer or a forecaster. He can dial a special telephone number and listen to a recording, changes made as often as required, giving current information over a wide range of stations. He can listen to transcribed weather broadcasts on special radio stations, at home or in flight. In flight, he can get weather information, again either from a briefer or a forecaster, and every ground navigation station broadcasts a regular weather summary every hour. In addition to all these services, designed especially for aviation, daily weather maps published in newspapers and daily weather reports on television are excellent broad-gauge guides.

The system takes some learning and requires some expenditure of time to get the most out of it, but any pilot who makes even a modest attempt to exploit it will never find himself trapped by weather. Moreover, the weather somewhere in the United States, during every month of the year, is pretty good. If this were not so, aviation would not have progressed nearly as far as it has.

Going back to the original question—"But what if a big fog comes up?" —the answer is that it won't, not if the pilot has done his homework.

Rain, rain, go to Spain. Student pilots are sometimes nervous of flying in the rain—but it can be fun, too.

STUDENT PILOT

Anybody may walk into a flying school and obtain flight instruction—in the beginning. But before he or she can be set loose on the first solo flight, a student pilot license is required. The flight instructor can usually supply the forms; they will be mailed to the FAA and returned in a few days with the "ticket" entitling the novice to fly solo. The FAA charges nothing for the license, though the flight school may require a small fee (about $2) to cover services.

Naturally, there are a few preliminary requirements. The student pilot must be at least 16 years old (or 14 to fly a glider). He must be able to handle the English language. And he must pass a medical examination ("third class," it's called) by a physician authorized to give pilot exams. (He'll usually charge $10 to $15.) The nearest FAA office can provide a list of doctors who give FAA medicals.

One last little requirement not directly connected with the license is a radiotelephone operator's permit. This is needed to operate a two-way aircraft radio. The FCC will issue one for $8. Again, the flight school can provide the form.

PRIVATE PILOT

The second legal pinnacle of flying is the private license. The student will be issued one when he has proved he is both well trained and safe in the art of flying. There are two hurdles along the way: a written test and a flight examination with an oral quiz. Before the student pilot takes the flight test, he must have passed the written exam and accumulated 40 hours of flying time (35 if from an FAA-approved flight school). A minimum of 20 hours must be solo flight time, and at least 10 of those hours must be on cross-country flight. During these cross-countries, the student must land at an airport at least 25 miles from home base, and during at least one flight he must down at an airfield 100 miles away from home. This is to ensure that he knows how to handle himself at "strange" airports well beyond his familiar home surroundings. One last requirement is a minimum of three hours of instruction flying strictly on the gauges.

Unless you are able to take rather intensive, almost daily flight instruction, don't expect to get your license within the 40-hour minimum. The national average works out to around 62 hours, because a lot of student pilots can fly only on weekends or occasional evenings when the weather is good. Naturally the learning continuity may be stretched a bit thin under such circumstances. There is no onus to taking even longer, depending on personal circumstances.

How long does it take to solo? Count on 10 to 15 hours of flying time as a rough average, again depending on continuity and the cooperation of the weather.

Anyone may take the written test any time he wishes—no matter how much flying time has been logged, or even before setting foot in the airplane, for that matter. The test, administered at the local FAA district office, has some 60 multiple-choice questions that cover flying regulations and air traffic rules, as well as probe the student's ability to recognize dangerous weather conditions and evaluate weather reports. They also assay his practical knowledge of cross-country flying, flight planning, map reading and emergency navigation aids, and communications procedures.

Seventy percent is a passing grade.

When he is ready for his "final" exam (the oral and flight test), the student will be quizzed by the examiner on a rather broad range of subjects such as airplane registration, logbooks, aircraft performance, and load-carrying ability. The flight test, which lasts about an hour or so, will expose him to a representative sampling of flying ability in all major skill areas.

INSTRUMENT RATING

Once you have a private or a commercial ticket, you may tack on various "ratings" to your practicing license. The most valuable of these is the instrument rating. Without it, a pilot is forbidden by law, not to mention common sense, from intruding upon any but the nicest weather. Thus the instrument rating will ensure far fewer frustrated trips and a much boosted sense of security, even if the only "bad" weather around is that annoying patch sitting over your departure or arrival airport.

If you have only a private license, you may obtain an instrument rating by means of the usual FAA route: a written exam and a flight test, plus a certain qualifying number of hours of instruction. The minimum number of hours of instrument time required is 40. At least 20 of these must be logged in an airplane; the remainder may be in either an airplane or a ground simulator or trainer.

The flight test will check ability to fly solely with reference to the cockpit instruments; the student must wear a visor, or part of the aircraft's windshield will be blocked off to simulate flying in "weather." The examiner will also test the applicant's ability to cope calmly and simultaneously with the flying and navigating and radio communications demands, plus a few emergencies thrown in to test his cool.

With equipment and procedures becoming more sophisticated all the time, the instrument rating is one every flier would do well to have under his belt, if he would consider himself a skilled pilot.

SEAPLANE RATING

Probably the quickest, cheapest (and most fun) rating any pilot can add to his license is the seaplane rating. There is no specific minimum number of flight hours required, though it may take five to seven hours to master the basic skills in a single-engine seaplane. There is no written test either. The only obstacle: an oral quiz and flight test.

MULTI-ENGINE RATING

As with the seaplane rating, there is no flight-hour minimum for the multi-engine rating, though most examiners expect to see at least 10 hours logged in the applicant's book. Also there is no written test. Instead there is an oral quiz and flight test emphasizing techniques of flying with one engine out.

COMMERCIAL LICENSE

After the private license, the next highest category is the commercial license, which a pilot needs if he wishes to fly for hire. But most pilots regard this paper plateau more as a significant mark of experience and ability, whether they plan to cash in on the commercial possibilities or not.

The commercial applicant must be at least 18 years old—two years older than for a private license—with at least 200 hours of flight time. There is also the inevitable written test. On the flight test the pilot must be able to do everything the private pilot can do, but he must do it better. He also has to demonstrate skill in several other new areas of precision flying, with special maneuvers such as lazy eights, chandelles, on-pylon eights. His instrument flying must also be of a higher order, though not as high as for the instrument rating. In addition, the applicant has to pass a medical exam ("second class")—a bit stiffer than for the private license.

AIRLINE TRANSPORT

The most exalted ticket of all is the airline transport certificate. The applicant must be at least 23 years old. A rather demanding "first-class" physical exam has to be passed. There is, of course, a written exam and a flight test. And the applicant must have logged at least 1,500 hours of flight time in the past eight years, with a minimum of 250 hours as pilot in command of an aircraft. Also he must have at least 500 hours of cross-country time, 100 hours of night time, and 75 hours of instrument time, to cap it off.

READING, 'RITING, AND 'RITHMETIC

One relatively gray area in aviation is that of the ground schools, which have proliferated at a tremendous rate in recent years.

Attending ground school classes is optional; there is no federal aviation regulation that requires a student to do so, and beginners often wonder whether it's worth the time and cost to attend such courses.

In assessing the value of ground schools, it must be realized that the cramped and relatively noisy cockpit of the average training aircraft is, at best, a poor classroom. Not only is it difficult to ask questions and understand the answers in this atmosphere, the learning process is complicated by the fact that, above all (no pun intended), the aircraft must be flown. This requires a considerable degree of attention and concentration from the student pilot, who has not reached the stage where his reactions are more or less automatic.

The classroom, on the other hand, is a quiet and relaxed place where the theories behind the practice can be studied and discussed. It is a place where, with the help of chalkboards and a wide variety of excellent audio-visual aids, it is easy to clarify even the more complicated concepts of aviation, making it possible for the new pilot to know *why* the airplane reacts in a certain way to certain control combinations or *how* to use the available electronic instruments to extract the greatest possible amount and variety of information.

As is true of any teaching situation, the value of individual ground schools varies to some degree with the expertise of the instructor. But the availability of audio-visual material (slides, filmstrips, records, and tapes) covering virtually any aeronautical subject has made it possible for even a relatively mediocre instructor to effectively present the information required.

Snow on the ground can mean beautiful weather aloft with visibility to the horizon. But snow in clouds can be sinister.

For those who prefer to do their studying in the privacy of their own homes, or who feel that the time or money involved in going to ground school (between $50 and $100 per course, on the average) is more than they are willing to devote, there are various books and home-study courses that present all the necessary information in lucid form.

The value of all this material depends to some extent on the individual's ability to absorb information—a capability that most of us possess to a considerable degree during the years immediately following school or college, but that we are prone to gradually lose as we get older and less attuned to the disciplines of formal study.

Since the books and other home-study materials available to aviators tend to carry some pretty healthy price tags, it is advisable to scan the comparable products offered by different publishers and to be selective before buying anything. We've appended a comprehensive list of books for pilots.

In recent years an increasing number of high schools and junior colleges, as part of their adult education programs, have started to offer aviation ground school courses that are frequently good and quite inexpensive. Inquiries as to the availability of such programs in your area should be directed to the nearest FAA general aviation district office or to the General Aviation Manufacturers Association, 1025 Connecticut Avenue, N.W., Washington, D.C. 20036 (202 296–8848).

COME JOIN THE CLUB

Within days of your first solo flight, you will probably receive letters from several aviation organizations inviting you to join their ranks. This is likely to be your introduction to the many organizations, clubs, groups, and associations that represent a number of divergent activities and interests among general aviation pilots. Whether or not you are a "joiner," you may wish to belong to one of these organizations, if for no other reason than to lend your support to worthwhile pro-general aviation activities.

To help you understand the character and goals of the major groups, here is a brief description of some of them:

The AOPA (Airplane Owners & Pilots Association) and the NPA (National Pilots Association) are organizations that appeal to all general aviation pilots. Of the two, the AOPA is the older (31 years), the larger (approximately 150,000 members), and the wealthier. The NPA represents some 10,000 pilots. It, like the AOPA, does a job of political watchdogging, but its often more diplomatic approach in dealing with general aviation problems has resulted in closer cooperation with the FAA and other government bodies. The $18 annual membership fee includes a subscription to *Flying* Magazine, a newsletter, and other benefits.

A second large group of aviation organizations consists of all those associations made up of members with common professional interests. There are the International Flying Farmers, Aviation Psychologists, Aviation Writers, Flying Chiropractors, Flying Dentists, Flying Funeral Directors, Flying Architects, Flying Physicians, International Flying Bankers, Lawyers-Pilots, Flying Priests, and a plethora of others. Most of these issue some sort of monthly newsletter and get together once a year at more or less lavish conventions.

A further classification of pilot clubs involves associations based on the type of aircraft flown or the kind of involvement of members in the different phases of aviation—the Antique Airplane Association, Experimental Aircraft Association, Helicopter Association of America, Soaring Society of America, Aerobatic Club of America, American Bonanza Society, American Navion Society, Convertible Aircraft Pioneers, Popular Rotorcraft Association, and organizations devoted to tail-draggers, to Cessna 195's, to Luscombes and Wacos and other nostalgia-producing aircraft.

There are also organizations devoted strictly to female pilots: the Ninety-Nines, the Whirly-Girls, and the Women's National Aeronautical Association.

In addition, numerous organizations serve any number of specific purposes, most of which are implicit in the names: the National Business Aircraft Association, Aerospace Education Foundation, Aerospace Industries

Association of America, Aerospace Medical Association, Air Force Association, Air Traffic Control Association, Airport Operators Council International, American Association of Airport Executives, American Institute of Aeronautics and Astronautics, Aviation Distributors and Manufacturers Association, China–Burma–India Hump Pilots Association, Early Birds of Aviation, Man-Will-Never-Fly Memorial Society, National Aeronautic Association (which, in cooperation with the Fédération Aeronautique Internationale, supervises all officially sanctioned competitions, races, and record attempts), National Aerospace Education Council, National Air Transportation Conferences (air taxis and commuter airlines), National Association of Flight Instructors, National Association of Flight Schools, National Aviation Trades Association, National Intercollegiate Flying Association, National Agricultural Aircraft Association, and so on, not to mention the many local, regional, and statewide pilot organizations.

A relatively new member of the family of organizations is GAMA (General Aviation Manufacturers Association), an industry financed group devoted primarily to promoting general aviation, to preserving and building airports, and to increasing understanding of general aviation by the nonflying public. Among its many activities is the production and dissemination of printed and audio-visual materials designed to aid in selling the airport concept to communities. In addition the association assists schools and colleges interested in adding aviation education courses to their curricula.

CHAPTER 4

Buying an Airplane

AFTER you have acquired your license and gleaned some valuable experience as captain in command, you might find yourself thinking of buying your own plane. The next appropriate decision, then, is whether to buy a new or used aircraft.

First, some words of caution about the splendid prospect of owning your own plane. Don't buy an airplane until you have at least a private pilot license. It sounds like fun to learn in your own airplane, and it might seem less expensive as well. Some dealers, continuing a practice which began with the Wright Brothers' first Army contract, offer free flight instruction if you buy an airplane from them. There are always special cases in favor, but in general the liabilities outweigh the assets.

The new student captain has more than enough to occupy his heart, hands, and head just trying to master flight techniques and ground school subjects. Learning to manage a flying machine on top of that is almost an impossible task. The flying school already knows how to keep an airplane fed, housed, and cared for, and is in a better position to obtain insurance coverage than is a brand-new student.

As to possible saving of money, the flying school earns part of its income by using its own airplanes, hence it is common practice to charge more for instructing in the student's own airplane. This basic business principle requires that the school's own airplanes be given priority in flight instructor assignments, so there is likely to be difficulty in scheduling instructors to fly. Finally, instructors are pretty finicky, and there are a lot of airplanes they simply do not want to use for instruction, if there is a choice available. Besides all that, the amount of money you could theoretically save by using your own airplane instead of the school's isn't enough to justify going to all that trouble.

BUYING A NEW AIRPLANE

That airplanes cost what most people consider to be a great deal of money will come as no surprise. Four-place single-engine airplanes start at around $15,000. There are a few two-seaters for between $5,000 and $10,000, but most experienced airplane owners think of $15,000 as the starting point for good new airplanes without much radio or other equipment. Since it is often the radio or avionics and other equipment that adds greatly to the utility of the aircraft, it is not unusual to spend between 20 and 30 percent of the cost of the basic airplane on avionics, flashing night lights, extra fuel tanks, and a variety of safety features. There are literally hundreds of "extras" that can be added to the basic airplane. Some are almost necessary to flight and some are simply creature comforts. All add to the cost.

Many airplane owners avoid the high cost of buying a new airplane by turning to used aircraft. The prices here start as low as $1,500 for older types and generally run up to between one third to one half of what a new counterpart would cost, and generally the price includes some avionics and extra equipment. Of course, in general, hidden problems may be found in a used airplane just as they may develop in a used car or house or anything else. These hazards are somewhat ameliorated by the fact that most airplanes are considered to have infinite life and, as mentioned before, since hours flown rather than simply the passage of time are the measure of wear and tear, most airplanes have a reliable hour meter on board.

It's almost invariably true that new is better—if you can afford it. For one thing, airplanes bought from reliable dealers include warranties that few used planes have. For another, you are comforted by the knowledge that if anyone is going to mistreat this airplane it is going to be you, and that if anyone is going to nick the prop or dent the wing tip you are going

N7277D

N9001V

N6540Y

N5413E

N8006G

N91017

Buying a plane is one of the most exciting experiences in life. The price range is almost without limit but it's much safer than buying a car since each plane is required to pass a stringent examination each year. High wing, low wing, fixed gear, retractable, single, twin—take your pick!

to know about it because you did it. The delights of buying and owning a new airplane can seldom be equalled by buying a used one, if all you have saved is money.

Whether you buy new or used, if you are buying for the first time, it's most important to choose the right airplane for the mission. Overbuying of first airplanes has been a major cause of disillusionment and subsequent abandonment of flying. The factors to be considered, besides the obvious one of resources, are number of seats, speed, range, and complexity. Generally a good first buy in an airplane is a single-engine, two- or four-seater with a fixed landing gear and fixed-pitch propeller. The speed will not be much more than a hundred miles per hour and the range something over 500 miles.

If you are considering buying a new airplane, you might find the wide variety of options available a little overwhelming at first. To make the task of deciding which craft is most suited to your purposes and pocketbook as pleasant as it should be, we suggest that you look over the following pages. After you've narrowed the range of possibilities to perhaps half a dozen, study the price and specifications of each. The next step is to check the yellow pages to learn which dealer is closest to you and how to arrange for a demonstration flight. From there on, matters will practically take care of themselves.

BUYING A USED AIRPLANE

Money and preference are important when deciding on whether to purchase a new or used plane. But there is another consideration to be taken into account. Perhaps you're able to luxuriate in a "fie-on-economics" philosophy and can picture yourself throttling along from city to city in a shiny new plane fitted out with all the extras that money can buy. If you're a newly licensed pilot, perhaps you should pause before fulfilling this dream.

The vital fact is that a newly licensed pilot is entering aeronautical adolescence and needs time to perfect his flying skills. In the company of a simple airplane, he has a better chance both of learning and of enjoying himself during the next couple of hundred hours. The fact that many such airplanes have short range is no real disadvantage; fatigue is a major factor in every pilot's early flying life, and frequent fuel stops allow for rest and relaxation.

In a year or two, you will make important progress toward aeronautical maturity. From having lived with your airplane, planned many flights, and flown a fraction of those planned, you will be able to see what various levels of improved airplane performance will mean to you. Moreover, your limited investment in an airplane which has already been fully depreciated will probably be retained. And after moving up two or three times, you may well have enough equity and understanding to buy your dream airplane and make full use of its long-range and instrument-filled capacity. Fortunately, there are now plenty of used airplanes to choose from, ranging from the simplest, two-place, pre-World War II trainers to early versions of excellent airplanes still in production. This pool amounts to nearly 80,000 aircraft, with prices ranging from $2,500 to $8,000. Naturally, some are in better condition than others, and the higher the price, the more useful the machine. But keep in mind that airplanes are designed for unlimited life and therefore even the least expensive are safe and reliable, and will quite probably be flying many years from now—unless somebody either destroys them or leaves them outside with no attention.

Prices are also affected by the type of construction and the kind of landing gear, so let's begin thinking about used airplanes by reviewing these. In the beginning, airframes were made of wood: ash, balsa, beech, bamboo, mahogany, oak, and spruce. The covering was cloth, either cotton or Irish linen. Wood struts and wire braces provided the structural strength. Gradually, metal replaced wood in the primary structure, first in the fuselage members, later in the wings. Finally, the outer covering was changed from fabric to aluminum. Very thin, very strong, aircraft-grade plywood was used for a while, as it was intermediate in cost, complexity of manufacture, weight, and life between wood and fabric and all metal. The Bellanca still uses plywood of a very high order of life and excellence in its wings. In most airplanes in production now, the entire airframe is aluminum. A small number still have some steel tube structure and some of these use fabric covering, but the fabric is quite different from cotton and Irish linen. Cotton and Irish linen do not last very long. Rain and snow are obvious enemies, but strong sunlight can be just as bad. Fabric-covered airplanes deteriorate faster when not flown than all-metal ones do. If the airplane can be kept inside a hangar, fabric life is longer. But there aren't nearly enough hangars, and those that are available are expensive.

There are several brands and kinds of synthetic-fiber fabrics, with much longer life than cotton and linen, which can be used as airplane covering. Some belong to the Dacron family; others are made of glass fibers. Any airplane originally covered with cotton or linen can be recovered with a synthetic (except perhaps some very old antiques). Many already have been, and many which originally had cloth covering have been reskinned, completely or partly, in sheet aluminum. It must be added that there are some models for which aluminum skin is impractical.

In the used airplane pool, the least expensive planes are usually cotton or linen covered, with four or five years having passed since the latest recovering. This is an important point when comparing prices. The same model, covered in synthetic, will cost more, and the top prices belong to those which have been reskinned in aluminum.

The type of landing gear—"conventional" or "tricycle"—probably has a slight effect on cost. In general the older designs have two main wheels set quite far forward, with one small wheel back at the tail. This is still called conventional, though the tricycle is now far more common. Airplanes with conventional gear rest on the ground in a tail-low position, leading to the nickname "tail-dragger." In a tricycle gear airplane the main gear is set behind the center of gravity, and the third wheel, which is sometimes as big as the main wheels, is up front, under the nose.

The tricycle design is actually quite old, but for many years it was abandoned in favor of the conventional. The Ercoupe, which will be described in detail, was the first modern light airplane to return to the tricycle idea, and was probably the strongest force in reestablishing it as standard.

The tricycle design has some disadvantages, but these are more than overcome by the vast improvement it gives in ground handling. Because the center of gravity is ahead of the main wheels, the airplane resists swerving, preferring to stay in a straight path over the ground, and because the wing is at a negative angle of attack when the nosewheel is on the ground, the airplane is resistant to being upset by gusts.

The improvement was so striking that manufacturers went too far in their praises. One said that the new landing gear "took all the skill out of landing and taking off." Another said, "You just 'drive' it onto the ground." The claims were easy to believe. The facts are that, at any level of pilot skill, the tricycle gear has a greater safety margin in ground handling than the conventional, but no landing gear invented so far eliminates the need for highly developed skills in the transition between ground and sky.

The list of airplanes which follows has been arbitrarily limited. Some have been omitted because they are not available in significant quantities, others because their selling prices remain higher than the highest listed. What remains represents a wide range of prices and performances, and a correspondingly wide choice for the first airplane.

AERONCA AND CHAMPION

Aeronca is the acronym of Aeronautical Corporation of America, which began building airplanes in 1928. Its products progressed from the ungainly C-2 and C-3 (called "Bathtub Aeroncas," now highly prized as antiques) through the K and KCA to the Chief and Super Chief. All of these had two seats, side by side, except the C-2, which had but one seat.

In the late 1930's the company developed a tandem trainer to compete with the Piper J-3. After World War II, a considerably revised version of this was put into production and named the Champion. When Aeronca decided to go out of the light airplane manufacturing business, their designs were sold to Champion Aircraft Company. The best known of these is called "Citabria," which is "airbatic" spelled backward. Its airframe is basically that of the original Champ, though its engine is much more pow-

ABOVE AND OPPOSITE. Sturdy little tail-draggers often provide pilots with an astonishingly good bargain.

erful. Most recently, a trainer version has been reintroduced, still called Champion. It uses a two-cylinder, 60-hp Franklin engine, and carries a base price (without starter or generator) of $4,995.

The Chief and Super Chief are quite comfortable for crosscountry, and the Tandem and Champion are good trainers. Aeronca also built a Sedan model, with four seats and a cruise speed of about 125 mph.

CESSNA

The first Cessna airplane was built in 1911, by Clyde Cessna, but the company did not begin producing until 1928. In the period before World War II, the Cessna Airmaster series was outstanding for performance, and quite a few of them still exist. They are not "first" airplanes, however, even if their prices, as antiques, do not cause dismay.

After the war Cessna built a delightful, light, two-place machine called the 120. Like the Luscombe, which will be described later, it was all metal (aluminum), except for the wing cover, which was fabric. It used something very new for landing gear legs: tempered and tapered pieces of spring steel, invented by Steve Wittman of Wisconsin. Unlike the Luscombe, the 120 had a wheel instead of a stick for pitch and roll control.

The follow-on model, the 140, was all-aluminum and had wing flaps, plus more power.

The Cessna 150, which went into production in 1958 and is still being built, has tricycle landing gear and 100 hp.

The first small, all-metal, four-place airplane built by Cessna was the 170, with conventional gear. It was replaced by the 172, with tricycle gear, in 1955.

The 120, 140, and 150 all have cruise speeds in the neighborhood of 95 to 115 mph. The 170 and 172 are between 125 and 130 mph.

ERCOUPE

The Ercoupe (E and R coming from the company's name: Engineering and Research Corporation) was one of the most unusual—and controversial—light airplanes ever built. It was designed by Fred E. Weick, one of aviation's foremost engineers, who decided to solve with one bold stroke the biggest single cause of aviation fatalities: the stall, followed by spin, at altitudes too low to permit recovery. The Ercoupe was designed to be stall-proof and spin-proof. (The same idea was executed, in a slightly different form, by Professor Otto Koppen, of MIT. His design, called the Skyfarer, was also stall- and spin-proof, but it never reached volume production.)

The Ercoupe could not be ignored. The wing was placed low, there were two vertical fins on a horizontal tail boom, and the third landing wheel was under the nose. This design flew in the face of all things known about proper light airplanes, which had high wings, one fin (and rudder), and a tail wheel.

The Ercoupe really is a nice little plane though some pilots (mostly those who've never flown it) don't think it's too respectable. Most owners love them.

Both the Ercoupe and Skyfarer were built in small quantities before World War II. After the war the Ercoupe came on strong, and was promoted as no airplane had ever been promoted before. It was displayed at state and county fairs, demonstrated at air shows, flown from shopping center parking lots, and even dismantled and reassembled inside department stores. The results were satisfying, to say the least, and Engineering and Research Corporation had to expand their production facilities several times before they could catch up with the demand.

All of this took place with absolute disregard of what aviation's oldtimers were saying about the airplane. Because of its tricycle gear, they called it "the flying milking stool." Because its ailerons and rudder were interconnected—there was only one pedal, for brakes, on the floor—the oldtimers spoke darkly about the problems of landing in a cross wind. (In fact, there were almost none: the landing gear was sturdy, and would accept a very high level of cross wind and a correspondingly low level of pilot skill.)

The Ercoupe was noticeably faster than its contemporaries and quite comfortable and easy to fly. One nice touch was that the cockpit canopy could be opened in flight (at some speed penalty), producing much the same sensation as driving a convertible with the top down. It was a nice-looking, all-aluminum machine, once one got used to its unconventional design. It was precisely true that it would neither stall nor spin.

Even so, it was soon found to have a serious fault. It would get into a high rate of descent (or "sink") which could only be stopped by full forward yoke and loss of a considerable amount of height. The usual result was a hard landing and expensive airframe damage. Injuries to the occupants rarely required medication, but the experience was unsettling enough to drive some new pilots out of aviation.

Fred Weick's goal of eliminating the stall-spin accident sequence was achieved, but the airplane was badly oversold. The high sink rate was never mentioned. In fact many salesmen were themselves surprised by it. The major thrust of the sales effort was "anyone can fly," and cases without end were cited in which pilots who had never had a previous lesson soloed in two hours, or three, or even one.

When the postwar airplane sales bubble burst, Engineering and Research Corporation was not alone in disaster, but unlike Beech, Cessna, and Piper, it did not survive. The Ercoupe itself refused to die and went through a series of revivals, with each new group of owners as starry-eyed as the last, certain that they could escape the fate which had overtaken their predecessors.

Unfortunately, none of the attempts succeeded, not even the most recent revival by Mooney Aircraft, who bought all rights, tooling, and parts from Alon Aircraft, which had been building a few at a time in Kansas. This time the resurrectors took the approach that the only thing wrong with the Ercoupe was its stall-proof, spin-proof philosophy. The tail was redesigned, using one fin and rudder. Rudder pedals were made standard. (A previous field modification had permitted adding rudder controls to the original.) All of the engineering tricks which had made the Ercoupe stall-proof and spin-proof were undone.

The Cadet, as the reincarnation was called, no longer looked odd: by now, low wings and tricycle gears had become commonplace, and that double fin was gone. The Cadet flew just like other airplanes, given small differences in handling. It would stall, and it would spin. The attempt failed: the Cadet didn't even show the small spark of life visible in the previous tries.

The unfortunate part of all this is that the Ercoupe is really quite a nice small airplane. The freedom from stalls and spins doesn't hurt, and anybody who wants to can have rudder pedals installed. The high sink rate can be avoided, as it is in all other airplanes, by proper pilot training and technique.

The one remaining Ercoupe problem is social: it is not thought to be a respectable flying machine. Most of those who have this attitude have never flown one and have no idea of its real assets and liabilities, but that does not lessen their scorn. The Ercoupe is worth looking at, even so.

LUSCOMBE

The Luscombe Model 8, which went into production in 1937, was years ahead of its time. It was entirely of aluminum construction, except for the wing covering, and it was one of the first airplanes in history to be built from what is now called "hard tooling." Its original power plant was 50 hp, but most of them used a 65-hp engine, and the top model, called the Silvaire, had 75 hp, with fuel injection, a rarity before the Second World War. Production was resumed after the war, but not for long.

The Luscombe is a very pretty airplane. Its controls are light, and its response lively. It is quite fast—the 75-hp model cruises at 110 mph. Its one serious shortcoming is lack of comfort. There is little leg room, and the seats are poorly designed and not adjustable. After a couple of hours, pilot and passenger begin to yearn for the ground and a chance to stretch the kinks out of their backs and legs.

The Model 8 Luscombe's fans swear by it and although it was designed in the '30s it still manages to awe by its delightfully sleek lines.

One criticism often heard, particularly from operators of J-3 Cubs, was that the Luscombe had a tender landing gear and that damage was more expensive to repair than on the steel tube and fabric airplanes. The unhappiness about repair cost is true enough, but the criticism of the landing gear is not. A Luscombe is not really hard to fly well, but it will not tolerate anywhere near the level of clumsy landing that the J-3 shrugs off.

Don Luscombe's first encounter with aircraft came as the driver of an ambulance during World War I. He used to tell a story, that he would trade cigarettes for a ride in aircraft being ferried to the front. He was so bitten with the bug he bought a surplus plane after the war and learned to fly it. But it was not until 1933 that he set up production of his first design—the Phantom Model One—in Kansas City.

At $6,000 in 1933 the Phantom was as much a status symbol as a Lamborghini is today. She had electric flaps, navigation and landing lights, dynamo, starter and battery. She was also supposedly fully aerobatic. She had one really bad habit. Because of poor forward visibility on landing and the narrow track of the mainwheels, she needed competence to get her down. If you were unsteady, you stood a good chance of a ground loop which would flip her over or damage the wing. About 25 were made in the four years the Phantom was in production and probably three remain.

The Model 8, on the other hand, was such a sufficient improvement on the original that it became stretched after the war to a four-seater, and continued in production until 1960 under the model name of Silvaire 8F. A Luscombe is a pilot's plane, but if you've been checked out in one, you'll make yourself very comfortable indeed. A pilot trained on Luscombes has no trouble flying a J-3, but the reverse is not always true.

Speaking of the Piper Cub, model J-3, there was a time when more pilots had received their first flight training in this airplane than all other airplanes in the world. The explanation was easy to find: the Cub was simple, rugged, easy to maintain, and inexpensive to operate. In the 1930's it carried the lowest price tag of any airplane, and during World War II with its heavy pilot demands, the J-3 was established as the standard primary trainer. It continued in production in one version or another throughout the war, and was one of the first to resume civilian production afterward.

J-3's were equipped with engines installed; and the present-day descendant of the Cub, called the Super Cub, is still in production, now with 150 hp.

The J-3 is of composite construction: steel tube fuselage, wood spars in the wings (changed to aluminum after the war), aluminum wing ribs, fabric covering all over. Interior appointments are spartan: simple slab seat cushions are supported on canvas slings; the floor is plywood; the brakes are operated by the heels (and often omitted from the front seat). It was long felt that heaters were unnecessary, with the result that even three pairs of socks, long underwear, and fleece-lined flying boots were insufficient on a cold winter's day. The J-3 is flown solo from the rear seat, and the rear seat pilot's legs are more exposed to cold air leaks than those of the lucky chap in front.

Getting into a Cub is an event. The right side has a most unusual door, which is split horizontally. The lower half drops down against the side of the fuselage, while the upper half swings up against the lower surface of the wing and is secured there (most of the time) by a spring clip. It is slightly easier to get into the back seat than the front, but neither is easy. Getting out is worse, especially for the front seat occupant, who is usually the instructor. In fact, it is sufficiently accurate to say that instructors fall out of Cubs when the lesson is over. People used to remark that the Cub is the only airplane in the world you have to take apart to get into or out of.

In common with all small airplanes (and even some large ones) of its day, the Cub had no electrical system. This meant that without battery and generator there could be no electric starter. The engine is started by swinging the propeller, a hazardous proceeding which has been done hundreds of millions of times, with an astonishingly low accident rate. Many pilots who lived through this are now very reluctant to lay hands on a propeller, no matter what the purpose.

If you call every small plane a Piper or a Piper Cub your generation gap is showing. Here are two Super Cubs, the original STOL (Short Take Off and Land) machine.

The engine-starting ritual was as fixed as the challenges and responses of a religious service. The man at the propeller, hands off the propeller, called: "Gas on. Switch off. Throttle closed (or 'cracked')." The pilot repeated, either doing each thing or at least touching each control to make sure it had been done. The man out front pulled the propeller through compression several times, carefully set it at the best pulling angle, wiped his hands on his pants, studied the ground carefully to be sure he had good footing, and called "Brakes and contact." The command "stick back" was often added, and if the airplane had no brakes, the cry was simply "contact." The pilot applied the brakes, closed the ignition switch, and answered "contact." The "starter" put both hands on the propeller, swung his right foot forward and leftward and himself back and out of the way, giving the propeller a brisk rotation.

If the engine failed to start after several tries, the assumption was that the engine was flooded. Now the prop man said "switch off, throttle open" and when he got the reply "off and open" he revolved the propeller backward several turns, the idea being to pump the excess gasoline out of the intake system. A man soon got to know which engines were likely to flood, under what conditions, and how much backward-turning it took to clear them.

Cubs were originally equipped with tail skids, which were fine on dirt or grass fields, and the drag of the skid made brakes on the main wheels unnecessary. Soon tailwheels appeared, connected to the rudder cables with birdcage springs for steering. The best design, which has become standard, is called "steerable-full swivel." Normally, the tailwheel obediently steers, but if the pilot wants to pivot, it unlocks from the steering mechanism and swivels like a caster. As soon as it returns to somewhere near center, the steering function automatically reengages. Brakes came along with tailwheels.

The Cub landing gear has one of aviation's oldest shock absorbing devices, called "shock cords." These are multiple thin strands of rubber, encased in woven fabric and made in the form of rings. They are installed between the wheels and the fuselage and in combination with low-pressure tires produce a very rugged assembly which enables Cubs to tolerate hard landings that would break the wheels off less sturdy machines.

It has become fashionable to say that the Cub was sensitive and very responsive to the controls, but compared to the Luscombe and Taylorcraft it was in fact coarse. It is also slow, with a cruise speed of about 75 miles an hour. It has little baggage space, and the tandem seating is uncompanionable. It is not an airplane to use at a busy airport: it simply cannot keep up with modern trainers like the Cessna 150 and the Piper Cherokee.

With all its faults, the J-3 has an appealing personality. It's a safe, reliable, inexpensive trainer and a good teacher. There are still a lot of them around, and it's virtually impossible to lose money by buying one, flying it for a year or so, and selling it.

The next most popular Piper is the Tri-Pacer, a four-place, tricycle

Big brother to the Cub was Piper's Tri-Pacer, an early, inexpensive and largely theoretically four-place family machine. Its detractors have called it the "flying milk-stool" and claim for it the glide angle of a brick when the power is off. Proper pilot technique *is* needed, and turns this Piper into quite a fun plane.

gear airplane. Like the J-3, a great many were built, and also like the J-3, it had its share of awkward design features. First is the matter of doors. There are two, one on the right side in front, the other on the left side in the rear. This makes for ungraceful loading. The battery master switch is under the pilot's seat, and so is the starter button. The fuel management system leaves something to be desired.

The first models had only 125 hp, which wasn't nearly enough. The change to 135 improved matters a little, but not much. When the power was increased to 150, the airplane was noticeably better, and the final change, to 160, made it quite respectable.

After many thousands were built, the market softened. Many trainer sales had been lost to the Cessna 150 because Piper had not developed a trainer to follow the J-3. So it was decided to modify the Tri-Pacer into a trainer by cutting it back to two seats and reducing engine power to 108 hp. This version is called the Colt.

The Tri-Pacer and Colt are useful airplanes, provided the pilot understands their quirks and limitations. They are not elegant in looks, and their handling qualities in the air and on the ground are not harmonious. They should be loaded more conservatively than the book figures allow.

STINSON

The Stinson Airplane Company built many excellent aircraft, rugged and comfortable, with all but one or two unusually handsome in appearance. Just before the Second World War, they decided to enter the light airplane field with the Model 105.

The 105 was not particularly good-looking; in fact its nickname was "Ruptured Duck." It was supposed to be a three-place airplane, but in fact it was barely large enough for two. The third seat, in back of the pilot's seat, faced sideways in the manner of seats in old cars called "opera seats." Seriously underpowered, with 90 hp, it retained the Stinson traditions of comfort and pleasant handling qualities.

Like the Luscombe, the Stinson has an ardent fan club. A good one is quite expensive since, when restored, they make good cross-country transport.

After the war it reappeared with 124 hp and was renamed Voyager. It was somewhat better, but still far from a satisfactory airplane. In time the power was increased to 165, and the name changed again, to Station Wagon. The 165-hp Station Wagons are very good airplanes, though not especially fast. They are still comfortable and pleasant to fly. After Stinson went out of business, the design was continued for a time by Piper. Many of those still in existence have been recovered in aluminum, some partially, some completely. An all-aluminum-skin 165 Station Wagon, with the late, large tail, is a very good family airplane.

TAYLORCRAFT

Charles G. Taylor was actually the designer of the Piper Cub. In fact, the Piper Cub began life as the Taylor Cub. William T. Piper, Sr., bought control of Taylor's company and Taylor himself soon started up again in his own business, now calling his airplanes Taylorcraft.

For several years the only Taylorcraft was a two-placer, side-by-side airplane, faster than all of its contemporaries except the Luscombe, with a cruise speed of 95 mph. Its model number is BC-12D. It is a nice-flying airplane, though its controls are not as well harmonized as might be wished.

The Taylorcraft is nothing more than a side-by-side Piper Cub. Mr. Taylor designed both and if you feel more comfortable with your friend at your right, buy this one.

It is a bit sluggish in roll and unexpectedly quick in pitch response. One soon gets accustomed to this.

A tandem trainer was introduced later, but it never reached the production levels of either the Aeronca Tandem and Champion or the Piper J-3.

THREE UNUSUAL POSTWAR PERSONAL AIRPLANES

When civilian production of light airplanes was resumed after the war, most of the models had either been in production before the war or were modified prewar models. (One exception was the Cessna 120, but although it was entirely new, it did not represent any major advance in performance.)

There were the Beech Bonanza, the North American Navion, and the Republic Seabee. The Navion and the Seabee were both products of companies which had never been in the light airplane market before, while the Bonanza came from a pioneer light airplane company which had never built purely military aircraft. For different reasons the Navion and Seabee did not survive, while the Bonanza became the all-time leader in light airplanes.

The Navion and the Bonanza were both all-metal, four-place, tricycle gear land planes, with speeds in the same range as the airline DC-3. They were worthy competitors, and between them they've set the pattern for the growth of light airplanes in all the years since the war. We'll have a close look at each of them later on, but first, let's examine the Seabee.

What set the Seabee apart from everything else was the fact that it was an amphibian. There was no doubt when it appeared that the Air Age had dawned at last, when Everyman's Sky Car would become a reality. The reasoning at Republic went a step further than that of any other company: since most of the earth's surface happens to be water, an airplane which could operate from either water or land would have an enormous advantage over one which could not. There were known disadvantages to amphibious designs, to be sure, the most serious being a lack of speed; but did that really matter? If, by using lakes, rivers, and harbors, the owners could depart and arrive closer to their destinations than they would if they had to use prepared airports, wouldn't this saving in ground travel time provide a heavy offset against higher speeds in the air? The argument sounded reasonable, and it is to the credit of Republic and its president, Alfred Marchev, that the decision was made to proceed.

The Seabee has to be one of the finest private planes ever built. It is immensely rugged but it did need extensive modification before it would provide the sort of performance needed. When modified, it can be used as a flying hotel, giving you hunting, shooting and fishing in the most exotic parts of the world.

The Seabee was based on an original design by S. L. Spencer. This was a two-place amphibian of conventional structure and unconventional design, powered with a 100-hp engine mounted with pusher propeller. As in the case of the Stinson 105, there was physically enough room for a third occupant, under light load conditions. The decision was made to increase the power a little, to 112 hp, so that three could travel all the time. The need for four seats was plain for all to see, and it was equally clear that, with still a little more power, four could be carried. The die was cast: power was increased to 125 hp, then to 150.

Aviation's classic problem had been recognized early in the program: the structural design was wrong for volume production. Airplanes of conventional design have too many parts and too many holes for too many rivets to hold the parts together. If the Seabee were to become the Model T of the air, it would have to sell at a low price, in addition to having good range and reasonable speed. The target price for a fully equipped Seabee was $2,995. For all these things to happen, there had to be a straightforward application of Henry Ford's laws: complete tooling, removal of every possible bit of hand work, volume selling, plus elimination of what were to become known as "airplane frills."

A major redesign program was begun, and in this, the Seabee design for production was very successful. There has probably never been such a strong airplane built with such an amazingly small number of parts. For example, there were no ribs in the wings; instead, heavy aluminum sheet was used, with external corrugations rolled into it to provide the same strength as ribs in ordinary airplanes.

Unfortunately, the heavier skin required more power, which needed more fuel capacity, which demanded a bigger tank. One staggering fact was that a 50-pound lead weight was needed in the nose to bring about some kind of balance. The final decision on power was 215 hp, which still wasn't really enough (more about that later).

Many of the parts involved in the cost-reduction effort turned out well, due partially to the fact that Republic was willing to buy in much larger

A fully modified Seabee can set you back the best part of $10,000 if you can find an owner who wants to sell. For the money you get the nearest thing to a "go anywhere" fixed wing plane. Don't expect her to break any speed records though; she cruises at only about 115 mph.

quantities than anybody else. There were charts showing how much each purchased part should cost, and what was allowed for each manufactured part. Only one, the engine, refused to yield.

Republic's solution was direct: if the engine makers wouldn't sell an engine at Republic's price, why not buy an engine company? Why not, indeed? Republic forthwith acquired Aircooled Motors Corporation, descendant of the company which built Franklin automobiles. It wasn't a good deal, as it turned out, but by then it didn't matter. What really happened was that "the dream" of the Seabee's possibilities didn't have a happy ending.

The way "the dream" was presented, you and your bride could get away from it all with that delightful couple next door, carrying with you sleeping bags, camp stoves, hunting and fishing gear, tents and toilets. You could stop at the last outpost flight strip for supplies and local expert advice, and be relaxing in front of the campfire, enjoying a mess of fresh-caught trout, before sunset the first day out.

The trouble with "the dream" was that it was supposed to apply to pilots with moderate skills, proficient in ordinary single-engine land planes. Such pilots could not manage the Seabee. It was a demanding airplane with difficult handling qualities and an unforgiving nature. It developed a bad reputation, which was more the fault of the advertising claims than of the airplane itself. When the postwar sales boom collapsed, the Seabee was one of the permanent casualties. This was too bad because its faults might have been corrected in the course of evolution.

Most of the 400 or so surviving Seabees have been modified in one or more ways and work better than the originals. Curiously enough, they still command prices in the $7,000 to $9,000 range, and some of the best ones are simply not for sale at any price.

North American Aviation had great success with two military airplanes in World War II: the B-25 and the P-51. Along with some of the other big airplane companies, they felt that the postwar future of general aviation was bright enough to be worth a strong effort. The North American entry was called the Navion, evidently a combination of the company initials and "avion," the French word for "airplane." (There is still a lively squabble over the pronunciation of the word. Purists hold out for the short, French "a"; the stronger preference is for the long "a," as in "navy.")

The Navion showed its P-51 ancestry: low wing, retractable gear, bubble-type canopy, squared tail and wing tips. Unlike the P-51, the third wheel was up front, and it was considerably slower than the advertising claims. Like the P-51, it was very strong. Some other similarities were unfortunate. As in the case of the P-51, one gets into a Navion by climbing up a step, sliding the canopy back, and stepping over the side. This required either standing on the seat cushions or lifting them out of the way and standing on the seat frame. With muddy shoes, this was messy either way. Getting into the back seat was worse. The whole affair was much too

Another one with a fan club. The original Navion was very strong but much slower than advertised. Modification of the original has produced a highly practical aircraft and it still seems possible that a modern version may be made once more.

athletic for women who, in addition, resented having a machine dictate to them what to wear—slacks. (However, fashion is having its revenge, and today most women who appear at airports wear pants—née "slacks.")

North American soon discovered that the Navion wasn't profitable and found a buyer in Ryan Aeronautical, who had built Lindbergh's *Spirit of St. Louis.* Ryan fared little better and sold the project to Temco, who in turn sold it to Navion Aircraft Company, a new concern founded solely for the production of this airplane.

The revised model was called the Rangemaster and offered several improvements, the most important being the replacement of the sliding canopy with a proper side-opening door. Wing-tip fuel tanks were standard, giving the airplane an endurance range of some seven hours. There was little success this time, either; but the Navion dies hard. Even as you read this, it may be going into production once again.

The Navion is comfortable, quiet for its time (good even by today's standards), stable, strong, and easy to fly. There is a large and active society of Navion owners, who have gone to great lengths to make sure that parts remain available.

Finally, the famous Beech Bonanza. When the Bonanza was introduced in 1947, Beech Aircraft Company had already invested $2,000,000 in design and tooling. Because of the company's long experience with general aviation airplanes, the comfort and convenience of the user had first priority. The occupants entered through a door on the side, and although this was not as convenient as getting into a car, it was reasonably close.

The Bonanza's outstanding appearance feature was (and still is) the unusual arrangement of the tail. Instead of a vertical fin and rudder, with a horizontal tail plane and elevators, the Bonanza tail is a V. This tail was given the credit for much of the airplane's speed, although many people disagreed. The argument is really of no consequence because that distinctive tail has become the symbol of excellence in light airplanes.

Some years ago Beech introduced a very similar model, the Debonair, which had an ordinary tail. Its sales were acceptable, but not startling.

TOP. The Beech Bonanza once more, this time with wing tanks for long distance flight. CENTER. Fast and speedy, the Mooney was born in Texas. A four-seat retractable, the Mooney Statesman shown here will cruise at around 180 mph. BELOW. Piper's Comanche has long been popular with the record-breaking crowd. Britain's Sheila Scott uses one (Myth Two) as did America's Max Karant. If you want to cruise in great comfort at 180 mph for up to 1,000 miles without long-range tanks, this could be for you.

Later, the Debonair was renamed Bonanza, but it still has nothing of the mystique surrounding the original.

It is said that there are only two classes of members of the Flying Physicians Association: those who own Bonanzas, and those who wish they owned Bonanzas. There are many pilots who find flaws in the airplane, and there are some faults. But what nobody can take away is the success story—which now spans almost a quarter of a century.

One of the most attractive parts of the Bonanza business is the fact that the untrained observer cannot tell the oldest from the newest, so that a man who can only afford $8,000 or so for an airplane can encourage people to think he just paid $50,000 for it. (Can you imagine such a thing happening with a 1947 Cadillac?)

USED PLANE ROUNDUP

The following table lists some vital statistics for most of the airplanes just discussed, their range of price, and how many are still in existence. The prices apply to airplanes which are currently in flying status, while the number in existence also includes those which are not now licensed. Some of these can be relicensed at small cost; others will need major work, probably including recovering. There is no way to show prices for these; all that can be said is that they will cost considerably less than flying airplanes. Don't forget that restoration costs will be quite high, and may well raise the price above that of an airplane already flying. On the other hand, knowing exactly what has been done is often comforting, and justifies the extra money.

USED PLANES

MAKE	MODEL	SEATS	SPEED	LANDING GEAR	AVAILABLE	PRICE RANGE
Aeronca	Tandem and Champion	2	85	Tailwheel	7,000	$1,250–5,000*
	Chief and Super Chief	2	85	Tailwheel	1,500	1,000–2,500
Cessna	120	2	90	Tailwheel	1,300	1,750–3,000
	140	2	105	Tailwheel	3,500	2,000–3,000
	150	2	115	Tricycle	10,000	3,000–9,500
	170	4	120	Tailwheel	3,600	4,000–6,000
	172	4	125–130	Tricycle	12,000	5,000–9,000 up
Ercoupe	415C	2	100	Tricycle	3,500	2,000–3,500
Luscombe	8 Series	2	95–110	Tailwheel	3,500	1,500–3,000
Piper	J-3	2	75	Tailwheel	6,300	1,500–3,200
	Tri-Pacer (includes 2-place Colt)	4	120–125	Tricycle	7,000	3,000–5,000
Stinson	108 Series	4	125	Tailwheel	3,500	3,000–5,000
Taylorcraft	BC-12D	2	95	Tailwheel	3,500	1,500–2,500
	DC-65 (tandem)	2	95	Tailwheel	600	1,000–2,000

* *Highest price is actually a new production Champion*

CHAPTER 5

Taking Trips

ON the surface of the earth, there is little difference in the speed of vehicles, whether they are private cars, buses, or railroad trains. Aloft, there is a very wide range of speeds, from the 600 mph of the airline and business jets down to the 100-mph range of the light trainers. The most numerous of the four-place family airplanes cruise at about 125, and the top speed of propeller-driven executive models is about 300.

So the question is inevitable: "After I get my license, what will I be able to do with a small airplane?" It's easy to go wrong in two directions. One is overestimating the airplane's ability as a travel vehicle—perhaps by comparing airplane and automobile speeds; the other is underestimating—by being too pessimistic about how far the small airplane falls short of jet transport speeds. You'll hear a lot of earnest talk, too, most of it to the effect that if you're really planning to go places in an airplane, you'd better have one that cruises at about 200 miles an hour.

Like everything else, that depends. What it depends on mostly is how far you are planning to travel and how long you can spend at getting from place to place. On short trips, high speed saves little time. On leisurely long trips, slow speed is no handicap. In a pilot's early stages, it is better to begin with a slow airplane and move up in speed after learning how an aircraft is used.

The small family airplane is the new time-stretcher and distance-shrinker. An airplane which cruises at 125 mph will take you and your family between two and three times as far in two hours as a car can. The more congested the area, the bigger the advantage. This includes the time it takes to get to the airport, load family, picnic basket, or baggage, do the preflight inspection, and climb out of the local traffic pattern.

There is another big advantage: comfort. Your car may be air-conditioned, but this doesn't shrink time—it just makes the time more bearable. Your light airplane is not air-conditioned, and it gets hot in the sun while it's standing still, but once you get up to your cruising altitude, it's as cool as you like.

CALIFORNIA

The time-stretching, distance-shrinking works anywhere, but for emphasis, let's look at what can be done in California, where it's as far from Los Angeles to San Francisco as it is from Boston to Harrisburg, with half a state still to go.

Nobody needs to be sold on picnics, so let's deal with only one place: Pismo Beach, California. This is a shade less than two hours' flying time from San Francisco, and a bit more than one hour from Los Angeles. Even from San Francisco, you can leave your house at 8:00 in the morning, have your toes in the Pacific by 10:30 or so, swim and play and eat and bask in the sun, and be home again about 7:30, after six hours on the beach. This

Circling over the airfield at Pismo Beach one can see close-by the magnificent sand dunes and the beach that is a clam digger's delight.

includes the drive to the airport, allowing half an hour each way.

The airstrip at Pismo Beach is on the edge of the ocean—hardly far enough away to be called walking distance.

A little closer to Los Angeles, and a little farther from San Francisco, is the town of Lompoc. In the spring and summer, Lompoc is a riot of color—it is one of the world's great floricultural centers. Don't take a picnic to Lompoc since there's a hotel with an excellent restaurant quite close to the airport.

Still in the same area, Santa Barbara has one of the sweetest harbors and beaches on the whole Pacific Coast, plus the famous and lovely Mission Santa Barbara, and an air of relaxation that is rare. Over the coastal hills from Santa Barbara is the little town of Santa Ynez, which also features one of the early Spanish missions, as well as two other fascinating attractions. One is the town of Solvang, founded and largely populated by Danes and their descendants. The architecture of the whole town is straight out of Denmark, and you'll not find as many Danish bakeries, restaurants, and shops anywhere else outside the mother country. The other attraction is the fabulous Alisal Ranch, a 10,000-acre working cattle ranch that takes in paying guests in attractive cottages scattered among the live oaks. The restaurant and bar are located in a separate building, and the food is a gourmet's delight.

While we're on the subject of dude ranches, it's appropriate to mention the oldest one in the United States—Wonder Valley. It's a few miles east of Fresno—almost exactly equidistant from San Francisco and Los Angeles—and it has its own 2,600-foot airstrip. Here, too, the atmosphere is lazy, the food is excellent, the cabins are restful and private. There is a pool to swim in and there are horses to ride. If you leave home on Friday, in the late afternoon, you can have two restful nights and lazy days, and be home again in comfortable time for Sunday supper.

A lunch trip to the Nut Tree restaurant, halfway between San Francisco and Sacramento, is popular with San Franciscans. It's too far for Angelenos, though a wonderful lunch stop on a longer trip. The Nut Tree has its own excellent airport and a miniature railroad train which runs from the airport to the restaurant. It's really an easy walk, but few visitors can resist riding the train. Inside, the dining areas are of a Polynesian bent. There are aviaries with live birds, screened so discreetly that you think you are outside and that the birds are free.

The old gold country is rich in history and nostalgia, and one of the very best places to visit is the town of Columbia, now a California State Historical Monument. Columbia's airport is 2,112 feet up the western slope of the Sierra Nevada foothills, and a fairly easy walk to town. But you don't have to walk; you can beg a ride or rent a car or wait for the stagecoach (runs a regular schedule during the summer), which is the best fun of all.

In addition to the old buildings—some shops, some museums—there is a theater, operated by the drama department of the University of the Pacific. On the edge of town, there is a comfortable restaurant which specializes in an ancient dish called "Cornish Pasty." This is a meat pie in which the crust begins life as a circle, and after the filling is put in, the crust is folded over and the edges sealed—making a thick half-moon—and baked. The recipe has been traced back to miners who came to Columbia from Cornwall, England.

On the west slope of the great High Sierra, the timber begins again. At the lowest levels, scrub oak dots the rolling pastures; but as the land rises, pines and firs appear, getting taller and denser the higher they go. In summer, cumulus clouds, like dabs of whipped cream, outline the top of the Sierra Nevada. In late afternoons they often build into thunderstorms, but the storms are quite local, and easy to see and avoid; their beauty, however, stays in your memory.

In a year of one-day and two-day weekend trips, carefully planned to cover the whole state, a pilot and his family can get to know more about California than an automotive family can in five years. And while they're at it, the airborne family will be sightseeing all the way, every minute, looking down on all the golden land.

FLORIDA

The special grace of the light airplane is clearly seen in a flight to Key West. Although this island at Florida's southern tip is a mere three hours from Miami by ribbon-straight road and causeway, to hurtle down the highway by car one misses much of the flavor of the Florida Keyes—the colors and quietude and lush tropicality that make this strange part of the United States unique. The aviator sees so much more, and in so much shorter a time: the emeralds and indigos of the balmy shallows; the hot, white sands of the quiet beaches; the still-unspoiled land beyond the concrete band of highway and motel and gas station; the sea birds soaring low over the water; and the bright, white sport fishermen thundering across its surface, outriggers set and conning towers high and proud in the sun.

The flight down the Keys is a delightful one at low altitudes, with the vivid water below and the peculiar, sharp Gulf/Caribbean cumuli dotting the scrubbed horizon. It's not a difficult flight for even the smallest two-seat trainer, for navigation is simply a matter of following the Overseas Highway, and there are even several airports en route to break up the trip or serve as safety stops. Total time from the Miami area shouldn't be more than an hour in the slowest of airplanes, and there's a vortac right at Key West to ensure that navigation will be no problem (with a powerful radio beacon at Marathon as a backup). The first airport along the way is just south of Biscayne Bay, at the posh, private Ocean Reef Club; it offers little for the casual visitor but a stiff landing fee (if they catch you—the airport office is often deserted) and the spectacle of golfers in bug-like carts scuttling around the course that abuts the runway. Next one along is the comparatively busy strip at Marathon—and a little farther away is the runway at Summerland Key. If you use them all, you'll get a lot of cross wind practice, for they're laid out according to the limited space available rather than the prevailing winds.

Unfortunately, many pilots avoid the trip to Key West simply because they think that the flight involves penetration of the Gulf of Mexico ADIZ (air defense identification zone). Even if this were true—and it is only if you make the flight direct from Miami, rather than following the island chain—it simply means you must file a DVFR flight plan, giving a relatively rough estimate of when you're going to enter the ADIZ. Better yet, keep the islands under either wing and you'll be within the wide limits of a corridor through the ADIZ, which obviates the need to file any sort of flight plan.

Key West "International" is that in name only, with the boom days of traffic to and from Havana long over. Tower and ground control are still there, the runway is wide and long (4,800 feet), and the terminal echoes to the occasional footsteps of a rental-car customer, but almost all of the activity at the field today takes place at Island City Flying Service.

Downtown Key West is only a couple of miles from the airport, and you can get there with the help of a rented car or a taxi. You might consider the latter, for the town is a walker's paradise, and anything farther afield—the beautiful, almost-empty public beaches near the airport, for instance—can be reached by bicycle (an ancient, honorable, and economical means of transport available for rental right in Key West).

Key West, Florida.

Key West is much like Provincetown, the artists' colony at the tip of Cape Cod, in Massachusetts. Both are a strange mixture of high-key commerciality and quiet pockets of rare beauty; both are hard-working fishing villages that go about their business despite the tourists and hippies thronging the streets; both have long attracted writers and artists as well as more temporary visitors; and both have a reputation for a kind of roll-with-the-punch ribaldry when the sun goes down. Key West is, by many standards, a honky-tonk town—full of sailors and tourists and saloons, a lot of bad paintings and a little good music—but it seems a solid, honest kind of honky-tonk when compared with the perishable plastic pleasures available up the road at Miami Beach and Florida's so-called Gold Coast (as they say, everything that glitters isn't).

Still, the side streets are never far away in Key West, and along with them, you'll find the palm-draped houses straight out of Tennessee Williams' plays, the lush Spanish gardens, the shady cul-de-sacs where perhaps a wrinkled old man delicately rolls cigars or a young artisan throws pottery on an outdoor wheel. You can tour Ernest Hemingway's old home and walk through the remarkably restored house in which John James Audubon stayed when he was doing research for his famous *Birds of America* folio. Turn back toward the heart of town and the list grows: ride a glass-bottomed boat out to the coral reef south of Key West or rent an aqualung and actually take the plunge; wet a line from a port boat or charter your own cruiser ($100 a day) for deep-water game fishing in some of the liveliest waters anywhere off the United States. Tour the turtle kraals ("corrals," in effect) and the aquarium, or take the half-hour flight ($25 per person, round trip) in the Tortuga Airways Cessna 185 floatplane to Fort Jefferson, an immense bastion halfway to nowhere, out in the middle of the Gulf of Mexico—the country's least accessible National Monument.

There are a good three dozen motels in town; the very active Chamber of Commerce will send you a list. (One to consider is the Pier House, a new, luxurious, and architecturally fascinating place right in the middle of town, on the waterfront and with its own little beach. The rates are from

$14 to $30, depending on the time of year. Their number is [305] 294–9541.) The ubiquitous Hilton, Holiday Inn, Howard Johnson, and Ramada also have outposts on the island. Key West is a let-your-hair-down town, where nobody stands on convention or formality—the sort of place where a mongrel dog climbs on to the bandstand with the musicians at a nightclub and gets a big hand of his own; or where the customers of an expensive French restaurant, finding themselves socked in by a cloudburst, take their shoes off and roll up pants and long skirts to wade home through the flooded streets.

If you can picture yourself doing that, you'll dig Key West.

THE BAHAMAS

While in Florida, you might want to consider a jaunt to the islands to the east, for island-hopping in the Bahamas presents a delightful dividend beyond the thing itself. After adding up the incredible scenic beauty, remarkable flying weather, resorts, rainbows, short flying distances, 30 or more airstrips, good fuel logistics, and adequate radio-navigation facilities, there's something more. Maybe it's those lengthy, untouched islands, emeralds in the sea, there for the taking. Glorious! Perhaps it's the exhilaration of ocean flying, the promise of near-high adventure without the probability of unusual jeopardy. Maybe it's the fun of mastering the special techniques to be learned while flying this salt-water paradise. Whatever, the total seems more than the sum of the parts.

Read the travel literature. Island-hopping "sounds" routine. Qualms soothe. If you think flying is sane even for types with responsibilities, you believe in the "unbelievable" statistical reliability of engines. What difference, you rationalize, over land or water? It's just mileage. Therefore, you might be inclined to check over your plane and go, as with any other casual crosscountry on a sunny day. No big deal. That's right, it's no big deal, but——

Imagine yourself over Fort Lauderdale's beachfront, climbing out. Your engine seems to roughen as you take a serious ocean heading. You concentrate on the "strange" sounds, finally deciding to continue. Suddenly, you become aware that Florida has disappeared, and you're no longer a statistical probability. You're you, *alone*, although you're still only 10 minutes away from an airport. If you haven't by now fetched an inkling of what Lindbergh must have felt, you haven't got the message. However, if you've done your homework, enormous odds say you should not be one of the handful of private aircraft (out of 25,000 annually, most of them single engine) the Bahamas Ministry of Tourism wishes had gone away some *other* way.

This flight isn't for the fledgling still bubbly from first solo; neither do you need 5,000 hours. With minimum cross-country experience—say 50 or 100 hours—and some preplanning emphasizing the special cares necessary for overwater flying, you're ready to launch with hardly a worry.

Island-hopping is the name of the game when you visit the Bahamas. But remember, you can never have too much fuel when you're flying over water.

As a starter, be prepared to use the maximum crosswind capability of the aircraft you intend to fly with the load you'll be carrying. *Reason:* Most landing places are single strips, and some of these seem to have been laid out at the whim of the bulldozer rather than on advice from the prevailing wind. This isn't all bad—it's just a challenge now and then.

When planning, figure your load with full fuel. Reserves should be 100 percent throughout. You simply can't have too much gas. Also, be positive you've got a sound compass. Next, arrange for air/sea rescue items: Mae Wests, inflatable raft, pocket-size emergency radio beacon. These are rentable at nominal daily rates from FBO's in Florida. For four people, they'll weigh about 25 pounds. A postcard to Red Air Service, Fort Lauderdale, or to Tilford Flying Service in West Palm Beach, will reserve the gear. Flares are also important; unless the Coast Guard knows that you have them aboard, they won't chase after you at night. Because the USCG covers the entire Bahama area, you can put them on 24-hour call by getting flares and writing the fact clearly on your flight plan.

As for Bahamian fuel, it's well deployed, carefully handled and stored, and frequently tested for contamination. Fuel costs much less at Nassau and Freeport than in the Out Islands.

You need a flight plan to cross the ADIZ (air defense identification zone), a 25-mile chunk of air offshore that is under constant radar and air-patrol scrutiny. This flight plan and associated radio procedure are straightforward, however; Florida FBO's will guide you exactly. They'll also fill out your customs/immigration documents and provide up-to-date charts plus a handy little folder done up by the Bahamas people. Called *Private Plane Flying,* it does a good job of pinpointing fuel and radio facilities. (The Bahamas Islands Tourist Office, 30 Rockefeller Plaza, New York City, New York 10020, will send you one free.)

Here's a slice of life while going over: Cleared for Nassau. The first checkpoint, Bimini, gateway to the Bahamas and a mere 53 nautical miles off Florida. The midmorning weather is typically good. At 4,500 you are just under cloud bases of widely scattered cumulus with tops of 6,500 feet.

The omni navigation aid is strong, Miami Radio clear, and you are fairly comfortable out over the briny.

Swing the heading toward Nassau, and see hues change according to depth of water, from deep purple to midnight blue in deep water and then on to turquoise, aqua, finally ending on the beaches in pale yellow and eggshell. See long, sweeping contours, deep cuts and shallow undulations defining age-old currents, channels, reefs, and shelves. Occasional barchans—wind-molded sand dunes—show prevailing breezes. Each shape reflects a different color. Now understand how to navigate by water color, as advised by an old hand: If lost, he said, fly in wide circles; steer for light water and track to a land mass.

Nassau International is a big well-run airport peopled with prompt customs/immigration service. Ask for and you'll get a transire, with which you can roam without serious interrogation from island officials you'll meet along the line. Jumping off from Nassau, you file flight plans and commit yourself to periodic check-ins. For example, describe a round robin, saying where you intend to stop and that you'll be calling in every hour while flying. There are remote radio receivers at Bimini, Rock Sound, George Town, and Marsh Harbour. The Bahamians are interested in air safety; their welfare depends on successful use of aircraft.

A must trip is the ride from Nassau to George Town, down the Exuma chain—those little emerald isles that some declare to be the most beautiful scenery in the world. At George Town there are several fine places to stay: Peace and Plenty, Out Island Inn. (When you write for trip-planning literature, ask for the Bahamas booklet listing all island accommodations.)

Once deep in the Out Islands, you sample a new kind of unicom radio service. At most island places, unicom doesn't reach the airstrip. Instead, the ground station is at the resort. You fly over, call the resort, make your reservation, and you will be picked up at the strip. In addition call your intended landing during the landing pattern—not to appraise the resort, but to tell other aircraft what you're doing. Someone else may be heading straight-in from the other direction.

Another particularly Bahamian use of the unicom radio is to call a passing plane from the ground for pilot-report weather. After a visit to Stella Maris, sampling George Friese's excellent island fare, you may use his unicom to call a passing airliner. The alternative is an expensive overseas phone call to Nassau. Incidentally, there is seldom any major weather. Rain showers are almost always widely scattered and easy to get around.

A phenomenon you'll notice is cloud build-up over islands. Each island is embossed with its own little cumulus. Whole chains are thus defined by their island in the sky. With practice, you can navigate, using clouds as landmarks. Obviously, this isn't reliable, but it can be helpful when conditions are right. Occasionally, build-ups get out of hand. The little island clouds grow, turning into standing thunderheads, which have been known to guard airstrips all day, especially in summer.

San Salvador, the first island upon which Columbus set foot, is worth a look from the air. There's a monument on the western side, marking the exact spot where he landed. You, also a navigator but with a godlike overview, can see as relatively few people have exactly what kind of monstrous problem he faced, standing off there with no charts, primitive instruments, and a disgruntled crew. He picked his way through impossible reefs for successful landings, here and all along his route. A near miracle. Proving the point, there's a wrecked modern freighter in the same kind of situation on Cat Island, next door.

Flying northward from Nassau, look over Great Harbor Cay in the Berry Islands. It's jet-set posh. Bring money. On Great Abaco, there are about 20 good places to stay; try Treasure Cay Yacht and Golf Club. Plenty to do, good food, beautiful, and air-conditioned comfort. If you like Americanized accommodations, there's Freeport (gambling) and the Grand Bahama Hotel at West End. The tourism people feel they have three different "products" to offer—old, colonial Nassau; new, swinging Freeport; and the Out Islands.

Next to last thing: Carry your own tie-down gear and a couple of quarts of oil—needs you may have in the Out Islands. Now, check over your airplane and go, as on any other casual crosscountry on a sunny day.

MAINE

Typical of the many quaint and lovely spots that abound in the northeast is the tiny coastal town of Wiscasset, Maine. You begin wanting the trip never to end. Flying from New York, you pick up the Atlantic shore just north of Boston—south of there it's just sand and suburbia—and you find yourself putting the nose down a bit to get closer to the constantly changing drama of hedge-clipped, crew-cut estates, rocky headlands and trim lighthouses, coves and harbors, and baronial nineteenth-century resort hotels.

The glacier-raked rocks lie in immense shelves, islets, islands, and peninsulas, all pointing the same way, all showing as fresh as though it were yesterday the passage of that vast earth-weight of ice. And the great hotels and manors . . . relics of an equally petrified past age, as grand and bleached as beached battleships from some Great White Fleet.

Wiscasset, Maine, is just a few minutes east of the Brunswick naval air station; just follow the highway and you'll see the airport right next to the road. Stay aloft and take a look at the town, though, about three miles farther on. It sits, foursquare and solid as a Republican in the statehouse, on the banks of a long, wind-streaked arm of the Atlantic that leads down to the sea. Here are the watch cupolas and widow's walks atop Wiscasset's incredible old homes, the weathered headstones of the captains not long out of their teens in the town's ancient cemetery, the two rotting hulks of lumber schooners that tower over the waterfront.

In the late eighteenth century, Wiscasset, tiny as it was, was a busy seaport—though you'd hardly know it from its somnolent present state. Yet it was for some time the largest American seaport north of Boston. The giveaway, as you walk its leafy, silent streets, is the row of crisp old houses, their blown-glass windows so clean they sparkle like diamonds in the morning sun, the dormers and fanlights and occasional—very occasional—frivolity of gingerbread molding still as sharp as the day they were hammered and pegged together. They are monuments to what once passed for wealth in a stern, struggling New England—the classic homes of the men

Once a bustling seaport, Wiscasset, Maine, today leads a quiet life.

who made money with clippers and schooners, coasters and dories. These homes are the pride of Wiscasset—the jewels in the diadem with which it crowned itself "Maine's prettiest village."

If it's blowing a near gale and you call on unicom radio to ask the wind force and direction, you might well get an answer like this: "Well, now, I don't rightly know, we don't have no gauge down here . . . but she's ablowin' right smaht, I'll tell you that."

Wiscasset Municipal Airport has recently been lengthened and vastly improved. You'll find it on the New York sectional chart, about 11 miles east of the Brunswick TVOR navigation aid.

If you've planned ahead, you'll have called Econo-Car in nearby Brunswick and asked them to leave a rental car at the airport for you. There's a single taxi and a small rent-a-car agency right in Wiscasset, but depending on the time of day, their mood, or whether or not it's duck-hunting season, they may or may not have any cars available. You'll also have called Frederick Engert to reserve a room at the homey Ledges Inn, right in the middle of town ($14 a night with bath, $10 without, all rooms are doubles). Engert, a pilot since 1935, used to do his traveling in a BT-13, but now he has an M Bonanza.

What do you do when you get there? Walk the gentle streets, look at the remarkable old homes, tour the 1807 Nickels–Sortwell House (open from mid-June through mid-October, Tuesday through Sunday). Visit the Lincoln County Museum, stop at the restoration of the town's old jail and at the Maine Art Gallery. Cross the bay to Fort Edgecombe, built to protect Wiscasset in the War of 1812 and now restored in all its toylike compactness. (After all, just how much of a fort does it take to protect a town across which you could then have pitched a well-tossed rock?) Look for antiques in the town's several shops, and sample contemporary crafts in the Independence Garage—not a repair shop, but an art studio founded by two local artists—filled with ceramics and paintings and metal sculpture and wood carvings and a small sign that says: "Please Touch. See With Your Hands."

Wiscasset is not a resort, with all the manufactured and organized pleasures that implies. It takes a little effort to appreciate it, for it is an unpretentious, stolid little town. Get beneath the plain surface, however, and you may be lucky enough to discover the town that *Esquire* magazine recently selected as one of the nine "happiest places" in the whole United States.

After a few pleasure trips in your own airplane, at your own leisurely pace, you'll doubtless want to try your hand at the greater demands of a business trip. Here the trick is to make certain you've left enough time for careful flight planning and to make sure you're not rushed. Should weather or some unforeseen problem detain you, you'll probably be surprised at the special deference with which you're treated when you call to delay that important appointment because you've made a precautionary landing in your own airplane.

An Ercoupe follows the shore line Baja-bound.

CHAPTER 6

Business Flying

BUSINESSES have long been using airplanes, though in the early days they were used more for publicity than for transport. One of the best-known publicity events was the sponsorship of Calbraith Perry Rodgers in competition for a $50,000 prize for the first transcontinental flight. The sponsoring company made a soft drink called Vin Fizz. Rodgers finally made it across, but few have heard of the soft drink since. About ten years later, another soft drink company hired pioneer pilot and airplane builder Jack Irwin to fly over downtown Los Angeles playing the opening phrase from "How Dry I Am" on an exhaust-powered aeronautical equivalent of a steam calliope. Nobody has heard of this company since then.

Perhaps the first extensive use by businesses of airplanes in the modern sense of transport of people and goods occurred in the 1920's. Not much is known about this since the heads of the companies involved wanted as little publicity as possible: the "passengers" were illegal aliens, and the "cargo" was illegal booze.

Promotional flying boomed in the 1930's, with the biggest users such oil companies as Gilmore, Pure, Shell, Standard, and Texaco. The Lorillard Tobacco Company introduced Old Gold cigarettes to the world by means of an airborne public address system which boomed "Old Gold—Not a Cough in a Carload." The "fi" of those days was not very "hi," and it's questionable how many people who heard the message understood what was being said.

Just after the Second World War, Milton Reynolds, the inventor of a ball-point pen which sold for $15 and wrote under water, promoted it by sending the late Bill Odom on a record-breaking flight around the world in an ex-military Douglas A-26.

BUSINESS FLYING

Even though promotional flying dominated the 1930's, at least one business executive was using an airplane as a flying office. J. H. McDuffee, general manager of the Prest-O-Lite Battery Company, would answer correspondence on a portable dictating machine while flying in the company airplane. He would then have the pilot fly low over a golf course, where he would drop a parachute-equipped package with the cylinders inside and mailing instructions on the outside, in the hope that some nearby golfers would promptly put it in the mail.

One of the better-known business airplanes of the late 1930's was the Beech Model 17-Staggerwing. This was a great success, but it was just the beginning. Beech sensed that business people wanted an airplane which compared closely to such airline types as the Boeing 247 and DC-3, and the result was the Beech Model 18, better known simply as the Twin Beech. Like the 247 and the DC-3, the 18 was all-metal and equipped with two engines. The first one was delivered to Ethyl Corporation in 1937. The Model 18 has been called the spark that set business aviation in motion. Production continued in several military versions during the war, providing a huge pool for reconversion to civilian use afterward. Although the passage of time produced faster and more efficient airplanes, the 18 was not phased out of production until the middle 1960's and, like the DC-3, 18's will be flying for at least a couple more decades.

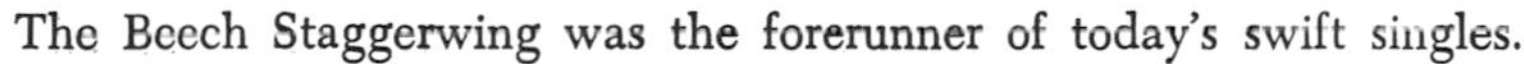

The Beech Staggerwing was the forerunner of today's swift singles.

The Twin Beech was probably one of the first aircraft to be taken to the bosom of the business community. It was introduced in the late '30s, and not phased out of production until thirty years later.

Since the Beech 18 had begun as a civilian airplane, conversion was really no more than restoring it to its original condition. But the postwar period saw many conversions of purely military airplanes, such as the Douglas A-20 and A-26, the North American B-25, the Boeing B-17, the Lockheed Vega and Ventura bombers, and even the Consolidated B-24.

One of the earliest serious contenders for the Beech 18 market was the Aero Commander, designed by Ted Smith, who had been responsible for the Douglas A-20. President Eisenhower gave Aero Commander a big boost by using one as his own personal transport.

The most visible part of business flying used airplanes with two or more engines, the primary advantages being speed and range. In 1947, however, Beech created another important airplane, the single-engine Model 35, better known throughout the world as the Bonanza. The Bonanza was almost as fast as the Model 18, lower in cost and upkeep, and easier to fly. It extended the use of airplanes in business farther into the small business field than the Twins could do; and though it is usually thought of primarily as a personal transport, many consider it the first effective single-engine business airplane.

The Douglas DC-3 went into business service too, through conversion of military versions at first. Later as companies bought phased-out airline-machines, larger and faster types were put into scheduled service. By modern standards the DC-3 is slow, yet there are still many of these wonderful old airplanes in business aviation. Like the Beech 18, they will probably be around for many years.

At the top of the pyramid are those huge corporations with large aviation departments, many operating the same jet airplanes as the airlines, with crews trained by the airlines, on schedules and routes comparable in distance and complexity to those of some of the airlines.

The list of members of the National Business Aircraft Association reads like *Fortune* magazine's 500 list.

These large corporation flight departments are easy to identify, yet they are really the smallest part of business flying. People have been trying for years with little success to find out exactly how many airplanes are involved and to what extent they are used in business. The reason is not hard to understand: as in the case of the private automobile, almost all of which have some element of business use, it is impossible to tell accurately just what amount of flying by which models of airplanes should be assigned to business. There are, however, at least 25,000 airplanes being used primarily for business flying, with some 1,000 of these million-dollar jets.

In the 1960 edition of the FAA statistical handbook, business flying was shown as 5.7 million hours and 855 million miles. In the 1968 issue these figures had grown to 6.6 million and 1,430 million, respectively. The fact of hours flown increasing by 15 percent while miles increased by 160 percent is explained by the great increase in the use by business of turbine-powered airplanes. Because jets are faster, they fly more miles. Because they fly more, they are more flexible and are used more often.

But there is an even more interesting factor at work: as each part of aviation grows and finds its proper place in the air transportation scheme of things, every other part is stimulated and grows too.

The scheduled airlines' very large airplanes are used best on long-haul routes where traffic is high. Travelers for pleasure can easily adjust to these schedules, which often involve long waits at intermediate points, while travelers on business cannot. As the long-haul routes settle down to serving fewer and fewer city pairs on fixed schedules, the demand increases for service of similar speed with complete schedule flexibility and the companion ability to reach cities poorly served by the airlines.

The same restraints of economics and efficiency which affect the airlines also appear in the operations of turboprop and pure jet business airplanes; and this gives a boost to light and medium twin-engine airplanes with piston engines. As distances get shorter still, many airports which are too small for even piston twins appear, and this stimulates the use of single-engine airplanes. The final step is the need to travel by air between points which don't have any kind of airport at all, and here is where the helicopter takes over.

From now on all phases of aviation for business will increase because at last we have in our fleet aircraft of every size, type, range, and speed, each with its own characteristic "best-service" range.

The compelling reason is personal convenience, which also explains why people use their own automobiles for every kind of surface transport, happily ignoring the facts of economy and speed. Men commute to work in large station wagons, whose prime function is long-distance transport of several bodies. Women drive pickup trucks with camper bodies a mile or so to the supermarket. This matter of personal convenience is at the bottom of the decline in availability of public surface transport systems. It is often said that Americans have fallen in love with the automobile; it may well be more precise to say that they have really fallen in love with what the automobile gives them: the ability to go wherever they want to go at whatever time they choose.

Exactly this same effect is now appearing in aviation. Once having learned what an airplane can do, the pilot is basking in the luxury of being able to come and go at his personal whim. To an instrument-rated pilot using our modern navigation system, the weather is less and less an interference; and even when the weather becomes a factor, the result is more likely to be adventure than hardship. There is a kind of frontier explorer atmosphere involved in having to spend an unexpected night or two in a strange town, and it matters very little that the accommodations may not be excellent. This is all part of the adventure of flight, and once the pilot becomes accustomed to freedom from outsiders' schedules, he thinks first of his own aircraft, just as the car owner thinks first of his personal car.

One of the problems facing many businesses today is how to choose a business airplane.

Let the model fit the mission is the best rule to follow. Recognizing this, manufacturers offer more than 70 models, and each can be tailored to specific requirements.

"Tailored" is an appropriate word for the business airplane. Just as there are wardrobes for different occasions, there are airplanes for different uses. Once the proper airplane is selected, it can be "altered" to fit the specific uses through selection of electronic equipment, seating arrangements, wheels or floats, and cargo or passenger configurations.

Probably the first considerations are: What will or can an airplane do for the advancement of your business operation, and how can you alter your business to take best advantage of this useful tool?

There are two steps, both of which should be taken before any serious consideration is given to a specific airplane.

First, a travel "profile" should be made of the company. Who in your company travels? Where do they travel and for what reasons? Do several persons go to the same destinations? What is the value per man-hour of these people? How long is the typical business trip? What percentage of travel is under 300 miles, under 500, under 800, over 1,000?

Second, a "projected" travel profile should be constructed. This differs from the current profile in that it seeks to determine what travel should be done that is not being done, and what opportunities could be explored that are being missed because of limitations. This second profile seeks to answer the question, "How can I alter my operations to take advantage of the airplane as a business tool?"

Such travel profiles can be constructed by airplane dealers or aviation consultants. From them not only the proper "fitting" of an airplane is assured, but also a realistic cost appraisal to compare to benefits is forthcoming.

There are, of course, several categories of airplanes, with those models within a category falling into broad general use patterns. But there are no rigid rules. For example, one company with 80 percent of its travel under 800-mile stage lengths may find that one or more single-engine airplanes personally flown by the company representatives best serves its interests, while another firm with the same stage lengths might better utilize a high-performance twin in a constant shuttle operation flown by a professional crew. Still others, who find they must frequently go in and out of rough rural airports, might find it wise to choose an airplane with STOL (short takeoff-and-landing) characteristics. This type of airplane is becoming increasingly popular because of its utility and practicality.

Because of this individual "tailoring," the following category outline of business airplanes represents only suggested types and typical uses.

THE SINGLE-ENGINE AIRPLANE

This category is usually flown personally by the small man of big business or the big man of small business. Its range is utilized best in frequent trips under the 1,000 to 1,200 mile limit, although it is capable of extended flight. A long flight requiring frequent business stops en route also is served well by the single-engine model. It has the capabilities of operating into and out of almost any type of airport. Since it is usually flown by the traveler himself, it saves the cost of a professional pilot. Yet, seating capacity ranges up to six passengers and a pilot. This enables teams of personnel to be used where needed, and two, four, or even more persons can be put into productive action for the same transportation cost as one.

Properly equipped, a single-engine airplane with a trained pilot is capable of operations at night and in limited weather conditions, although it is not recommended that the plane be operated in *both* bad weather *and* darkness. Icing conditions will restrict use to a small degree in some sections of the country because of the absence of anti-icing equipment.

Since most of the operations are usually over short stage lengths, the speed of one model over another frequently is not the most important consideration. Over a 300-mile distance, for instance, an airplane traveling at

The Cardinal RG—the RG stands for retractable gear, seen here folding away—is a versatile machine for the independent businessman. Cruise speed around 170 mph with a range of 700 miles makes this attractive at the price.

150 miles an hour will take two hours to complete the trip, while one having a speed of 180 miles an hour will do it just 20 minutes faster.

Turbocharging in engines of many new models raises both the speed of the airplane and its ability to operate at higher altitudes. This makes possible some "over-the-weather" flying and permits taking advantage of more favorable winds. All of this adds to the utilization for longer distance travel and begins to place a premium on speed when longer distances are a consideration.

Convertibility of most single-engine models to cargo configuration enables carrying of displays, samples, and similar equipment.

It is with the single-engine category that most businesses "get their feet wet" in the use of an airplane. One manufacturer's customer research indicates that from 60 to 75 percent of its single-engine purchasers use the airplane for business. Many times this beginning originates with an employee who uses his personal airplane just as other employees use their own automobiles. From this use comes recognition of the benefits, which are translated to other employees in similar situations.

In cost the single-engine models range from about $5,000 to $50,000.

THE LIGHT TWIN

More than an additional power plant is added onto the twins. Utility increases many times over. In the twin field, night and weather travel take on added meaning. While seating capacity and payload of the light twin do not vary much from the high-performance single-engine models, the added power plant expands its use during darkness and adverse weather. On some light twins de-icing or anti-icing equipment may be added for convenience.

Seating ranges from four to six. The light twin sometimes is flown by a professional pilot; at other times it is piloted by the individual businessman making the trip.

Since a flight over long distances is more likely to encounter varying weather conditions, the twin increases mobility for the company whose travel profile includes a fair percentage of trips to different parts of the country.

Some light twins are available at prices that are less than those for some of the high-performance single-engine models. Operating costs run higher though, both on fuel and maintenance.

In the light twin category, choices range from the tandem-powered model, which provides easy transition for single-engine pilots, to turbocharged types with speeds in the 250-mile-an-hour range.

THE MEDIUM TWIN

When the company has as many as a dozen people traveling over the same routes; when in-flight conferences for several, or ample desk space for a few, are required; or when all-weather operations are a matter of routine—that's when the company turns to a medium twin.

Customized interiors to fit the specific needs and desires of the owner are found in this range. High-density seating in some models provides airline comfort for 10 or 12 passengers. Fold-over tables, side-facing seats, or

Additional power in the form of an extra engine provides increased utility. Your payload rises, and there may be a useful increase in cruising speed. The Beechcraft Baron shown here will seat up to six people and cruise 1,000 miles at 230 mph.

These light twins are functional, but can provide a surprising degree of comfort in so small a space.

The Beechcraft Duke is pressurized and designed to cope with most weather conditions. Note the de-icing equipment on the leading edges of the wings and tail unit. Pressurization means airliner comfort above the weather and a cruise of around 275 mph.

swivel seats make for a mobile conference room. Divans offer seating for several or bedroom comfort to let an executive arrive at his destination thoroughly refreshed.

The medium twins usually are flown by a professional crew. Their all-weather capability, range, and speed give great flexibility for short- and long-distance flights. Although used many times for direct and return flights with the same passengers, the medium twins often work the shuttle and pickup runs, dropping and adding passengers as destinations and needs require.

The medium twins, with speeds approaching 300 mph, carry price tags from about $90,000 up. Cost of operation usually must include one or more crews.

THE TURBOPROP

The turboprop features the best of two worlds—the lower costs of propeller driven airplanes combined with some advantages of the jet. Falling into the "medium twin" category, the turboprop usually is professionally flown. Its jet power and pressurization make it well-suited for medium and long trips at speeds over 300 mph, yet it operates efficiently on short runs.

While the cost of jet fuel is less per gallon than that of gasoline, consumption per hour of flying is greater, but so too are the distances covered. This is just another example of why "the travel profile" is important to cost-benefit. Initial purchase price is higher than for piston-powered twins, but still under the pure jet.

At present less than a half-dozen manufacturers are offering turboprops designed for the business market. Prices range from $150,000 to $1,250,000.

The turboprop can operate into and out of smaller airports than required by the pure jet. This can be a consideration for the business whose travel patterns are more variable.

Virtually mini-airliners, turboprops are fast, pressurized and comfortable. More important, they cost less than a pure jet.

THE PURE JET

At the top of the business fleet is the pure jet. It rivals the best of the airliners in speed (well over 500 mph) and the best of the piston-powered planes in flexibility.

The mission of the business jet is to compress great distances into short expanses of time. Almost invariably professionally flown, the pure jet moves the big men of big business to widely scattered points and returns them in a matter of hours. For the man with a jet, a morning meeting in New York, followed by lunch in Miami, an afternoon appointment in Detroit, and home by evening is not unusual.

The environment of the jet is high altitude; for this reason it is most efficient for medium- and long-distance travel. Because of its speed, the jet, probably more than any other business airplane, is used most frequently in the "drop and pickup" pattern, even though company travel may be spread over widely separated miles.

Starting at about $700,000, models of the pure jet range over the $2.5 million mark. At least eight business jets, both American made and foreign imports, are available. Some businesses even use medium-range airline models with business interiors.

A Cessna Citation fan jet actually costs less than some turboprops, yet offers higher performance, with a cruise speed in excess of 400 mph. Unlike many other jets it is able to get in and out of small airports.

The archetype of "bizjets," the Learjet was created by millionnaire inventor Bill Lear, whose current interest is the steam engine. Its cruise speed is more than 500 mph and, depending on the load, its range can be nearly 2,000 miles.

The only four-engined "bizjet," the Lockheed Dash-8 Jetstar has full transatlantic capability. It's a relatively big plane which seats up to 12. Cruise speed is 500 mph plus.

The Beechcraft-Hawker BH 125 is one of the few jets to coolly handle the arctic frosts of north Alaska. A versatile machine, its cruise speed is in excess of 500 mph but pilots like its very slow landing speed

The Grumman Gulfstream II is—with a price tag of more than $3 million—a plane for the very rich. David Rockefeller has one. With a high cruise speed of more than 600 mph, the Gulfstream II is the fastest of the small "bizjets"—faster than most airliners.

Perhaps the ultimate in "bizjets" is Hugh Hefner's Playboy Bunny, a McDonnell-Douglas DC-9-30 airliner adapted to the Playboy lifestyle. Hefner's private quarters include the famous elliptical bed, and the bathroom boasts a small paddling pool. Further forward there's a mini-discotheque, with quadriphonic sound, movie projector, screen, cassette TV and so forth. Complete price tag was well in excess of $6 million.

THE HELICOPTER

This is one vehicle which is enabling business aviation to build a corporate transportation program to utilize the convenience of outlying fields with their shorter runways, thereby eliminating the time delays at congested metropolitan airports.

While its maturation as a private transportation tool has been slow, the helicopter's use has been directly proportionate to its acceptance by the communities to and from which the executive must travel to conduct his business. But now a pattern of acceptance is evident: in 1961 there were fewer than 350 heliports and helistops in the United States; today the number is close to 2,000 and growing. This is a significant breakthrough in the forging of an air way into city centers, while alleviating the problems being experienced at the commercial airports.

The advent of the small turbine engine designed specifically for use in the helicopter has resulted in the aircraft's increased utility. Capitalizing on the inroads made into the executive market by the piston-powered helicopter, the compact turbine engine now allows for the added convenience of having the helicopter cabin designed as a complete unit for the passenger. Most of this new breed allow for more spacious passenger area and fuselage shapes more in keeping with the jet age.

What the development of the advanced piston and turbine engines have done for the helicopter industry is seen in the optimism of manufacturers and market analysts alike. By 1975 they estimate business helicopter sales will grow to about 1,000 per year.

The present turbine-powered helicopters are generally faster than piston-powered models by 40 to 50 percent. This doubles their range or allows for higher payloads. Current estimates in operating costs are lower than for piston-powered helicopters by 35 to 45 percent per hour.

The reduced weight of the engine also increases the lifting capabilities of the aircraft—capitalizing on the combination of cabin design and available space and weight. This new generation of turbine-powered small helicopters is capable of providing a substantial increase in luggage space.

ABOVE. The helicopter is finding increasing acceptance with businessmen because of its door-to-door capability. A small car park is a landing pad for a chopper. The Bell Jet Ranger here has a cruise speed of 135 mph and a range of nearly 400 miles.

RIGHT. The pilot is enthroned in solitude, the instrument pedestal to his left, and clear-view panels all around. Note the clean, almost ascetic appearance of the strictly functional working environment.

These small helicopters range in price from $40,000 for the two- and three-passenger piston-class to almost $150,000 for five-place, turbine-powered machines. The cost effectiveness of a helicopter is unique because it cannot be measured along with the standards imposed by the aviation industry as a whole. The cost-per-seat-mile normally employed is not valid in the context of helicopter utilization, and must be exchanged for an economic or budgetary appraisal on the basis of time saved. The "close-in" time—the periods spent either in ground transit or waiting at major air terminals—and its value placed against the worth of the man involved must be the yardstick used to determine the economic worth.

The immediate future of the small helicopter has never looked brighter. At last its place in business aviation has been more clearly defined.

Business aircraft statistics are on the rise. A Federal Aviation Administration study indicates that by 1975 the business fleet will number 32,150, a gain of 52 percent over 1964. Utilization of business airplanes will also be up to 301 hours per airplane, an increase of 23 hours over 1964. Total hours flown will be up 65 percent.

The number of four-place and over single-engine planes in the business fleet will jump to 17,500 in 1975 compared to 12,598 in 1964. Most of this growth is expected in the large, higher horsepower, single-engine group. The smaller twin-engine planes are expected to increase by nearly 75 percent to about 9,000. In 1964 there were 5,200 of this type operating.

Turbine-powered aircraft being used for business will also increase. Government forecasters predict that by 1975 this fleet will number 3,100—1,900 turboprops and 2,200 jets.

No matter what category is chosen, the purpose of business aircraft is the same: to put productive people where they can do the best job in the shortest possible time. Because requirements vary within companies as well

Outside its duties to businessmen, the roles for the helicopter are almost limitless. Agriculture, forestry, public health, traffic reporting and general police work, pipeline laying and patrolling, working offshore oil rigs, public utilities maintenance—all these and many other missions are performed efficiently by helicopter.

as from business to business, selecting the proper airplane becomes a specialized action.

It is common practice for companies to trade-in rapidly. Rather than an indication of bad judgment in original selection, it is a reflection on the recognized value of the airplane, as well as a move to gain increased benefits from increased utility.

Whatever the model, the business airplane is a slave driver. It no longer permits the luxury of missed appointments or unplanned meetings. It removes the "later's" and "maybe's" from business vocabularies and supplants them with "now."

CHAPTER 7

Flying for a Living

ONCE upon a time, the flight school was the coffee-spotted waiting room alongside the line shack, with a sofa made from the back seat of a Buick, and, next to the washroom, a classroom that nobody ever seemed to use: it had a chalkboard on which could still be seen the dim outlines of a traffic pattern, and beside it a pile of empties from the Coke machine. The instructor flew occasional charters in the Twin Beech, and wore a shiny, old tanker jacket. He sat under the wing with you, making formations with his hands and slipping his palm gracefully to a cross-wind landing in the summer dust.

You idolized him, and knew there was no more skillful Pan Am four-striper, carrier pilot, or pin-striped Learjet jock alive. Perhaps you pumped gas to buy flight time, and maybe you washed an airplane or two. In any case, you had plenty of time to consider, for the airplane meandered in from student crosscountries half a day late, and it always seemed to be down for a hundred-hour just when the wind was straight enough to let you solo.

That was once upon a time. Today, the prototypical flight school of the future is the immense, computerized, systematized, sanitized Burnside-Ott Aviation Training Center, an all-business, by-the-numbers outfit in Florida dedicated to the pursuit of a solid profit while turning out above average lightplane pilots and embryo airline officers.

There are a dozen or so such schools in the country today, and they vary only slightly in the quality and thoroughness of their methods: Embry-Riddle in Daytona, Florida; Spartan School in Tulsa, Oklahoma; American Flyers in Fort Worth, Texas; and Parks College in St. Louis, Missouri, to name a few.

Your old school had a direct line to the FSS? Burnside-Ott has its own weather radar to broadcast the bright splatters of Gulf squalls via closed-circuit TV to students checking weather in the main lobby. They have three Cherokees and an Apache on the line down at the local airport? Burnside-Ott has 83 Cessna 150's and 172's, two Lake Amphibians, eight Twin Comanches, a Twin Beech, two DC-3's, a Cessna 310, and an IFR partridge in a pear tree. The last instructor you flew with looked at the tach, took into account some taxi time, and called it an even hour? Burnside-Ott has a Univac 9300 computer that fills a room and figures out everything from how close to foreclosure student #1392 is to the mean life of the cylinder barrels on the Continental 0-200 engines in the fleet.

Gone is the line shack with the ashtrays made of run-out pistons, and gone with it is the instructor with crow's-feet in the corners of his eyes and those suntanned hands pantomiming the mysteries of flight. In their places, at Burnside-Ott, are modern buildings bustling with clerks and secretaries, young students, and not much older instructors of all ages, nationalities, and sexes. In a rare quiet spot near the admissions office sits a Swiss instructor giving an oral exam to a young Lebanese undergoing the mental anguish of trying to remember the difference between control zones, control areas, and airport traffic areas. In a room down the hall, three-winged robin's eggs —Link Gat I trainers—silently pirouette and bob under the sweaty ministrations of students practicing instrument approaches, and around the next corner, a roomful of young men await airplanes, ground school classes, and buddies in front of a scheduling board that resembles the war room of a fighter squadron rather than the aircraft roster of a general aviation flying school. Upstairs, a lengthy lecture in meteorology is under way—given by a professional, who makes meaningful the threat of a roll cloud and the power of wind shear, rather than resorting to the time-honored technique of teaching that "the answer to question number 27 is 'three' and remember it until 30 seconds after having completed your FAA exam."

On the ramp at Opa-Locka—an airport just outside Miami that has more runways (12) than most flight schools have instructors—the Burnside-Ott Cessnas and Pipers drone in and out constantly, getting plenty of high-density traffic practice: "Report left base for Nine Left . . . there's a Helio over the highway on final for 12, he'll be very slow so maintain proper spacing . . . and Aztec 922, you're cleared to land Nine Center . . . Cessna 641, cleared immediate takeoff Nine Left, traffic on one-mile final. . . ." You'll spot the Burnside-Ott airplanes, incidentally, for they have vertical fins, which effectively eliminates the almost irresistible temptation to buzz Florida beaches: the flat-hatters are too easily recognized.

It is easy to criticize the sheer impersonal bulk of Burnside-Ott—the "Let's go, Number 367, today we're going out to practice page 13 of the syllabus" feeling that the place gives—yet the efficiency, professionalism, and ceaseless activity of the school are signs of its success, as well as important elements in its training procedures. Burnside-Ott is based at three Miami-area airports—Opa-Locka, Tamiami, and Fort Lauderdale/Hollywood—and it includes not only the flight schools but a complete engine-overhaul shop, an avionics-repair center, aircraft painting facilities, and an air-taxi service. Courses are given for the middle-aged private pilot who wants to add a seaplane rating to his ticket (in a Lake Amphibian, at $35 an hour) and for the youngster who comes aboard with zero hours and a burning ambition to become a working pilot (for a minimum of $3,685—probably more—and four and a half months of 30-hour weeks, for a commercial license with an instrument rating). Burnside-Ott caters to the airline copilot who wants to get the airline transport rating he needs to become a captain ($175 an hour for dual in the DC-3), and it has a summer camp for 13- to 16-year-olds who are too young to solo but too impatient to stay on the ground ($495 for two weeks of flying and fun in Florida).

Everywhere you turn, the emphasis is on career piloting. Ride with an instrument instructor and his student, and hear the instructor say, "Now don't roll out of a turn, figure out whether you need more of a crab and then roll out of a second turn—it's uncomfortable for the passengers. Figure out your new heading while you're turning, and roll out just once." The halls, lobbies, classrooms, and cafeterias are dotted with airline posters suggesting the joys of Paris and Hong Kong, the beaches of Bermuda, the bright lights of New York, and the excitement of Africa—though, to be fair to the youngsters who face long hours of dogged work with air-taxi firms or regional carriers, there should at least be some shots of Wilkes-Barre, Pennsylvania, in a freezing drizzle or Dothan, Alabama, when the temperature is 120° F. on the ramp.

Nonetheless, everywhere there is the feeling that this is a school, not a hobby shop where one buys a new game to play. The students are mostly young men intent upon careers, not suburbanites who have clipped $5-ride coupons and want to see what airplanes are all about. If you don't believe it, take a look at the bulletin board in the lobby, where you'll see "for sale" notices reading, "My loss your gain. Must pay for lessons. Selling perfect '68 Roadrunner, with tape deck and wide ovals. . . ." These are young men and women with a lot at stake.

Though the per-hour airplane rental rates at Burnside-Ott are fantastically low for modern equipment (starting at $16.50 an hour dual in a Cessna 150, with Piper Twin Comanches renting for an equally surprising $45 an hour, including instructor), the school is by no means cheap. Burnside believes in charging for everything: If a student is dense and needs oral coaching, he'll do it upstairs in a classroom, at $6 an hour—not sitting under the wing for free; if he's slow to pick up the intricacies of holding patterns or VOR navigation, he's welcome to play with the school's audio-visual devices—at $3 an hour. If he wants to buy a logbook, write home to Mother, give his girl a Burnside-Ott ring, or replace his toothbrush, the school has a well-stocked store to sell him whatever he needs. Burnside-Ott is fully self-contained, with facilities to bed and board the student, get him a quick loan to pay his tuition, provide him with the books he needs and all the instructors he could desire, both ground and air. All for a price, of course.

What else does the money buy? Entrance to a school that, since its inception in 1964 with a huge bankroll from a pair of wealthy young Miamians, has always had the best equipment—and more of it than anyone else; that has turned out perhaps 15,000 pilots in the last seven years; that allows the student to set his own schedule, at his own speed, at his own convenience. Classes begin anytime at Burnside-Ott; ground school courses are continuous, and can be entered at any point; and flight instructors are ready to fly whenever you are, however often you want to. The school is open from seven in the morning until seven and often even ten at night, seven days a week; and whenever you arrive, you won't be lonely, for the school presently has a grand total of 1,500 students enrolled.

One of the more valid objections to the Burnside-Ott method is that the rapid pace can indeed give a green student his private, commercial, instrument, and multi-engine tickets in six months, but that the speed with which this is accomplished gives the knowledge precious little time to sink in. When a 20-year-old and his parents are spending $5,000-plus to get him started in a career, there's little time or money to spare for the niceties.

Since real knowledge in aviation is acquired only through variety and experience—built upon a base of solid primary instruction—the process will hopefully be augmented by the years the new Burnside-Ott graduate will doubtless spend as a flight instructor, air-taxi copilot, handyman for a charter outfit, even as a lineboy.

This, then, leads to that most basic of caveats to be offered young men considering a career in aviation. Despite the advertisements showing that empty right seat in the 747 waiting just for you, despite the grinning young man who went from carpenter to copilot in a year, despite the faraway places with strange-sounding names in the posters lining the halls of Burnside-Ott, there is no easy way to get a glamorous job in aviation without a lot of hard work, starting at the bottom and working up, and being in the right place at the right time.

Each year, hundreds of young men write to the editors of *Flying* magazine, hurt because they've spent many months and more dollars, and won all the right ratings—and they haven't yet been hired by the airline of their choice. Somehow, the feeling has grown that it is a breach of faith if a pilot is not hired by the airlines as soon as he meets the minimum standards set forth by them. Though good schools exist, designed to prepare one for a career as a professional pilot—the word is "prepare," not "guarantee"—

simply attending one and logging the ratings and the hours does not mean that aviation henceforth owes one a living.

Walk the halls of Burnside-Ott and look at the faces you pass, many of them under shoulder-length thatches of hair, eventually to disappear in a copilot's crew cut. They are your competition, and there are more of them —plus the graduates of Embry-Riddle and Spartan, FSI and ATE, Florida Institute and Sierra, Bartow and American Flyers, and a dozen other good schools—than there are top jobs. Those that eventually slide into the left seat will be the ones that work hardest, persevere longest, look deepest for the opportunities, and jump quickest when the big ones come along.

THE AIRLINE PILOT

The flight instructor on the Boeing 720 was a graying forty-seven, with 30 years of flying behind him—everything from crates before World War II to the Training Command during the war; the airlines after the war (starting at $180 a month as copilot on DC-3's, quitting after a few years and watching those who stayed fly 20 years in the right seat), working at this and that while flying fighters in the Air Guard; then, happily, going back to the airlines as a professional instructor on the pistons and then the jets.

Resetting his stopwatch, the Captain readies for the next leg. A stopwatch is useful when making a landing on instruments.

The young man to whom he had just given a qualification ride as copilot on the big jet had fewer than 250 hours—total! But he flew the huge bird as though it were welded to his backside.

The older man couldn't fight back a thin rise of jealousy that crept up in his throat. The boy, who had already served a year on the airlines as a second officer/engineer, was now a proud new first officer/copilot, exactly on his twenty-second birthday. By the time he reached twenty-seven, he'd be a 727 or 737 captain; by the time he was thirty-seven (with 23 years of airline flying still ahead of him if he kept his health), he'd be an SST captain, at perhaps a shade under $100,000 a year.

Born 30 years too soon? Possibly, the older man thought wryly, remembering the years of pinching pennies; married 20 years before he could buy a new car. He had seen this boy's car—a new Porsche, about $6,000 worth.

But, he thought, I wouldn't have traded any of it: a pilot before the war, in an age that idolized pilots; the great days of open cockpits; then silver wings in the old brown-shoe Air Corps and the pride at seeing that star out there on the wing of an Army plane; the DC-3 days on the airline, when there were so few liners that if you passed another at night, you flashed your landing lights in camaraderie; the unalloyed thrill of your first jet fighter, the P-80. And, later, the deep joy of accomplishing the rating in the great DC-8. No, he wouldn't have traded any part of it.

Then the grizzled instructor thought of his own tall sons: one, cum laude from college, with all the desire but eyes not good enough for the service or the airlines. The other, nineteen years old, with 50 hours in Cessnas, but only one year of college so far. What would his chances be?

Slim. Most of the airline slots would be filled for years to come by veterans of the Vietnam conflict, prematurely old youngsters with 2,000 hours of F-105 or F-4C time, plus four years of college. This boy who had just qualified on the 720 was a rarity. In addition to brains and ability, he had golden luck going for him. When he started with the line, he had hit the famed "pilot shortage" just right (the over-publicized shortage that had lasted for only a few short weeks several years ago). The instructor wondered if the young man would properly value his good fortune; something easily won is lightly valued. He remembered a captain with whom he'd flown after the war, who had had considerably less time, in much smaller planes, than he—the copilot—had logged. This man had learned to fly in Cubs during the war, had gotten onto the airline seniority list just before the end of the war, and had made captain as soon as he got 1,200 hours. It had all been so easy that he had begun to itch for "big money." He quit the airline and invested his money in a harebrained scheme that soon put him on the streets, penniless.

The old instructor hoped this young man would be smarter. He had been in the right place at the right time with what it took. He was the finest the airlines could find on a certain day. And at twenty-two, he was home free. The instructor's own 19-year-old wouldn't—couldn't—fare that well. Time and circumstance were against him.

But what do you do if you're bitten by the bug—if you "just have to fly"? Say that you're twenty-five, an accountant, married with two children, bored with your job, no good for five minutes after a plane passes overhead? You want the uniform, the pay, the glamour, the fringe benefits of airline flying.

Well, there's an answer that has always proved to be true, with qualifications: No one—repeat, no one—who desired a good flying job ever failed to find it, if he persisted, if he stuck it out all the way. In some cases this presupposes an acre of pain, a pond of tears. It might mean mortgaging the old homestead or spending two years flying "bush" in Central America or seeing a good wife grow old early trying to make one dollar fit where a hundred are needed.

Yet aviation is booming—no doubt about that. Airplanes don't fly themselves, and men like the old instructor get older, and trifocals replace bifocals and the ground gets harder to find on rainy nights. And finally, they sneak off to the rocking chairs of their memories.

The curve of World War II pilot retirements on the airlines is peaking right now, and the exit of veteran pilots will continue at a high rate for

15 more years, just in time to cross over the peak of Korean pilot retirements, and so on ad infinitum.

Lots of jobs, and they'll go to the most qualified men—a major share of them men with good military time in their logs. But there will always be never-say-die civilian pilots in the group who came up via instructing or "flying pipeline" or logging 3,000 hours of copilot time in a corporate Sabreliner.

As always, the trunk carriers will get the cream of the military and civilian troops. The supplementals and feeders will take what they can get, with the third-level carriers culling for winners.

These are the top jobs, but right behind them will be more and more corporate jobs—some in jets, many in reciprocating-engine craft. Here's where the young man who won't be denied can get his log enriched for a later jump to the airlines. Perhaps he'll even find a home there.

The helicopter and convertiplane field will develop into a colossus in its own right. Fixed wing can only, if you pardon the expression, go up. Pick your area and work 20 hours a day to become better at that work than anyone else. Become "the expert," and the world will construct a runway that leads to your threshold.

There is a job explosion in the making: crop-dusting, pipeline patrol,

To the uninitiated the maze of dials and switches in the cockpit of an airliner is meaningless. To the men who fly the big jets each has its use. To aid in-flight monitoring systems, alert lights provide visual warning of malfunction. For preflight checking, lists of more than 150 items are provided—and actually checked—before the big ship thunders down the runway for takeoff.

cloud-seeding, fire-bombing, bush-flying (from Arizona to Alaska), sales of aircraft and flying/selling jobs peddling everything from toothbrushes to skyscrapers, instructing, air-taxi, "bird-scaring," advertising (both skywriting and towing signs), "bug-dropping" (live insect drops for pest control) —these are only a few of the myriad jobs in aviation, with more imaginative ones being dreamed up and implemented every day.

Getting into aviation is costly and takes character. A commercial license requires at least $3,000 (time payments can be arranged), an instrument ticket costs a minimum of $500 more, ditto for an instructor's rating. But the military veteran has an advantage through the GI Bill. After the private license, which he must pay for, the government pays 90 percent of other ratings, depending on how much eligibility he has accrued.

So, with all his licenses but the ATR, the ex-accountant starts to hunt for a flying job, while his wife works, and Grandma (if they're lucky) takes care of the kids. He soon finds that he can't ring the gong on a job because of his lack of "time." He doesn't have a log full of hours, naturally, so who wants him?

If he's lucky he catches on to instructing (to build his hours) on a monthly guarantee, plus so much an hour. More likely, he can't even find a job that guarantees a minimum of $200 per month. Perhaps he has to go to the eager-beaver expedient of renting or leasing someone's Cessna 150 and hustling up his own students. With enough students, he can fly 100 hours a month and bring home $500 a month.

The picture often looks bleak. And the guy who loves his wife and kids more than flying gets out and goes back to the green eyeshade. The bitter-ender stays with it, and sooner or later (maybe much, much later) the break comes. Or maybe the break comes the first day.

Let's suppose another of those three-week pilot shortages happens. And say, suddenly, an airline looks at him, he passes all the hurdles, and is hired. Valhalla, Excelsior, and what was the name of that Cadillac dealer again, dear? I'm an airline pilot now.

Perhaps after three years on the line, however, he finds that crewing a skybus isn't really what he thought it would be. Sure, there's a future, but the present salary isn't too hot, some of the old captains can't be pleased very often, and the glamour and gold seem a far day away. He doesn't think he'll ever make copilot, much less captain—and digging ditches in the air seems to be letting his talents and brains go to rot.

That really—the boredom of it all—was why the old instructor quit line flying years ago—and to this day is much happier with the challenge of teaching in a schoolroom that moves along at 550 knots. Instructing, whether in Musketeers or Stretch 8's, is often a headache but never a bore. It's sometimes downright dangerous, much more dangerous than flying from A to B with four engines turning, but then one man's steak is another man's strychnine.

How about the captain of the airliner? Is he a happy man? The neighbors see him lying in the hammock all day or heading for surf or turf, and they say: "Does he work? Where does he get his money? Oh, an airline pilot! Tough life. Three 'thou' a month and plush hotels and swimming pools and pretty stewardesses, trips to Europe and a condominium at Waikiki."

Got It Made. Four stripes on the sleeve and eggs on the brim of the cap and sitting proud and tall in the office of a 707 at the terminal gate. Glamour on the half shell.

But the captain knows the other side of the coin. He knows it when he takes the annual physical, when he looks in the mirror and sees the network of wrinkles around his eyes. Airline flying is tough, hard work, and the responsibility is pressure squared and condensed. Ten, 15, even 20 years as copilot, coming after a stint of combat in the Big War, before he got the left seat. Years of getting up in the little hours, flying on holidays and Sundays, looking down at all those lucky people who could sleep eight a night and have normal holidays with their wives and kids.

Nobody builds a uniform, a plane, or a terminal that looks glamorous at three A.M. The airport is dusty and dead at that hour, stirring only with sleepy soldiers trying desperately to get comfortable on Swedish-modern contoured chairs. Flying all night isn't too glamorous either, and the "duel in the sun" that follows is hardly worth the money to many pilots. Throw in wind and rain, thunderstorm and tornado, and you have to have the dedication of a monk, a bottom as tough as a turtle's top, and a constant source of Tums to survive.

And how about the well-heeled corporate jockey tooling his plus Jet-Star around the world? Good pay, lots of time off, and maybe a new car each year thrown in to sweeten the pot?

Actually, most corporate pilots fly something with propellers, like an Aztec or a Queen Air, for moderate pay—and buy their own cars. And if the company controller says, "We have to tighten the belt this year," it isn't the janitor who goes, it's "that airplane" and its pilot. Even if the job is solid, things aren't all beer and skittles either. You are on call at any time (after all, the only thing a company plane can offer to compete with the airlines is availability for a "now" departure). You have to find the right day to have a drink—when you're sure you won't be flying for awhile. You have to be pilot, mechanic-supervisor, and superpurser. The boss will want you to tackle any weather when he's in a hurry—and chicken out when it's ceiling and visibility unlimited. You'll get awfully tired of trimming the ship as a boozy party swerves fore and aft in flight—and when you land, it'll be your job to get immediate repairs if the mahogany is scratched, the seat cushions are sopping with bourbon, and the ceiling is smeared with lipstick.

Naturally, this is only a small corner of the corporate picture. Most bosses are considerate, and the things noted above rarely occur. You could be lucky enough to fly for a straight-arrow operation. Lots of guys do, and wouldn't trade it for anything.

Every job—be it crop-dusting (get lots of insurance), instructing, or flying an atmospheric research plane—has its strong points and its drawbacks. Like any other way of making a living.

Sure, often it's digging ditches. But it's also the satisfaction of making a perfect instrument approach in zero weather or of seeing the majesty of Mt. McKinley through a sudden opening in a winter sky or of descending into Beirut over a Mediterranean splashed by silver from a full moon. It's the realization that your hands on that wheel hold the lives of up to 300 people, who at that moment depend on you for absolutely everything.

It's pride in that uniform, in that lovely plane, in a lifetime of hard-earned goals that has distilled a quiet confidence that whispers to you: "I can do this thing as well as or better than anyone on earth."

You wouldn't sit at a desk for anything in the world. Because you are a pilot.

THE BUSH PILOT

Meet Weldy Phipps. Other men have claimed to be "the last of the bush pilots"; if they're right, we'll have to call Weldy the first of the Arctic operators—and if he's not the first, everybody knows he's the best.

Welland W. Phipps runs an outfit called Atlas Aviation Limited, based at bleak, bitter Resolute Bay, on the northernmost fringes of the Northwest Territory, in Canada. He is certainly the world's northernmost charter operator, and probably Canada's best-known bush pilot.

Weldy Phipps—a bushpilot's bushpilot.

Resolute is a 6,000-foot-long gravel strip, an assortment of low buildings erected by the Royal Canadian Air Force when they built the runway after World War II, a bristle of antennas, a clutter of small tank farms, and a tiny Eskimo settlement of tin shacks. A bare 100 miles from the magnetic North Pole and so far north that there's nothing between it and the true Pole but a few more Eskimos, some scientists, and a number of lonely oil-exploration crews, Resolute is also home base for three Atlas de Havilland Twin Otters, a single-engine Otter, a Beaver with tires the size of a DC-3's, an Aztec owned by Weldy's chief pilot, a woebegone Atlas Apache with more snow in the cabin than most stateside airports ever have on their runways, and a Super Cub.

When Weldy first came north, in the late 1950's, he did so not to cash in on the oil boom, which hadn't yet started, but because he loved the country—"and because I was curious." Phipps had been a flight engineer in the RCAF during the war, but didn't learn to fly until he was a civilian again. He wasted no time, though, and was soon making a specialty of buying surplus equipment and converting it for high-altitude photomapping, a job that showed him much of the Arctic from 35,000 feet.

After a decade of work with various aerial-survey and Arctic-specialist firms, plus stint flying for a small feeder line, Weldy struck out on his own. He took a four-wheel Cub north—more on a lark than anything else—with a cinematographer who was making a movie about the Arctic. There, he met a geologist who was laboriously roaming Ellesmere Island with dog sled and—when the ice melted—canoe. Weldy soon had a job flying the surveyor around in his Cub.

The next year he borrowed $30,000, bought a used Beaver, and sold his house for operating capital; Atlas Aviation Limited was in business. In 1961, Weldy won the McKee Trophy, a cup given annually "for meritorious service in the advancement of aviation in Canada." Phipps got the award for the development, testing, and certification work to produce the immense tires that are now a standard part of Arctic and Alaskan flying. The Phipps wheels and tires make it possible to land anything from a Super Cub to a Caribou on just about any snow or ground you can walk on without sinking.

A de Havilland Beaver, one of the few aircraft able to take an arctic beating day after day and come back for more.

The deep Arctic is difficult to describe, for it both exceeds and falls short of the popular images. It sometimes gets colder on the farms of Canada's western prairies, and Resolute Bay, far north of northernmost Alaska, has at times been as warm as a Maine summer resort. Polar bears are hard to find, and there's not a dog sled in sight; the Eskimos all drive snowmobiles. But when you hear the story about the bear last seen lumbering across the snow, its arms wrapped around the approach-light pylon that it had torn out of the ground, or when you see from the air a lonely herd of musk oxen that live out most of their lives in cold that fractures metal—you realize that the Arctic is something else. And when it does get cold in Resolute, it's searing, wind-driven bitterness that penetrates every layer of clothing and touches your face like a hot iron. Forty below is no rarity, −65° F. is the present record, and a spring day when it gets up to −10° F. is considered absolutely balmy.

Thankfully, though, "cold" is relative. If you're a mechanic working barehanded on an engine in −20° F. and 20 knots of wind, it's like puttering about in a suburban basement workshop once you get the jug off and into a semi-sheltered shop warmed by body heat and a blower to perhaps

30° F. And for the copilot loading and preflighting in the early morning (the pilot is in the office, staying warm), when the wind is up and the temperature down, it's luxury to climb into the cockpit, which is probably still so cold you dare not touch metal with bare skin.

The Arctic's real extremes, though, come in its flight conditions, not its temperatures. During the winter, the sun never appears from the beginning of November to the end of January, and for almost three months, the pilots literally fly blind. When the ice melts and the rocky hills are bared, though, the fog starts—fog so thick you can't see the wing tips from the cockpit. More than one Atlas pilot has had to land his ship on the beach and walk home when he couldn't get into Resolute.

The fog can come in with startling suddenness. The Resolute runway is rare for the Arctic in that it has high-intensity strobes on the approach. Weldy doesn't consider the fog too bad if he can let down to 100 feet over the strobes and pick them out one at a time as he comes up the approach. One approach technique is to make his procedure turn on the southernmost of the two Resolute beacons and let down until he sees the water in the bay. Then he flies inbound until he picks up the Eskimo camp about three miles south of the runway. With full flaps, lots of power, and the nose down like a preoccupied anteater, he trundles the Otter on up the approach, following the road from the camp to the airport. Using this technique, he can usually get in under a ceiling as low as 50 feet. (The Atlas Twin Otters carry radar altimeters, of course.)

Smog has yet to afflict the Arctic, but the polar region serves up every other kind of fog known to temperate man—and a few that are not: radiation fog, advection fog, up-slope fog, frost smoke, ice-crystal haze, ice-crystal fog, and blowing snow, to name the most common. Ice crystals are often present in the Arctic air—invisible motes that glint like cut glass if you get the sun at the right angle; if you do so from an airplane, they can cut horizontal visibility to five miles or less. More spectacular yet, they will adhere to any airborne particle receptive enough to serve as a nucleus for an even larger ice crystal. Make a low pass at a runway or run a snowplow down it when conditions are right, and your exhaust pipe will paint a curtain of ice crystal fog thick enough to shut the airport down.

In the spring and the fall—otherwise the best times to fly—icing is a hazard, for it gets warm enough then even for freezing rain. The ice usually shows up in low-level stratus (it's rare that an arctic pilot isn't flying in the clear at 5,000 feet), but occasionally it will be solid on up to 10,000 feet. The Twin Otters can punch through the layers, but the singles aren't so tough. "You take a loaded Otter through a thousand foot icing layer," says Weldy, "and you may make it through, but you'll be so heavy that you'll sink right back into it."

When there's a cross wind at Resolute, it's a beauty—70 degrees to the runway, like as not, with gusts as high as 85 mph and a steady state of 40 mph considered quite ordinary. Phipps tells of landing his Twin Beech—a truculent airplane even in a dead calm—in a 70-degree, 70-mph cross wind. He says, with a laugh, "That was the only time they had all the fire engines and crash trucks out at the same time at Resolute. My wife was sitting in the right seat, and I had to ask her to lean way back so that I could keep the runway in sight out her window on final."

Polar expeditions are one of the peculiar burdens that Phipps must bear, and he considers any year during which nobody tries to ski, walk, flap, or jog to the Pole a good one, for he's the gent who has to find them when they go astray or keep them supplied when they don't. One year, some eccentric decided he had to parachute onto the Pole, and he hired Weldy

Fuelling's no joke where the cold freezes metal. Touch a surface ungloved and you'll leave your skin behind.

to fly him up. ("They weren't anywhere bloody near the Pole when he jumped," opined one of the Atlas mechanics.) Upon his return to civilization, the chutist embroidered his tale by telling how they were so low on fuel during the return trip that Weldy had to add a quart of cognac to the tanks. Since Weldy's number-one Twin Otter has his initials as registration letters, one story about the expedition was headed, "Whiskey-Whiskey Papa, the Alcoholic Twin Otter"—a legend that was quickly stenciled onto the otherwise sober de Havilland's cockpit door.

Navigation in the northern latitudes is surprisingly simple, though undeniably crucial. While the magnetic compass is meaningless (variation is 80 degrees west at Resolute, and no indications are to be trusted within 1,000 miles of the magnetic pole), and though landmarks are hidden during the winter and so numerous and uniform as to be almost useless during the summer—an infinitude of lakes, a limitless dullness of tundra—the primary rules are to trust your dead reckoning, hold the best heading you've ever held, and not believe your ADF until you are sure you're close enough to the station for a firm lock-on.

What about precession of the gyrocompass? All Arctic aircraft carry a simple device called an astral compass, which looks like a tiny surveyor's transit, mounted on a homemade tripod bolted to the instrument panel; set the local hour angle and approximate latitude into it with two little knobs, aim the instrument's rifle sights at the sun, read off your true heading, and reset the DG. During the dark winter months, they take star sights with mariner's sextants.

"With the beacons, and the sun and the moon—and we even have a VOR up here now—I don't see how anybody could get lost," said one of Weldy's young copilots. The simple, reliable, largely forgotten technique of ADF navigation is a finely developed art among Arctic pilots; all of the Atlas ships carry two, sometimes three, ADF's.

Fly above the glistening icecap for awhile and you'll begin to notice (it's hard not to) the burnished skeletons of downed aircraft—modern-day mastodons trapped forever by the ice. There's a Lancaster, and you wonder why it never made it to the airport just over the ridge. A B-24, polished by the wind to a luster as bright as the day it left Willow Run. A Hughes 300 helicopter, one pontoon in the air like a beetle on its back. A Fairchild F-27 on the plateau south of Resolute, so clean that it looks as if you could get her home with a ramp tug; but her back is broken. (The pilot made his procedure turn off the beacon north of the runway, rather than the south beacon, and that brought him down over rocks and snow instead of open water.)

There are 42 aircraft down just on the islands of which Resolute is a part, and whichever way you go, you won't go far without being reminded that the Arctic is rough country.

Weldy Phipps' two top pilots—Dick de Blicquy and Jan Backe—are said to be the two best-paid pilots in Canada, earning more than even transocean captains for Air Canada. This would put them somewhere above $30,000 a year. They work for their share of the profits, though, and while Weldy straight-facedly insists that none of his pilots flies more than 120 hours a month, the legal maximum, the truth is closer to 190 or 200 hours a month during the busy summer season. Weldy is privately of the opinion that a healthy man might just as well fly as sit on the ground, as long as he gets a solid eight hours of sleep the night before.

The Atlas crew works as a team, a tight coalition, rather than a company with a boss and employees. De Blicquy, for instance, has bought an Aztec that he flies under the Atlas colors—but to the profit of de Blicquy and whichever Atlas pilot happens to be driving it that day. There are times when it takes trade away from Weldy's Otters, but Phipps encourages this sort of enterprise.

"I'll never go back to airline flying," Backe says. "It's too boring. You're just a number on a scheduling board. With an operation like Weldy's, you're really part of something, really contributing to it."

Nonetheless, Weldy has trouble finding good people to come north and work with him. Some sign up, stay awhile, and quit. Others take one look and hop the next flight south. The Arctic is a harsh yet pure land that either repels instantly or appeals irresistibly, and for those who can see it only in terms of featureless frigidity or numbing boredom, there is no way to communicate its appeal and challenge.

The world seems full of young men with "all the ratings" and 2,000 hours in Cessna 150's, every one of them convinced that fate has dealt them a kidney punch because they can't step straight into the right seat of a golden-route 727 or at least a corporate Gulfstream. If they were truly ambitious, they might be able to load mail and preheat engines and bulldog oil barrels for Weldy Phipps for a while, and if they were truly lucky as well, he might take the time to teach them how to be real pilots. One of Weldy's young copilots, Hans Hollerer, came to him with a lot of ambition but not much time, none of it in anything bigger than an aging Apache; another is an Eskimo—the only Eskimo pilot in the eastern Arctic—who Weldy taught to fly. Both of them know what they're doing.

Weldy Phipps is a good man, and he has a good life, up there in the barren Arctic. There are mornings when you'll hear him muttering, as the wind tries to tear a rudder batten from his mittens, that anybody who chooses to make a living in the Arctic has to be soft as a grape. But still, but still . . . the Arctic is so clean and quiet that it gives new meaning to those words. Weldy has his family around him, working with him, involved in his life and his skills in a way no suburbanite's brood could ever be. His work is his pleasure, for it's all-consuming, infinitely variable—and exciting.

There are those who put up with the frustrations of a massive city for the sake of convenience or a kind of transient excitement. There are those who put up with stultifying jobs so they can fill their weekends with golf or skiing. Weldy puts up with the cold.

If you're stopping for more than a few minutes you wrap up the engine to keep it warm. That searing, wind-driven bitterness penetrates everything.

CHAPTER 8

Flying for Sport

RACING

IT wasn't long after airplanes first flew that people began to wonder how long they could stay up and how far they could fly. Endurance tests were devised—the first one of real note being the Blériot flight across the English Channel in 1909. Once it was established that airplanes could indeed stay aloft for several hours, the question became how fast could they go. The first air race on record was held in 1910 at Rheims, France, where a handful of airplanes staggered around a ten-kilometer course. The winner was an American, Glenn Curtiss, who achieved a speed of 47 mph in his Golden Flyer.

The first truly international competition took place in 1913. The Schneider Trophy race attracted entries from many countries, including Italy, France, England, and the United States. The trophy was finally retired in 1931 when the British flew a Supermarine S6B, the ancestor of the famous Spitfire, at 340 mph.

Interest in air racing in the United States grew during the middle 1920's until in 1929 the Cleveland air races became the major annual racing event in the country. Both military and civilian pilots and aircraft competed in this colorful spectacle, and although the military invariably defeated the best the civilians could muster in the early years of the contest, by the middle thirties the more advanced designs of private owners consistently won. Roscoe Turner, Jimmie Doolittle, and Wedell Williams were a few of the outstanding winners.

By 1940, after a series of calamitous accidents during the Cleveland races, they were discontinued and the golden age of air racing came to a close.

Time spectrum and the biplane. An early Wright brothers' Flyer and Mike DuPont's modern Pitts Special. The appeal of the biplane is perennial.

After the war sporadic efforts to revive air racing were made, but it wasn't until 1964 that the right combination of promotion, organization, and prize money brought racing back to life. Credit for this must go to a Reno, Nevada, rancher, Bill Stead, who did most of the organizing and promoting and put up much of the purse. Bill Stead understood racing from his days as a world-champion hydroplane driver. He loved airplanes, such as the Bearcat he flew off dirt roads on his 270,000-acre cattle spread. He lost his life several years ago in the crash of a Formula One racer that he was testing.

The crowds at the first Reno races justified his confidence in the appeal of the sport, and the races at Reno have been the major event in air racing ever since.

Every September, for a week of sheer delight, to this improbable area come the most dedicated air-racing enthusiasts in the world. From early morning till nearly sundown, they absorb every movement and sound and smell of wild airplanes and peaceful desert.

The Reno Races start deceptively slowly. Bit by bit, the large hangars begin to fill with Formula Ones and Sport Biplanes flown or trailered in from long distances (the majority, from nearby California, insist on waiting until the last minute.) The Unlimiteds, which are parked in front of the grandstands as they land, are gradually shoved down to their pit area, eventually filling the near half of two parallel lines along the half-mile ramp. The T-6's, SNJ's, and Harvards are parked in the far half of the ramp.

Along with its fabulous desert setting, the unique aspect of the Reno meet is the presence of the Unlimiteds, for this is the only place they are still raced. And one could hardly ask for a better site: the sheer size of the vast Lemmon Valley and its surrounding mountains cries out for the fastest machines in all of power racing. Unlimiteds means P-51's and Bearcats and others, but mainly P-51's.

A P-51 is a fine-looking airplane. Its form is full of character; every fairing and duct is shaped in a way that arrests the eye and delineates a personality, just as the details of a face do. The scoop below the spinner, like a sheepishly smiling little mouth above a receding chin, stays in your mind; later, you need to see only that to flash "P-51." The larger scoop below the trailing edge of the wing, resembling a bull's stock in trade, is the strongest characteristic, of course; even an idle observer remembers it as the hallmark of the Mustang.

On your marks . . . engines roaring. When the flag drops, the little racers shoot away across the grass to become airborne in seconds. The holding crews usually collapse upon the ground after straining to keep the nearly brakeless planes steady and in place.

When you think about it, there is scarcely a part of the plane that one could mistake for part of any other—the spinner, the scoops, the cowling, like the body of a 1950's fountain pen, the understated exhaust stubs; the wings with the unmistakable thin-nosed profile and the slim fairings over the aileron actuators; the conservative, straight-edged vertical fin with the horizontal tail placed well ahead of it; the bubble canopy and, in the early

Classic: a P-51 banks around a pylon in a race. The plane is flown low since any unnecessary distance takes more time, and competition is intense. Miss Candace, seen here piloted by Cliff Cummins, has—alas—since been destroyed.

versions, the thick hump of the old turtledeck. Scarcely a contour or a shading that does not come instantly into the mind and say "Mustang."

That is one of the reasons people go to the Reno races. They come from hundreds of miles off to see the Mustangs. Despite the greater variety and larger number of contenders (and, often, better sport) in the other classes, interest in the Unlimiteds outnumbers the others by 10 to one.

Engines are extensively modified for better performance, crankshafts balanced, ports polished and shaped to provide better breathing. A P-51 here gets checked.

In the last couple of years, there have been signs that the Grumman Bearcat would replace the P-51 as the characteristic racing unlimited. The Bearcat has personality, too; not quite so much as the P-51, perhaps, but a lot nonetheless. Its nose is not too distinctive, but then its fat fuselage (like a cambered avocado), its unnaturally tall vertical tail, and its rakish ground angle speak well enough for it.

'51s and Bearcats in close action in the unlimited racing class at Reno.

There are also Corsairs, P-38's, and a Hawker Sea Fury—all honorable old airplanes, though the P-38 seems ill at ease, like Bogie among Hell's Angels. Eventually, there will be an Aircobra or a Kingcobra with an oversized engine. They will all move in on the P-51; it may become the airplane in which you would be sure not of a second place, as now, but only of a fourth or fifth. Even so, it will still be the airplane that brought air racing back and the airplane that will always be associated with Reno.

The second fastest class at Reno is Formula One. The F/1 specs outline basic requirements for engine type, wing area, landing gear, cockpit size, visibility, and a few other odds and ends. Reading them, one becomes aware of the patchwork nature of the class. Since the rules have become more strict with each passing year as the purses got bigger, competition more serious, and lawsuits more frequent, they are full of little exemptions for planes raced before such an such a date and not modified since. A number of current contenders fail to meet the requirement of unobstructed visibility from a point 140 degrees up and aft of the cowl line. Bill Falck's handsome Rivets, which was originally designed for a prone pilot position, probably does not meet the spirit of the cockpit-size requirement (pilot reclined no more than 20 degrees from vertical; no mention is made, however, of the size of the pilot). Steve Wittman's Bonzo races on a waiver, since it weighs less than the 500-pound-empty minimum. And so on. Speeds in this class exceed 200 mph. One of the special favorites at Reno is the Sport Biplane class, for it was born here in 1964 when a group of local Experimental Aircraft Association members convinced Bill Stead to have a race for them. It worked and has continued to work throughout the country, but Reno always draws the biggest and fastest fields.

Coming up soon will be the development of a completely new class of homebuilt racers. With the supply of ex-military Mustangs and Bearcats steadily shrinking, the future of the Unlimited class is none too bright. In view of this, the Professional Racing Pilots Association is investigating a variety of ideas that could produce racers that might capture the interest of the general public as did the Thompson Trophy racers of the 1930's. Under consideration are homebuilt Unlimiteds, and totally new classes based upon such power plants as piston engines of up to 550 cubic inches, small propjets, smaller turbojets, and even Wankel free-piston engines.

Still another new class idea that has been struggling for breath these past five years is Formula Vee—small sport racers with 1,600 cc. Volkswagen car engines. If this class makes it, one result could be the spread of small regional races—minor leagues of air racing—with opportunities for new planes and pilots to get experience before entering the big time.

The town of Reno rewards predawn walks with the sight of countless

ABOVE LEFT. Air racing enthusiasts seem somehow more eclectic than their cousins at the motor racing track. The hot smells of oil and gas and rubber seem much the same but the colors and the machinery itself are somehow more vivid. And who can forget the biting snarl of these engines singing their way around the sky?

ABOVE RIGHT. The telephoto lens makes these racers seem closer to each other than they really are, but they are separated by only thirty or so feet—close enough at high speeds.

old ladies in rapt psychic communication with slot machines, silent before them with wattles heaving at every pull of the arm. A cab is easy to find, and it takes you up the winding road out of town, around wide bends, and then down the incline into the valley where the former Stead Air Force Base is a cluster of cryptically colored buildings struggling to disappear into the morning twilight.

The place has an abandoned air—pennants fluttering in the breeze, scraps of paper hurrying down the walks, the gaunt loudspeakers mute statues against the empty bleachers and the encircling mountains. As you look west toward the white hangar of Lear Reno, the foreshortened rows of Unlimited racers face one another across a taxiway down which a lone man

From P-51s, Bearcat Specials, the popular T-6 class, special homebuilt racers to a pair of stock Mooneys—air racing has something for everybody.

with a little child is taking an erratic stroll. The airplanes are most eloquent in this isolation and silence. They look down on you as you walk between the rows, haughty and impassive as sphinxes and stone kings. You are always looking up at them, and they in turn up at the brightening sky.

You look at them and wonder whether and where they fought, and under whom, and for what; how many times that sleeping crankshaft has shuddered with anger; over how many miles those scoops have slid, like rocks in a stream, while the Merlin roared ahead, its cranks and cams and rockers humming and clattering in the oil darkness. Which will win?

Yet it's not curiosity about which will win that probably brings people to Reno. It is, rather, an uncritical passion for the airplanes—the Unlimiteds particularly—with their immense propellers, their weaving taxi and coughing idle, and the snarl as they slide past the stands in brief array at 400 miles an hour. There are enough people for whom the line-up at dawn is worth a year's wait and for whom vacation is a trip to this gambling town in the Sierras to watch fighters bore by. Such people are sport aviation's hard core, and certainly they are the backbone of air racing. It is for them that racing returned after its long dormancy, and it is from among their ranks that the racing pilots come.

AEROBATICS

For centuries man watched with envy the flight of birds and dreamed of being able to match their skill and grace. The unsteady, shaky flight of the earliest aircraft was a far cry from the effortless soaring of the birds, and far from being satisfied with their efforts, men still yearned for the same ease of control and maneuverability, which persistently evaded their grasp.

Better aircraft with more reliable engines began to appear, with the pilots of these machines vying with one another at early flying demonstrations to prove the superiority of their craft. It was during such a meeting in 1910 that the Frenchman Pégoud performed the first aerobatic maneuver when he looped his Blériot.

The First World War was responsible for a very rapid advance in the design of aircraft. Very soon it was found that the pilot with the more powerful and maneuverable aircraft would emerge victorious in air combat. At this time, too, pilots began to realize that the control, strength, and power of the airplane could be made to conform to their will, to produce an intricate pattern in the sky, giving them a sense of freedom that no man before them had ever enjoyed.

They were flying with the ease of birds, and the sport of aerobatics had been born.

Aerobatics soon became synonymous with stunt flying, unfortunately, and for many years was regarded as the wicked lady of aviation. Yet the lure of the pure aerial ballet remained, and between the wars, only a few timid pilots could resist the temptation to learn the art of aerobatics. At that time the biplane reigned supreme, and unfortunate is the man who has not stopped to watch a tiny silver biplane, high among the cumulus clouds, the sole performer on a stage of infinite breadth and indescribable grandeur. The roar of the engine is muted to a far-off drone, no louder than a bee in the summer sky, while the sun glints and sparkles on the wings and cowlings as the aircraft loops and rolls with lazy grace.

How many thousands of unknown spectators are the audience to this performance? The pilot, oblivious to the envious watcher, sits behind a small wind-screen, his hands and feet resting lightly on the controls. The air is crisp and clear, and he is alone in the sky.

The sound is very different here; the muted drone is a deep-throated snarl that blends with the roar of the slipstream and the howl of the bracing wires. To the pilot this is no mere machine, but a living creature, quivering with life, eager to repond to every pressure on the controls. The slipstream thunders around the cockpit, tugging mischievously at the pilot's leather helmet and goggles. The propeller is a whirling disk, shimmering in the sun, and the instruments, trembling, tell their own stories—airspeed, altitude, engine rpm, oil pressure and temperature, fuel contents, sideslip. The pilot scans these at a glance, not really studying any one of them, but knowing that all is as it should be.

A slight back pressure on the stick and the aircraft soars upward, stick and rudder smoothly coordinated, and the little biplane is poised on a wing tip, the slipstream dying to a sigh while the engine noise becomes harsh and strident. Now the nose is dropping and the slipstream rises to a shrieking crescendo, drowning even the engine's blare. The controls become heavy as the airspeed indicator shows the speed rising toward the maximum. The

The choice of champions—the Pitts Special in action, with Bob Herendeen at the controls. The combination of the virtues of the Pitts and the talents of their pilots enabled the U.S. team to bring home the Nesterov Cup (awarded to the best team in world aerobatic competition) in 1972. In addition, Charles Hillard—also in a Pitts—won the Aresti Cup in the men's competition, and Mary Gaffaney in *her* Pitts won the women's. Some plane! Some team!

pilot's movements are quite small now, for the aircraft responds very quickly to the slightest pressure.

Slowly the nose comes up, and as the aircraft comes out of the dive, the pilot presses back harder on the stick. The machine arcs upward, the flying wires tight with strain, while the landing wires, relaxed, vibrate until they are blurred. The G forces press the pilot down into his seat, and his muscles are tensed as he combats the rising acceleration. Now the climb is vertical, as the pilot looks up and back for the horizon to appear. The pull force is easier now, and as the top wing comes into line with the horizon, he eases the stick forward until the airplane is inverted. With hardly a pause, the stick is pressed to the right and the horizon revolves slowly. A touch of right rudder and the roll off the top is complete. Another wing-over, this time soaring above the snowy peak of a towering cumulus cloud, before diving again for a lazy, flowing slow roll, so beautifully controlled and easy that the watchers on the ground are unaware of the months of practice to achieve it.

For most pilots the sense of achievement and freedom is sufficient reward in itself—coupled with the knowledge that a pilot skilled in aerobatics is a much more accomplished flier, since he knows the limits of his airplane and how to get the best out of it. The art of aerobatics brings confidence and increases skill, touch, and an understanding of the finer points of aerodynamics—in a way that cannot be accomplished in any lecture room.

It is inevitable in such an advanced form of endeavor that those who excel will become interested in competition, for this is one way of determining just how good a pilot really is. Competition flying is not a relaxing business, though, and many good aerobatic pilots prefer the enjoyment of flying for their own recreation, rather than undergoing the pressures of contest flying.

For those who do enter competition, there is all the color and drama that anyone could wish for. At international meets, pilots from 15 to 20 countries arrive at the contest airfield with brilliantly painted airplanes.

Then comes the most enjoyable part—the training period, during which each competitor is allowed two practice flights over the airfield. Pilots walk up and down the lines of aircraft, renewing old acquaintances and making new ones. Occasionally one finds an airplane with a diagram of its pilot's aerobatic sequence attached to the panel, and these are studied with interest. Some pilots with strong senses of humor have been known to leave impossible sequences fixed to their aircraft, and then to retire to a safe distance and watch the expression on their rivals' faces.

The waiting is the worst, especially for the first round of the competition. Many pilots at this stage ignore their rivals' performances and try to relax in their tents. Once in the aircraft, with the engine running, the initial nervousness disappears and one becomes impatient to get airborne. Preflight checks are usually carried out three times each, because there must be no mistakes at this stage.

The task is to perform a series of predetermined maneuvers in a diamond-shaped box of air above the competition field. There is a floor and ceiling to the box, and the longer of two axes usually running the length of the airport is marked by two datum points on the ground. Midway along this course is a cross axis, also marked by two ground-based datum points. The judges, on the ground, will observe how swiftly, smoothly, and precisely the maneuvers are performed as well as how well they are "framed" within the prescribed course.

The starter's flag drops and the stopwatch is started. All nervousness has disappeared as the throttle is opened for takeoff. The climb is initially straight ahead, with a careful check that gear and flaps are retracted (one never sees a pilot showing off at a world-championship event). The climb pattern has been planned to put the pilot at the correct height directly over the start point, marked by a cross on the ground. During the climb, a check is made to see if the four datum points are clearly visible on each end of each axis, and the engine instruments are monitored.

The pilot rocks the wings—the signal that he is about to begin—and rolls the aircraft into a dive straight above the main axis. Now he is almost over the center of the field and can no longer see the axes. The plane has reached the full power selected. The pilot makes small and instinctive corrections for turbulence, and after a quick check of airspeed, the stick comes

The Pitts precisely marking out an eight-point roll. Each station is held fractionally before moving to the next.

back hard and the aircraft shudders as the needle on the accelerometer peaks on the red line. The pitch is checked sharply as the aircraft hits the vertical, and full right aileron is applied. The wing tips race around the horizon, which is blurred because of the high rate of roll. The datum points flash past—one, two, three, four—and the roll is checked exactly on the last one. The vertical climb is held until the speed is no longer reading, and the power is cut right back to idle. As the aircraft starts to slide backward, the stick is eased back a little, and rudder and stick are then held as firmly as possible. The controls are trying to snatch over, and the pilot hangs on grimly. Suddenly the nose goes down hard in a vicious whip stall; as it does, he applies full power, and as the engine roars back to life, the pilot hits hard rudder and forward stick for a vertical diving outside snap roll. He cuts the power again and recovers after one turn, checking that the flight path is exactly vertical and noting that he is exactly over the intersection of the axes.

So the sequence goes on for up to 30 maneuvers of exacting precision flying, so different in concept from the antics of the little biplane high above the clouds, but equally as rewarding. The combination of the two styles is probably the most exacting and difficult to achieve, and is the ultimate in aerial ballet. The effort is great, the concentration intense, the work load high, and the rewards infinite.

But even when we have mastered all the maneuvers, we will still watch the flight of birds and admire their grace and perfection.

HOW TO DO AEROBATICS

First, a Warning: There are Federal Air Regulations that govern aerobatics, and they are sensible ones. Anyone who breaks them is not only illegal, but an idiot. Briefly the regulations allow aerobatics only in airplanes certified as aerobatic (or approved experimental types); only with parachutes worn, if carrying passengers; never below 1,500 feet or when visibility is less than three miles; never in an airway, over cities or towns, or over open-air assemblies of people. (The experts you see at air shows doing aerobatics operate under a special waiver of the minimum-height rule, and they have to demonstrate their skill to the FAA to get one.) If you stick to these rules—and most notably the first three—it's hard to hurt yourself. We'll add two of our own: Get a grounding in basic aerobatics with an experienced aerobatic instructor before you try them by yourself. Use a double harness in case one comes open or lets go.

The Loop

The most basic maneuver. Clear the area for other traffic, then dive gently to about 20 percent above cruising speed (the airplane manual will give you the recommended entry speed), and ease firmly back on the stick. You may have to throttle back during the initial dive to stay under maximum rpm; if so, ease on full throttle by about the time you are going vertically upward. As you approach inverted flight, ease up on the G; your air-

LOOP. Start with a gentle dive. Watch your rpm—stay under redline. Ease firmly back on the stick. As your speed begins to drop, apply full power. Over the top, relax back pressure, and check your wings are level. Coming down, close the throttle. Not too much G on the pullout. You should finish with roughly the same airspeed and altitude you began with. Path followed wants to be a circle.

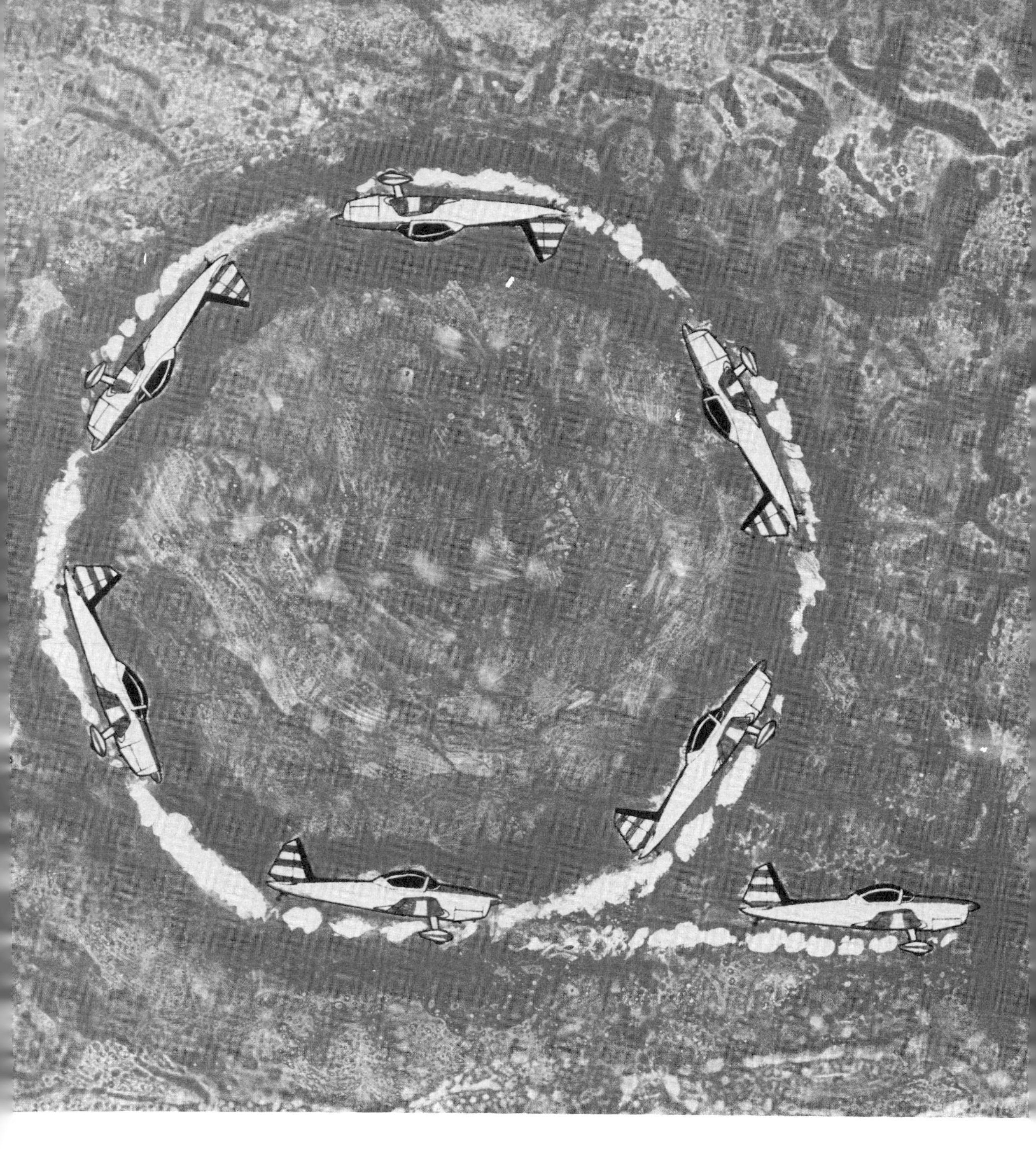

speed is dropping fast, and it is easy here to get into a high-speed stall. Over the top, you should just be gently held in your seat by G, but no more. As you start downhill, close the throttle, and again avoid too much G on your pull-out—you may be surprised how quickly you gain airspeed here. In calm air an accurate loop will give you a solid jolt coming down, as you hit your slipstream from when you were going up.

A good loop looks round from the ground. Get a friend to watch yours and tell you how they look. Recovery speed should be about the same as entry speed. Rudder and ailerons should be used for trimming the airplane only. Practice loops lined up with a road or railway, and check that your wings are level—though inverted, of course—as you come over the top.

The Slow Roll

This is harder than it looks. First, make sure your harness is tighter than tight, for hanging loose in your straps three inches off the seat is really unpleasant. Start in level flight or a hair nose-high, at maybe 10 mph above normal cruise. Full throttle, then full ailerons. As you reach a vertical bank, add top rudder—quite a lot of top rudder—to keep the nose from dropping. Leave on full ailerons. As you reach inverted flight, don't—no matter what—let the sensation of inverted flight throw you; if you decide to chicken out and pull through, you are surely going to go well over airspeed redline. Apply forward elevator—just enough to keep the nose maybe a little above the horizon. Don't be too violent with that forward elevator because with all that rudder and aileron, you can start out on an inverted snap roll a little earlier in the program than you'd intended to try one. As you roll through inverted, you slowly change the rudder; you are going to need top rudder the *other* way as you roll into a vertical bank on the other side. As you approach level flight, ease off the rudder and ailerons. Practice slow rolls left and right lined up with a road or section line, and check that you are maintaining altitude. Again, a friend on the ground can be asked to tell you whether the airplane looks as though it's rolling level, or rising and falling through the maneuver. When you get more proficient, you can use less than full aileron, but at first things go much more easily if you roll as fast as possible.

The Snap Roll

This goes more easily if you do it with torque. In some airplanes it goes so easily *with* torque that you may prefer to do it *against* torque till you are sure you can cope. You had better be highly proficient at spin recovery because a snap is nothing less than a high-speed spin done in a forward rather than downward direction, and if you overlook it, a regular spin is what you will end up in. So practice spins a while first.

Use the entry speed recommended in the manual. (Try it slower, and the airplane may not snap at all. Try it much too fast, and you could break something; snaps put a considerable strain on the airframe.) Use full power, and start by pulling the stick quite sharply back. An instant later, add full rudder, and hold full rudder and full rear stick for about three quarters of the way round the roll. Then apply full opposite rudder and a modest amount of forward stick to stop the snap. It will take fully a quarter turn to take effect. Aileron to help the roll may or may not be needed; it depends on the type of airplane. Your instructor will know. The snap is the one maneuver that varies much from one type of airplane to another, and what works most crisply with one may leave you hanging soggily on your back in another. Practice, they do say, maketh perfect.

The Hammerhead

This is surely the prettiest of the basic aerobatic maneuvers to watch from the ground. Start at a little above cruise, with full power, in level flight. Pull the airplane firmly but smoothly into a vertical climb and hold it there, still with full power. As the airplane runs out of upward airspeed, kick on full rudder to cartwheel it over sideways. You may need some aileron to keep it an exact cartwheel. Just before you start coming vertically down, ease back on the stick till you are once more in level flight. You should be at the altitude you started with, and at about the same airspeed.

SNAP ROLL. Start at recommended airspeed, with plenty of power. Heave back on the pole, and a moment later kick on full rudder. Keep going. Aileron may or may not be needed. As you reach the three-quarter position, opposite rudder and forward stick to begin recovery. Recover to level flight, neutral controls.

SLOW ROLL. Start slightly nose-high, with full power. Apply full aileron. As you reach the vertical, add top rudder. As you roll through inverted, still full aileron. Gently forward with the stick to hold the nose up. Change over rudder to top rudder the other way. As you approach level flight, ease off rudder and aileron.

Sounds easy? It isn't. There are several tricks to a good hammerhead. The first is judging when you look to be going exactly vertically upward. Your wing is set at an angle on the fuselage, and it is the fuselage that you want to be vertical to the ground. So the wing, as you check the angle it makes with the horizon, should look as though it is a hair *past* the vertical. (Sounds odd, but that's how it works out.) You must also glance out at both wing tips to make sure one is not higher than the other. The next trick is judging the moment to kick on rudder—the moment when you are motionless in space. Your airspeed indicator has a lag in it, notably at low speeds, and it will probably still be indicating 30 or 40 mph when this moment arrives. If you wait till it indicates zero, you will actually have started to slide backward, and you had better have a firm grip on the controls because the reverse airflow is going to whang them against the stops. Tail slides are strictly for experts, and at that, many experts avoid them. Start by pushing the rudder over deliberately early, so you do a kind of a wingover, and slowly reduce the speed you rudder at until you think you've got it right. The only way to know if you have captured that magic moment is to get someone on the ground to watch you, and tell you how it looked. *Another thing:* Torque and slipstream effects contrive to make it much easier to hammerhead one way than the other. With most American engines, it goes best to the left, so leave right-hand hammerheads till later. (You may find that, to do a halfway decent right-hand hammer, you actually have to reduce power as you cartwheel.)

These four basic maneuvers are the building blocks of aerobatics; almost everything else is either a variation on one of these or a composite, with two maneuvers or parts of them added together. Any good aerobatic textbook will fill you in on the details. We recommend *Modern Aerobatics and Precision Flying*, by past national champion Harold Krier, in the Sports Car Press series ($2.45) or *Roll Around a Point*, by Duane Cole, published by Ken Cook, Milwaukee; obtainable from Duane Cole, 201 Lester Street, Burleson, Texas 76028; $3, plus 25¢ handling charge.

The one exception is a maneuver called the *lomcovák*. It is the toughest aerobatic of all, and we tell you how it is done here not in any way to suggest that you try it. If you go to air shows, you are bound to see it done by such experts as Art Scholl and Ed Mahler, and you will want to know what is going on. The *lomcovák* is hell on props—particularly Aeromatic props—crankshafts and engine bearers, not to mention the pilot. The *lomcovák* is strictly for experts, and even they don't attempt it below 1,500 feet. And you are a brave man if you try it in an airplane that you haven't watched someone else do it in first.

There are various methods of entry, but basically, you begin with the airplane going upward at about 110 mph, at which point you apply forward stick as if to begin an outside loop. Then you add to this (in airplanes with American engines) full left aileron and full right rudder, to initiate an outside snap, and you hold it there as you embark on the wildest ride of your aeronautical lifetime. At first, the nose will track around the horizon, while the airplane hovers; then, the axis of rotation changes and the airplane will begin to tumble end over end, rotating forward about the axis of the wings. Maintain full power and leave everything in the corner until the airplane begins to run out of rotational momentum and slows or stops. Recovery is the same as from an inverted spin; full back stick, full left rudder. Ideally, you will be pointing straight down as you come to a stop; then, you simply center the controls, cut the power, and ease out of the resulting dive. If, when you stop rotating, you are pointing straight up, you are going to tail-slide, and must firmly hold all controls to stop them from banging against the stops. (Art Scholl's Chipmunk Special tends to go into an inverted flat spin at the end of a *lomcovák* if prompt recovery action is not taken.)

The negative G, the buffeting, and the rate of rotation in a *lomcovák* would utterly astonish you. *Note:* The *lomcovák* only works when done with engine torque helping. Try it the other way and almost nothing happens.

THE ARESTI KEY

Sistema Aerocriptografico Aresti, it is called in its native Spanish, and it is nothing more or less than a system of writing down an aerobatic se-

HAMMERHEAD. Start with full power. Pull firmly into a vertical climb. Wing will look to be *past* vertical. As you run out of momentum, apply full rudder. Coming back down, close throttle, ease out of resulting dive.

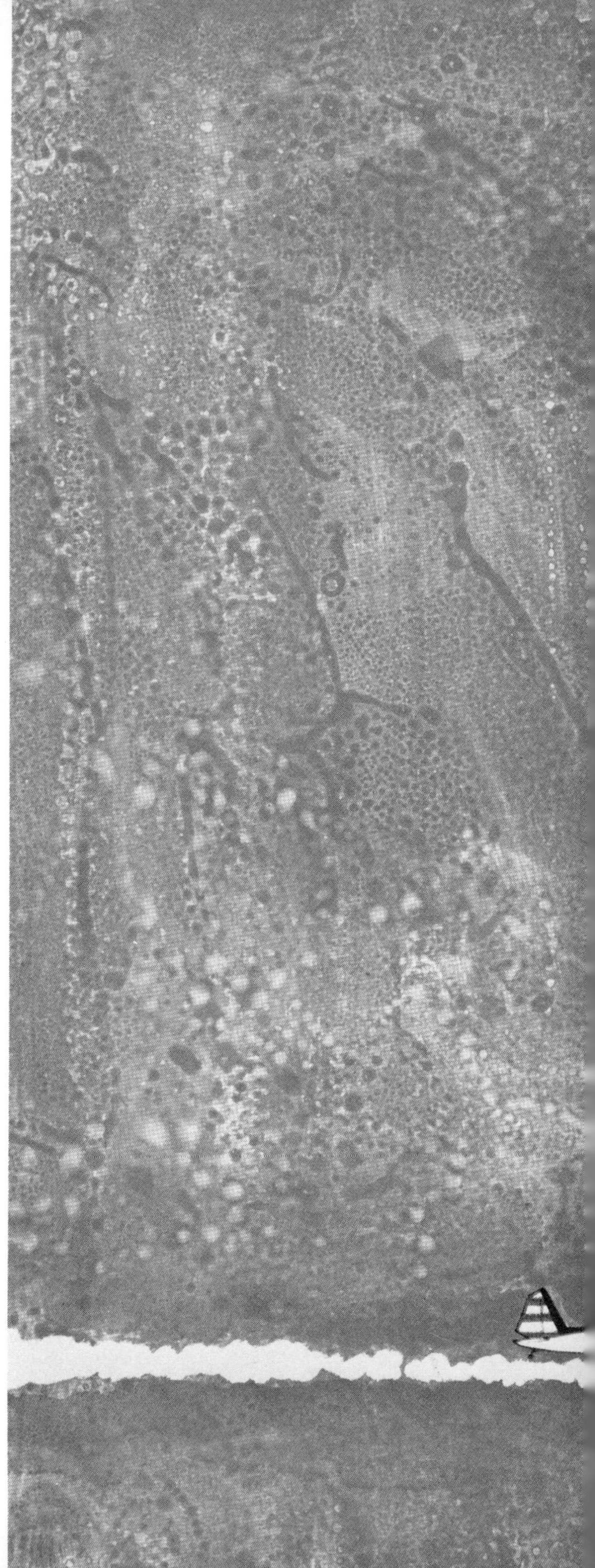

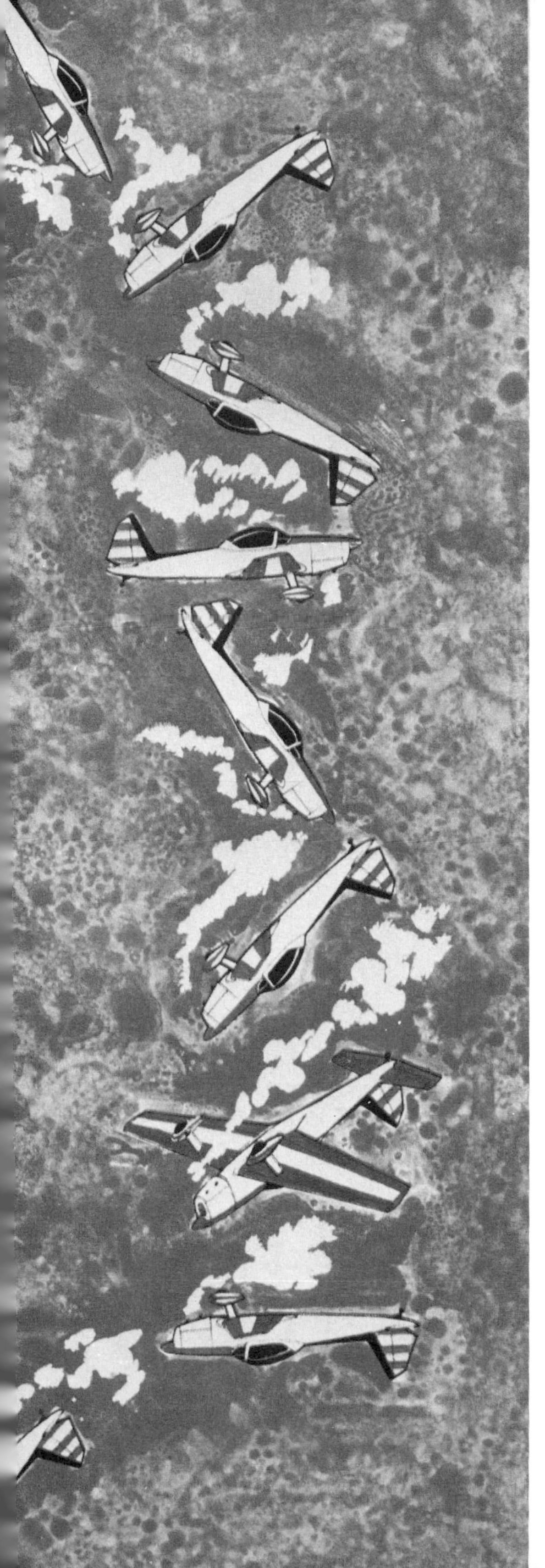

LOMCOVÁK. Start from 45-degree climb. Push forward stick, full left aileron and full right rudder to initiate outside snap. Nose first tracks around the horizon then drops and airplane starts to tumble end over end. When you begin to run out of rotational momentum, stick back and full left rudder. Airplane wants to do inverted flat spin. To recover, centralize controls, ease out of dive.

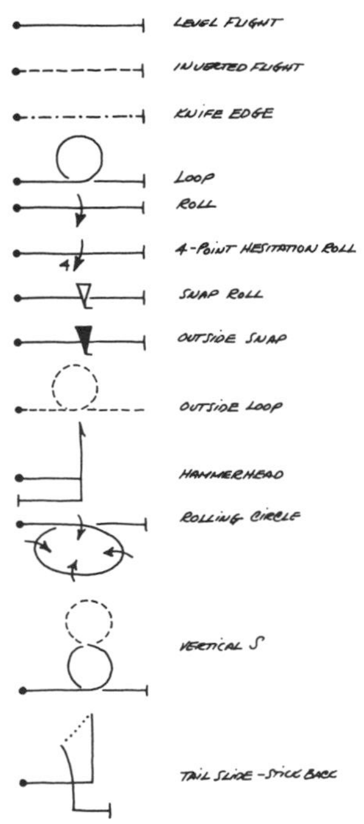

Bob Herendeen's second-highest scoring free group, World Aerobatic Contest, Magdeburg, German Democratic Republic, 1968.

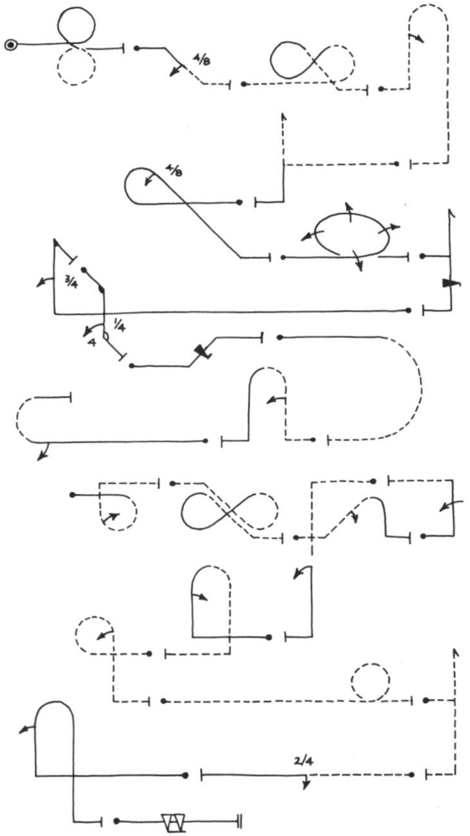

Harold Krier's top-scoring free group, U.S. National Championships, Oak Grove, Texas, 1968.

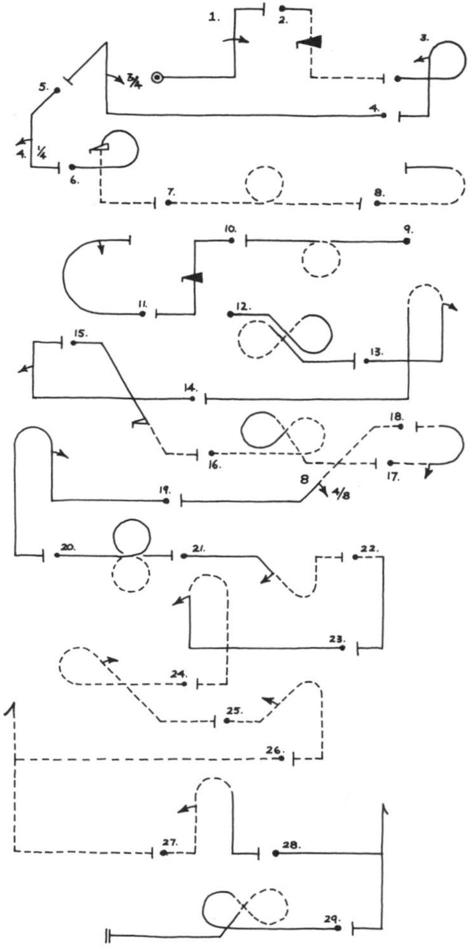

LEVEL FLIGHT
INVERTED FLIGHT
KNIFE EDGE
LOOP
ROLL
4-POINT HESITATION ROLL
SNAP ROLL
OUTSIDE SNAP
OUTSIDE LOOP
HAMMERHEAD
ROLLING CIRCLE
VERTICAL S
TAIL SLIDE—STICK BACK

quence, much as you might write down a piece of music, as indeed a well-flown aerobatic sequence is in the same realm of things as a fine violin solo. José L. Aresti is Spain's old master of aerobatics and one of the world's great Jungmeister exponents. His aerocriptographic system is the beautifully thought-out culmination of years of work and development, and it has been welcomed and accepted for use in contest rules by the Fédération Aeronautique Internationale, the Aerobatic Club of America, and almost everybody else.

Like the notations of music or mathematics, the Aresti Key transcends language barriers, enabling aerobatic pilots from many countries to compete on equal terms though they speak not a word of each other's languages. Here is Aresti's own dedication of his system: "To all pilots fond of aviation that with their ardor, enthusiasm, and great sportiveness did contribute to the graphical representation and actual perfection and development of the Artistic Flight all over the World."

The basic elements of the key are shown here. (Each maneuver starts with a dot and ends with a bar.) From these definitions of the *basic* aerobatic maneuvers, you should be able to work your way through the two full sequences shown—Bob Herendeen's high-scoring freestyle routine from the World Aerobatic Contest in Magdeburg, East Germany, and Harold Krier's free sequence from the 1968 U.S. Nationals, where he emerged national champion. (It is freely allowed to use the hands in following a sequence through; even the experts do.)

Scoring is something else again. Basically, each maneuver has a "difficulty coefficient," or "K factor," which Aresti spelled out, and this K factor is multiplied by another factor that defines how well the judges thought the competitor flew that maneuver. More about scoring and the Aresti Key can be found in the Aerobatic Club of America's contest rules, available for $5 from the A.C.A. at P.O. Box 11099, Fort Worth, Texas 76110. (It is free to A.C.A. members.) Aresti's own tome on the subject, in three languages, is $20 from Frank Price, American Tiger Club, Municipal Airport, Waco, Texas 76709.

SOARING

"Okay, if you're ready, we'll go up in the 2-22 over there." The lineboy was attaching the towrope behind the Super Cub. After all, I thought, air is our most vital element. And when something is vital, it's familiar and safe. I kept this thought firmly in mind as I strode with Bernie Carris toward the sailplane, resting awkwardly with one wing leaning on the ground. We were at the Schweizer Soaring School on Chemung County Airport in Elmira, New York, and I was getting ready to take my first soaring lesson.

Climbing in was like mounting a horse, only from the right side since the opened plexiglass canopy blocked the left. In the mood of the occasion, the sailplane became the noble white stallion of legend, ready to challenge the four winds. (Bernie observed that it was a calm, hot day.) I was soon harnessed into the front seat, and Bernie into the instructor's seat behind. After an exchange of signals among Bernie, the lineboy (who runs alongside the plane and holds the wing tip off the ground), and the pilot of the tow plane, we were off!

A Kirby Gull lazily circles a thermal off the wooded slope beneath it.

We started with a jerk and bumped along the ground for a few seconds before being airborne. Bernie explained that the object of handling the plane in tow was to keep it in position behind the tow plane, preferably above the slipstream caused by the propeller. Because the towplane bobbed up and down in air pockets while climbing, constant attention was needed here.

I was assigned the task of watching the altimeter, and as soon as we reached 3,000 feet, I was to pull the release knob which would free us from the towrope. A little awed by this responsibility, I kept my eyes glued to the altimeter. (We were already at 1,500 feet . . . halfway there!) Also, there are dual controls in the 2-22, and though Bernie was flying, I kept my hand lightly on the stick and my feet on the rudder pedals to follow their movements.

So far, I felt a little cheated. There were so many distractions that it was impossible to absorb what was happening. The odd sensation of being pulled helplessly through the air by a plane that kept ducking in and out of sight up front was a bit unsettling. Also, the groaning of the towrope was both distracting and ominous. The rudder pedals and stick moved back and forth with a will of their own, and I hardly dared take my eyes from the altimeter to peek at the changing scene below. We had been aloft for about ten minutes, heading for a fat cloud, when the needle hit 3,000 feet. "Okay. You can let it go." Bernie's voice seemed uncannily calm compared with my own excitement as I reached for the red knob marked "Release." I pulled it, and with a bang I saw the towline dangle like an empty trapeze from the tow plane. The Cub swooped steeply to the left, landward bound. We were free. Free . . . and 3,000 feet above the ground!

Suddenly all was very quiet, as if a window somewhere had closed, leaving only the muffled sound of rushing air. The terrain remained comfortably distant, and more beautiful and still than I had ever seen it before. We were a huge kite, fluttering over a giant fairyland of farms, bridges, roads traveling to the towns, and a silver river hugging the trees.

It's important for a sailplane pilot to know at all times the location

The absence of power controls and the variometer (a sensitive vertical speed meter, upper right) mark this the cockpit of a glider. Note cable release, oxygen and 24-hour clock.

of the airport, his approximate distance from it, and his altitude—if he expects to return there for a safe landing. When Bernie asked me to locate it, the geometric design of the airstrip among the curving lines of the landscape was easy to find.

It had become very hot in the plane. The clear canopy which offered such wonderful views of both earth and sky offered no protection from the sun's rays. (I made a mental note that a peaked cap should be a required part of my wardrobe in future.) Though there was an air vent in the cockpit, it did little to cool us on such a hot day. The temperature on the ground was 90° F.

"We've hit a little lift here," Bernie was saying, "Let's let it work a while." The horizon tilted, the plane rolled to the right, the wing—that endless wing—pointed earthward like a vaulting pole, and we began to circle round and round. More importantly, up and up. My new task was to keep a close eye on the variometer, a simple, sensitive instrument for measuring rate of climb. It was astonishing to learn that we had gained 600 feet in just a few minutes. We continued to spiral—and to climb.

So this was soaring. Soaring on invisible columns of rising air (thermals). Soaring like the birds when they circle for endless moments with wings motionless.

If a power plane were here you might wonder what he was up to. But the glider pilot knows he'll find lift off these sun-warmed slopes.

Thermals are columns of hot air rising from the earth's surface. The air which creates thermals becomes heated when the earth it rests upon is heated by the sun. As the warm air rises to the higher atmosphere, it cools, and drops of moisture condense to form clouds. Most thermals are capped by clouds, and the clouds become the sailplane pilot's signposts for finding lift.

Once a plane enters a thermal (a pilot knows this by checking the variometer or, if he is expert enough, he can sometimes sense it as the plane begins to climb), the pilot spirals his plane until he either climbs as high as he wishes or the thermal dissipates. Then he levels out and continues flying straight in the direction he wants to go, searching for more thermals on the way. Thus, thermals become the glider pilot's stepping stones across the sky.

The next 10 minutes were a time to relearn relatively simple words: horizon, attitude, bank, turn, shallow, relax—but with new meaning. Again, we hit lift, and again it was like striking gold. This time, I took the controls (somewhat tensely) and tried to roll the plane into a left bank. Too immediate! The left wing pitched so violently toward the trees below that it threatened to catapult us out of the sky. But my expert companion guided me into shallowing the turn, joking about my "short right leg" as he did so.

Then, at last, a magic moment amidst the confusion: we were, indeed, flying straight and steady—wings level, nose on the invisible spot on the horizon, airspeed 50—and I was alone at the controls! Rhapsodic phrases of aviation came to mind, of jubilant freedom, of elements conquered, of being one with the universe, of—— But this was not yet to be. The rains came. We skimmed in for a landing ahead of the squall and quit for the day.

This first flight of a young woman and, in fact, the whole world of aviation is based on work done by the pioneers in the art of gliding, men who were inspired by watching birds stay aloft with their wings spread and motionless.

Otto Lilienthal in Germany and John Montgomery in the United States were among the most influential of these pioneers. Both began with wings alone, and hung their bodies beneath them, controlling their path of flight by shifting their weight around. (This delightful primitive art, called "hang gliding," has been going through a revival recently.)

Wilbur and Orville Wright thought that control by shifting the body was very poor technique because they felt the response time was much too long. They had already observed that birds controlled their gliding and soaring flight by twisting movements of the tips of their wings. The Wrights developed their control system first by trying it in soaring flight, before using it in their powered airplane.

Powered flight was such a compelling idea that gliding (now more often called soaring) was neglected. A few people saw it as a challenging sport, but there weren't many of them. The greatest stimulus powerless flight ever received came about as a result of a provision of the Versailles Treaty following the First World War: Germany was prohibited from having anything to do with powered airplanes.

It has long been known that the Germans took to the air in gliders and that the entire German *Luftwaffe* grew from the training of thousands of glider pilots. Unfortunately, it still has not been widely noticed that one of the reasons for this success is that gliders are in many ways better flight trainers than powered airplanes.

The art of soaring has come far since the early days of two-, five-, and ten-second flights. The altitude record is 46,267 feet; the world distance record 716 miles. The Soaring Society of America and the Fédération Aeronautique Internationale no longer recognize endurance flights: with modern aircraft and up-to-date knowledge of where slope soaring winds are continuous (as at Dillingham Airfield on the island of Oahu), endurance flights depend almost entirely on the pilot's ability to stay awake, and require very low skill.

The top award of the Soaring Society of America is the Diamond Badge. To qualify, a pilot must make an endurance flight of five hours, a cross-country flight of at least 500 kilometers (310.7 statute miles), a flight of at least 300 km (186.4 statute miles) over a triangular or out-and-return course, and a flight in which at least 5,000 meters (16,404) is gained from the point of release. There are gold badges and silver badges, with less stringent requirements.

Achieving a diamond badge is comparable to running a four-minute mile; and even the gold and silver badges require an exceptionally high degree of skill. But the training and skill needed to share the joy and satisfaction of soaring are well within reach of most people. Best of all, glider training is a delightful improbability, like finding strawberry shortcake on your reducing menu. It is not only fun, it's good for you: the art of flying a sailplane polishes your control touch, and learning about vertical currents will add importantly to your safety in powered flight.

Compared to the rest of general aviation, the field of soaring is quite small. At the end of 1970, there were a little over 11,000 pilots licensed to fly gliders. Two thirds of these were also licensed to fly powered aircraft, leaving not quite 4,000 with glider-only certificates. The total number of glider pilots amounts to only about 1.5 percent of the total number of pilots of all kinds in the United States. This is in part a result of the same sort of antipathy that exists between men of sail and men of power on the water. A much larger factor is the conditioned reaction deeply trained into all pilots of powered aircraft: in single-engine airplanes, engine stoppage brings on an immediate forced landing, the precise immediacy of which depends on how much altitude the pilot has when the engine quits. Power pilots don't like to think about engines stopping, and it's but a short step to associating that dislike with a similar dislike of aircraft which don't have engines at all. A captain who flies Boeing 747's for United Air Lines takes a different view: "Since every landing is going to be a forced landing, why not relax and enjoy it?" He is a Gold Badge holder.

In actual operations the size of the problem is much smaller than the power pilot perceives it to be. Sailplanes are very light, so they can be stopped in a short distance after touching down: much less landing run is required than for all but a handful of powered airplanes. More important is the fact that sailplanes are equipped with means to reduce the lift in the wings and thus can descend quite steeply. In this, they are very much easier to manage than conventional fixed wing airplanes. All of this becomes clear to the power pilot once he begins taking glider training.

Once the power pilot is in free flight in a glider, he is struck by the quiet of the cockpit, the feeling that flight is effortless, and the fact that events seem to be happening in a most leisurely way. For the first time he is able to converse with his instructor in living-room voice levels; and at the end of the flight, he is surprised to find that he is not as tired as he had expected to be.

The real reason for the small size of the glider pilot population is the inconvenience of getting an unpowered flying machine into free flight. There are several ways, all but one of them awkward or expensive or both.

Lilienthal and Montgomery ran downhill into the wind, lifted off, and floated to the bottom of the hill, landing as best they could. Lilienthal built himself a conical hill, so that he could always face the wind no matter how it was blowing. Montgomery didn't have that problem because the mesa on which he worked outside of San Diego had an almost constant prevailing wind blowing off the Pacific.

Only a few feet off the ground, the glider pilot has already raised his ship a few feet higher than the tow plane.

Pilots without either of these advantages used launching crews, who took hold of ropes attached to the gliders and ran with them into the wind, for all the world as though they were lofting kites, which indeed they were. Some people used long lengths of multiple-strand rubber cable, called shock cord, prestretched between stakes on the ground, hooked to the glider, and then released by a trigger.

The modern ground launch methods are winch tow and auto tow. In the auto tow the sailplane is tied to the tow car with a long line, and the car accelerates to a predetermined speed. As the aircraft leaves the ground, the pilot pulls back on the stick, which increases both speed and climb, and releases as he reaches a point almost above the tow car. Winch tow works the same way, except of course that the winch doesn't move. Sometimes the auto tow system is modified, where straightway distance is short, by running the towline over a pulley. The pilot's technique is essentially unchanged.

By far the most common and effective way of launching sailplanes is by aero tow, in which the glider is pulled into the air, to whatever altitude the sailplane pilot wants, by an airplane, most often a Piper Super Cub. For landing practice, this is 700 feet, with the sailplane positioned on the downwind leg for landing. For airwork, the altitude may be as low as 2,000 feet above the ground or as high as 5,000 feet. If the sailplane pilot wants to soar, or engage in a badge task, he stays on tow, directing the tow plane pilot either by radio or by standard aeronautical signals to spots where he thinks lift is to be found.

The technical flexibility of aero tow is badly offset by its cost; in a typical example, three tows to 3,000 feet, at $6 per tow, will be required on a day with no lift to get in an hour's practice. A Schweizer single-place 1-26 sailplane can be rented for only $10 for that hour; with the three tows, the total cost turns out to be $28. This makes soaring more expensive per hour than powered flight by a wide margin; yet if you look at the actual costs involved, the tow plane charge is quite a bargain. The trouble, of course, comes from the fact that it takes two airplanes and two pilots to get one of them into the air.

For the power pilot learning to sail, the hardest part is the launch. Auto and winch tow are easier to learn than aero tow, even though the technique seems to be entirely backward. The problem with aero tow is that the pilot is in a familiar environment, but the sailplane does not fly at all in the same way it does free—or the way his familiar powered airplane does free—while under tow. Glider instructors have a tendency to make the newcomer spend too much time in the early stages in learning the required maneuvers while on tow, leaving little opportunity to savor the splendor of quiet gliding and soaring. It is likely that an important number of potential soaring converts from power have been lost in the first lesson because of the unnatural "feel" of the flying machine while being towed.

Now imagine bolting some kind of a small engine onto a sailplane, with just enough power to take off and just enough endurance to permit a climb to a reasonable altitude, plus the ability to restart in flight and further endurance of maybe half an hour. This surely seems a modest problem, now that we have proved that we can put men on the moon and even take televised pictures of their departure.

A SOCATA Rallye, a sturdy French machine, seen here providing a multiple tow.

At one stroke this would solve almost all of the tactical problems facing both existing soaring pilots and power pilots converting to sail. It would allow for the principle of one pilot/one airplane. Sailplane pilots would be independent of tow planes, their costs and their scheduling problems; they could maneuver themselves, at very low fuel cost, into the places where lift seemed likely. Failing to find that lift, they could return gracefully to base, refuel, and wait for more favorable conditions.

The benefits to power pilots are even greater. They would be freed from the demand of mastering the tiresome tow maneuvers and from their deeply trained concern about engine-out forced landings.

This solution would also go a long way toward eliminating another clumsy problem: the present necessity of having a trailer on hand. Sailplanes must travel on trailers to or from home and special soaring areas, as well as each time they land away from their home airports. Pilots on cross-country flights have to be "retrieved" by a faithful ground crew, who must find their way as best they can to wherever it is the pilot has come to earth, help him take the flying machine apart and stow it in the trailer, and bring all home again.

In a lot of cases, the presence of the minimum engine would allow the sailplane to be flown home again. No matter that the speed would be low: it would still take less time, and cost less, than ground-based retrieval.

More and more pilots are finding the answer to their problems in the powered glider. Takeoff with the engine, climb to your start altitude and switch off. If you can't find those thermals, start up the motor again and head for home.

Finally, a lot of cross-country flights end in an off-airport landing because the pilot ran out of lift short of his destination and had to land as best he could. With the air-start ability, this, too, would pass. So would waiting for a tow, at which sailplane pilots often spend more time than they do soaring. And soaring could spread everywhere, even to places and at times where there is no lift at all, because a lot can be learned and a lot of enjoyment can be had simply by sailing down from a height of 5,000 feet.

This is not a dream: there really are sailplanes with small engines. They have been known as "powered gliders," but lately a more stylish name has come into favor: "self-launching sailplanes." No matter what they are called, progress has been amazingly slow. The Soaring Society of America's 1970 U.S. Sailplane Directory shows only 27 active, and although it's possible that there are others belonging to pilots who are not members of the association, it's hard to imagine that there could be very many.

One of the earliest of these was the Nelson Hummingbird, designed by Harry Perl and Ted Nelson. Even though the design is now twenty years old, the Hummingbird is still elegant and its performance remarkable for its day. The engine, mounted on a pylon, extends for powered flight and retracts concealed within the fuselage for soaring. It takes a keen eye to see the joints where the engine covers meet the fuselage when the engine is retracted. Only seven were built, and six are still flying. Nobody who owns one has the slightest intention of selling it, no matter what the price. There has been a lot of talk by several groups about putting the Hummingbird into volume production, but nothing concrete has resulted so far.

Most of the other self-launching sailplanes, such as the Scheibe Motorspatz and SF-27M, and the Schleicher AS-K 14, are single-place, unlike the Hummingbird, which seats two. The Scheibe Falke SF-25B also seats two, and Schleicher has announced the two-place AS-K 16.

It's hard to understand why there has been so little progress in the field. Perhaps the biggest factor is inertia, but there are some practical problems as well. First of these involves achievement of goals: a pilot who reaches the silver, gold, or diamond badge level in a pure sailplane has accomplished something remarkable. Without carefully written rules, a powered sailplane could easily cheapen these feats. The rules have been written, but it's still too soon to be sure that they have done the job precisely.

Second, the FAA is wrestling with the matter of defining a self-launching sailplane. A glider—but if a glider has an engine, does it remain a glider, or does it become an airplane? If it becomes an airplane, the soaring regulations are in for some changes. The most important of these is the matter of a physical examination for glider pilots: none is required now, not even for the commercial pilot level. This might perhaps be solved simply by requiring anyone who wants to fly a powered glider to take a physical; but it certainly seems better to find some way to define the machine. In view of the small number of people now interested in the subject, there is little pressure on the FAA to expedite this.

Aggravating they may be, but these are small matters, easily capable of resolution. And when they are, we will see an expansion of the art of soaring beyond everything that has happened up to the present.

One of the aircraft which may start the boom is the Caproni A21J, from the Italian pioneer aircraft builders. This is a two-place machine with side-by-side seating and outstanding sailplane performance. The news is in the suffix "J," which stands for "jet."

The preliminary figures for this aircraft show a glide ratio of 43 to 1, a theoretical absolute ceiling under power of just a few hundred feet less

Another example of the power approach to gliding. This is a Ted Nelson Hummingbird, introduced in the early '40s, and powered by a simple 2-stroke.

than 50,000 feet, and a speed of 208 mph at 42,500 feet. For people who prefer no power, the same airframe will be available as the A21, with a slightly higher glide ratio (45 to 1).

On this side of the Atlantic, a man named Dick Tobey is hatching an even more exotic machine in California. Called Invicta, it will also be jet powered and will offer two sets of wings easily interchangeable—a long set for soaring and a shorter pair for travel.

Soaring is a clean, lithe, lively, and lovely sport, and its machines include some of the most beautiful things man has ever made.

BALLOONING

A hot-air balloon consists of a two-ton bubble of air heated to some 200 degrees or more, held captive within a light fabric bag, from which is suspended a cab or gondola usually made of fiberglass. Between the bottom of the bag and the top of the basket, which are six or eight feet apart, is suspended a kind of metal table containing one or more burners. The burners are fed propane from cylinders carried within the gondola, and the flame is controlled by a valve—operated by someone in the gondola—located on the underside of the metal table.

Balloons first impress by their size. They arrive on a small trailer, the entire balloon and all its equipment squeezed into the gondola. When the balloon is removed from its canvas carrying bag and stretched out downwind of the gondola, it seems enormous—about 40 or 50 feet long. Then the mouth of the balloon is held open by sticks and crew members, and the burner flame is turned on and directed into it.

The 10-foot-long flame roars mightily and radiates enough heat to make one uncomfortable several feet away. The balloon immediately begins to swell, revealing a cavernous interior, and billows rapidly upward until it is the size of a small house. Crew members tug at cables and shroud lines, keeping the rim of the mouth away from the flame, and sometimes running inside the balloon to push and lift its rolling skin in the proper directions.

Soon the balloon is filled, and its underside begins to rise from the ground. The crewman handling the burner has one leg inside the gondola. At once all the others let go the lines and the bubble lifts, tipping the gondola upright with the crewman inside. The burner is shut off. The balloon, inflated but still "heavy"—that is, not sufficiently buoyant to lift the gondola—stands now a good 40 or 50 feet high and 30 feet in diameter.

The passengers hoist themselves over the waist-high sides of the gondola and pull helmets down over their ears. There are several reasons for wearing the helmets: one is the possibility of a rough landing spilling everyone out pell-mell; another is the danger of the burner table hitting the passengers on the head during a moderately hard landing; yet another is simply to blunt the roar of the burners.

Everyone aboard, the pilot opens the burner valve. The flame shoots up with a great whoosh into the mouth of the balloon, which swells and distends. After half a minute, the gondola rocks slightly and drags a little along the ground. The burner is shut off.

The next step, you might think from *Up, Up and Away* and *Around the World in Eighty Days,* is for the balloon and its occupants to soar rapidly skyward, shrinking to a sun-sized spot and drifting off behind the hills. What happens is quite the opposite. With a delicate, magical levitation, the immense thing lifts itself a few inches above the turf and moves slowly away.

It is only a few minutes past dawn. The wind is nearly calm, and there is still a slight chill in the air; except for the occasional chirping of birds, everything is still. Like a submarine moving slowly across the bottom of the sea, the balloon slides along—silent, level, graceful. In the gondola the passengers converse quietly. Their words are almost audible to the crew, who trail along behind the balloon, kicking the wet grass. From time to time, the pilot fires the burners for a few seconds, and then silence closes in again and the balloon is still floating eerily along.

Two hundred yards off, the balloon settles with a little bounce to the ground. Passengers change, handing helmets and cameras back and forth.

Some say that the hot-air balloonist of today has even more problems than 200 years ago. Certainly there are more obstacles to avoid, but modern technology has introduced considerable factors of safety that the pioneers of flight never did enjoy.

When the new crew is aboard, the balloon ascends again, this time to 20 or 30 feet. It moves more rapidly now, passing through the tops of trees and skimming over a windmill and some power lines. The ground crew walks back to the car and sets off after the balloon.

In the gondola, one looks down, from a small height, at the fields and hedges below, and is suddenly aware of the life filling them. Everywhere there are rabbits, scampering frantically back and forth when the burner roars overhead. A feral cat prowls alongside a row of low bushes. A dog trots purposefully down a dirt road. Off a little behind the balloon, the ground crew is coming along the same road. Most of the farmhouses are still asleep, but occasionally, as a dog sets up a great yelping and tries to dig its way under a woodpile at the approach of the fiery monstrosity overhead, an old man or a small girl comes out on a doorstep and looks about for the cause of the excitement, never thinking to look overhead as the balloon glides silently along.

The balloon drifts among low hills. The chase car, stymied, stops at a fence, hesitates, and then doubles back to look for another road. Because of a Venturi effect, the balloon moves faster over ridges. The pilot aims to just scrape the bushes along the ridge, while the passengers lean against the back of the gondola in anticipation of the jolt, which, if it were hard enough, could spill them all out onto the ground and leave the lightened balloon to travel on alone.

It is impossible to steer or even to make the balloon revolve; the fortuitousness, isolation, and lack of control are much of the charm of balloon flying. With nonchalant egotism, the balloonist drifts off, indifferent to the world except as a sort of terrarium into which he peers curiously, while the ground crew, for the moment his serfs, follow doggedly after him. When fuel runs low, he looks for a place to land—preferably a valley, downwind of a screen of trees, but any clear spot of 50 yards' diameter will do—and, coming up to it, he opens first a small gate in the side of the balloon to let some hot air escape and steepen the descent. Then, when the landing is assured, a rip cord is pulled that detaches an entire panel of the bag and lets the bubble of hot air escape rapidly. As the balloon sinks, the burners are shut off and, time permitting, the fuel valve is closed and the lines emptied. The passengers brace themselves, their knees slightly bent like parachutists' and their hands gripping the sides of the basket. Everyone secretly tries to be behind someone else in order to land on top in the melee. The gondola hits and tips over; the balloon, deflating rapidly, falls beyond it. The passengers tumble into a heap like scrimmagers as they pick themselves up and dust themselves off. Curious locals arrive in pickups or afoot to ask questions—which are always the same, with a few surprising variations—and gape at the huge collapsed balloon.

Shortly, the ground crew arrives in the car. The balloon is milked of its remaining hot air and stuffed any-which-way into its bag, which in turn is loaded into the gondola. With one man at each corner—including, generally, some drafted local help—the whole affair is carried to the trailer, everyone piles into the car, and then it's off to breakfast at the local diner.

Ballooning is a sport in which, even more than in skydiving, much effort and preparation is put into a comparatively brief and delicate result. While it is possible to do it by oneself, it is much more practical to have three or four people along to help with the struggle at beginning and end. For those in the gondola, however, for as long as it lasts, ballooning is, of all kinds of flying, the most reflective, artistic, and soul-satisfying; it lulls the mind to rest, brings a philosophic calm into the heart, and gives an intimate view of a world which is that of birds, household gods, and low-flying ghosts.

CHAPTER 9

Homebuilts and Experimentals

THERE are always those to whom the conventional is anathema; they avoid the mainstream. In aviation these people gravitate toward such pastimes as homebuilding, antiquing, and experimenting. Some design and build their own aircraft. Others are devoted to the idea that the perfect airplane is one in which the human leg muscles are the most efficient source of motive power. For most of these people, the airplane is not a vehicle in which to go from here to there more quickly than by any other means; it is quite simply a device in which to *fly*.

Two of the most active and exciting aspects of general aviation involve antique and homebuilt airplanes. They have a lot in common: most antiques have been discovered "in shreds," stored away in old barns and all but forgotten, and need at least as much hand labor as it takes to build a homebuilt airplane from the beginning. Both require dedication and mechanical aptitude, lots of free time, and space to house them while the work is in progress. In fact, it's possible for an airplane to qualify as both an antique and a homebuilt: the official definition of an antique airplane is either an original or replica of an airplane built originally more than thirty years ago. Thus a replica of a Thomas-Morse World War I fighter, even if it is itself only two years old, qualifies as an antique if it is a faithful imitation.

Both branches have national organizations: the Antique Airplane Association, of Ottumwa, Iowa, and the Experimental Aircraft Association, Hales Corners, Wisconsin. The EAA has a much larger membership (35,000 worldwide members) than the antiquers' club, a fact which is understandable: except for occasional finds of forgotten machines and construction of faithful replicas, there is no way for the population of antique airplanes to expand. The homebuilders are, in contrast, capable of unlimited expansion.

What is the attraction of the antique and the homebuilt airplane? Is it that for the owners it's sort of getting back to basics?

The do-it-yourself airplane idea has plenty of precedents, including the fact that the first powered airplane was built in a bicycle shop in Dayton, Ohio. If you decide to start such a project, you'll find that you are not alone. It has been estimated that there are some 7,000 homebuilt aircraft now under construction in the world, most of them in the United States. More than 2,000 homebuilts are now flying.

Building your own is neither easy nor the fast way to become an aircraft owner. First, you must be thoroughly proficient in and dedicated to one or more of the mechanical arts. Woodworking is a good one; so are welding and sheet-metal fabrication.

Next, you must be an extremely patient man. We know of airplanes that have been built in six months, but they are exceedingly rare. Like time payments, some of the homebuilt projects stretch to eternity. All the while your garage is filled with bits and pieces, shavings and slivers of metal, and oily engines.

Is homebuilding the inexpensive way to aircraft ownership? This is a controversial question. In actual dollars spent for the airplane hardware, it is inexpensive. Six hundred is about the bottom. From there, it depends on how much airplane you want. In general, materials for the aircraft itself are cheap enough. One firm advertises a basic materials kit for $1,190. If you are a scrounger, a scavenger, a wheeler-dealer—and if you become a homebuilder, you will learn to be all three—you can cut the basic costs to around $200.

The incidentals mount up, however. Engines, for example. You can find them for $50 or $75. Volkswagen engines or power plants used on military target drones can be had for $150 and up. The more likely price, though, for an aircraft-approved engine in airworthy condition with necessary accessories, begins at about $500 for one of less than 100 hp. A man with a yen for a big or speedy airplane will pay about $2,000 for an overhauled 250-hp engine.

After the engine come instruments, with altimeters costing $40 and up, a compass $17.50, an engine tachometer $20. Then you'll need wheels and brakes at $50 or so, and a propeller, tires, paint.

No victory parade—merely proof that these WWI aircraft have perennial appeal.

The bright side to all this is that most homebuilders do not reckon their labor or overhead—extra depreciation on a car sitting outside a year or so, automotive gas consumed chasing after parts, electricity to power building tools.

So, give or take a few hundred dollars, you can build your own for somewhere between $1,500 and $10,000, depending on how fancy and elaborate your dream plane is. Plus, of course, one to five years of your leisure time.

Is it worth it? A lovingly crafted homebuilt is the most envied possession in all aviation. There is a pride in flying a self-made plane, an appre-

Modern experimentals come in all shapes and sizes and surprisingly diverse mission profiles.

ciation for the ability to fly, that is denied the person with a store-bought one—even the fancy, twin-engined, dual everything models. And there is a greater feeling of security, too. You'll learn, as you build, that no matter how careful the craftsman, things do not go together perfectly. And each flight you'll be thankful that you know every imperfection in your machine, while the fellow who bought his aircraft can only squirm in the knowledge that they are there, somewhere.

Finally, the man who builds it himself has the prerogative of changing things around if he doesn't especially care for a feature—something Federal Aviation Administration regulations forbid you to do to assembly-line products.

How do you get started? First, mail a check for $10 to the Experimental Aircraft Association (P.O. Box 299, Hales Corners, Wisconsin 53130). This will tap a perpetual fountain of comradeship, advice, and encouragement from fellow EAAer's, all of which you'll need as time passes. Second, select the type of plane you wish to build and buy a set of plans for it. Then, you can dream for a few months, scheme how to get the money and convince your wife it's really as easy as—and no more risky than—putting together the kids' swing set from the bits and pieces and cryptic instructions that came with them.

Finally, find a place. Suburbanites always have the garage attached to their house; some are even lucky enough to have an old outbuilding. City dwellers have a bigger problem. Some have solved it by going to the suburbs and renting a building that they visit on weekends. A better solution is to find an old basement that can be leased cheaply. And here's a far-out idea: One man's boss allowed him to build an overhead platform at his machine shop, to which the employee flew like a cliff swallow at each coffee break and lunch whistle.

The main thing is to have a firm grip and a long lease on the nest in which your bird will hatch. You'll be abiding in it at least three times as long as you now contemplate the project will take.

But don't let this cloudy thought dissuade you. As the fuselage and

Antique means more than thirty years old. This Grumman Goose, although antique, still earns its daily bread flying passengers between the various Virgin Islands in the Caribbean.

wings and interior appointments take shape, the silver lining will appear. For the flying buff, there is no greater sense of fulfillment and excitement than the final days of a homebuilt project.

FLYING AUTOMOBILES

One of the more exciting, recurrent aviation dreams involves Everyman's Skycar, or the Flying Flivver. It is the aeronautical equivalent of the family automobile, equally at home in the air and on the highway, able to rise and descend vertically from and into a handkerchief-sized backyard. The most versatile form of transportation ever conceived, the flying automobile can be used for family vacation travel, outings at the seashore or the mountains, commuting to work, or even going shopping. Freed from the congestion of highways and safe from the hazards of bad weather, it is swift, safe, and economical—and once it goes into mass production, it will be priced like an automobile rather than an airplane.

However, there are difficulties in this delightful dream. Airplanes are inherently more expensive than automobiles; mixing functions, of both air and ground, will result in a machine which is an inefficient compromise for either; and not enough people would buy the Skycar, hence the economic gamble would carry intolerable odds.

Furthermore, many pilots shudder at the thought of a sky black with aircraft, and it is indeed true that there would be a considerable increase in collision hazard. There are already practical means at hand to reduce this to acceptable limits, but the real problem is that it isn't the sky that is crowded—it's the ground.

There aren't many airports. A recent figure lists about 12,000 of all kinds and sizes, of which one third are not open to the public. That leaves only about 8,000 public facilities, including small airports, seaplane bases (very few), and airports large enough for airliner use. There are 3,735 publicly owned airports in the United States, and only 2,474 of these have paved runways. At the bottom of the scale, there are fewer than 500 airports which have even one airline arrival and departure a day. The rest of the airports range up to the large terminals, and there is where the congestion is.

Since most air traffic flows between the large airports, and since even the largest facilities have a small number of runways, the traffic inevitably funnels into the air space leading to one or two precious runways. The result is delays in flight, while the air traffic control system provides safe spacing to all flights.

This explains how the system will become less crowded as more runways are built and—if we ever do have Everyman's Skycar, able to land on a relatively unprepared or, at worst, a small paved strip—how we will be able to accept a very large increase in total air vehicles before anything like saturation will occur.

A fundamental analysis of the subject finds another condition, or pair of conditions, which go far to explain the absence of the Flying Flivver. Not only has the market been limited, not only has surface traffic congestion only recently been accepted as a serious restraint to further growth of the automobile, but, finally, neither the airplane nor the motorcar people have had any interest in each other or in the development of a combination machine.

There is very little to suggest that these conditions have changed as yet, but let's look at one man's solution, all the while keeping in mind that the automobile makers are now fully aware of the limitations in dollar sales and growth and that the airplane people have been going through a serious

pause in their own growth. The idea of a flying automobile, or a roadable airplane, has inspired countless dreamers and a few aircraft designers. But for all its appeal, only one design has ever won full approval from the Federal Aviation Administration. That one is the Aerocar, designed and built by Moulton B. Taylor in a small, neat building in Longview, Washington.

Moult Taylor is no attic inventor. He is a professional aeronautical engineer, with a long and successful career in many phases of aviation design. Certainly he has been more dedicated to the flying automobile than anyone else, devoting imagination, ingenuity, time, and money to the concept for over twenty years. Though he has at present only one flying article to show for it, his enthusiasm remains high. The latest version is called Model III.

In sharp contrast to the boxy, old-fashioned look of the earlier versions, the Model III's ground half looks like a sports car that might have come from one of the great European *carrosseries*. It is also quick, responsive, and marvelously comfortable; and when Moult Taylor hurls it across double railroad tracks at 80 mph, holding both hands in the air, you are convinced that it has remarkable handling qualities. It's not as quiet as a

OPPOSITE AND RIGHT. An unlikely story! But the camera is not lying. This is the passenger's view from the cockpit of Moult Taylor's Aerocar. On the ground you fold away the wings, untuck the fuselage and drive away.

Cadillac, but what sports car is? And what sports car was ever disqualified for making competent, purposeful noises as it went about its work?

The other half of the machine is a trailer, complete with wheels and hitch, composed of all the ingredients needed to accomplish the metamorphosis from car to Aerocar. It takes about five minutes to knit the two halves together ("Less time than it takes to carry your bags from your car to your airplane," says Taylor). Positive, fail-safe interlocks are provided at each attach point; if you haven't made everything secure, you can't start the engine.

The engine—a Lycoming 0-320 derated to 143 hp—is at the rear, driving forward to the front wheels, and is provided with an aft coupling to the propeller shaft, which extends through the tail to the rear-mounted propeller.

These are the bare ingredients. When you study the details, the Aerocar emerges as a magnificent monument to Taylor's ingenuity. Among other things, every federal auto safety and FAA standard has been satisfied.

"What do you have to change when you want to fly?" is the question everyone asks. Moult Taylor has his answer ready: "All you have to change is your mind." This turns out to be quite true; the mixing of ground and flight operations has been done so carefully that a pilot adapts quickly. If the ramp is blocked ahead, you shift into reverse and let the wheels back you out. If you want to taxi away gently and not blow down the folks behind, put it in low and it drifts away. You find yourself using the foot throttle in taxiing; but after the run-up, you change naturally to the hand throttle.

On the takeoff roll the Aerocar feels much the same as it does rolling down the highway. You maintain direction in the same way—with a steering wheel.

There is one small source of amusement at takeoff. After the wheels leave the ground, the speedometer winds down to zero, while the airspeed indication rises. The airspeed meter is a proper round aircraft type, while the ground speedometer is rectangular, so there is little chance of mistaking one for the other.

The Aerocar has a rather pleasant, swooping style of flight, something like a sailplane and something like a helicopter. Visibility is great, seating position and comfort excellent (even though the seats are not adjustable), and the noise level delightfully low.

Frontal view emphasizes the considerable care given to aerodynamics. The wind-cheating shape is reminiscent of the Jaguar.

The Aerocar has one flight characteristic which is not possessed by any other airplane anywhere near its class, and few of any kind, except radio-controlled models. A very desirable characteristic; were it universal, many of the problems of instrument flight would be eliminated. This is known as spiral stability, or lateral stability. Airplanes turn by banking, or putting a wing down in the direction of the turn. Unlike automobiles, in which the steering wheel must be held in the direction of the turn to keep the turn going, turning pressures in airplanes are applied only during turn entry, and then removed.

In conventional airplanes the pilot must manipulate the controls, once a turn is established, to keep the turn going at the same rate and to keep from losing altitude. If he does not do so, the airplane will put its nose down and begin to speed up. This in turn will cause the down wing to go down further, which will cause a further speed increase. The Aerocar is exactly opposite. If the pilot lets go of the controls after entering a turn, the airplane will roll itself back to a level, upright position.

In landings, again unlike conventional airplanes, you can stand on the brakes the instant you touch down, just as you do if you want to stop quickly in a car. "After all," says Taylor, "these are big wheels, and the steering and suspension are designed to go 100 mph on the ground. You're not going to break anything."

Speaking of wheels, they have three positions: fully extended for takeoff and landing, retracted for cruise, and in-between for road operation. Suspension is by torsion bars, so positioning involves only more or less twisting of the springs. Operation is electric. The engine starts and stops like the engine in your car. Taylor has achieved this miracle by the same means used by automobile engineers long years ago: the spark is retarded on starting and advanced by a centrifugal mechanism in proportion to engine shaft speed. Conventional airplane engines are not so equipped, although they could be, and starting would become much easier.

Beyond the design and performance, which are measurable, the Aerocar requires considerable mental adjustment, and this can only come from

Moult Taylor himself. He is the man with a dream. "The Aerocar is not just another airplane, or just another car; it's a whole new kind of transportation machine. It's the only vehicle that can go from your house to my house at over 50 miles an hour," he points out. "Airplanes haven't changed their ways much since the first ones flew: they can still go only from one cow pasture to another. The only differences are that airplanes have become faster, and most of the cow pastures are paved.

"I used to think that maybe helicopters would be the answer, but now I think not. They are very expensive, and they suffer from serious artificial restrictions that will probably get worse. You can't really run down to the store in one.

"There isn't any way to compare production of airplanes and flying automobiles. If we can't sell, in our first year, at least as many Aerocars as the whole light airplane industry sells airplanes in its best year, then my conception of the idea is wrong. For any distances between 30 and several hundred miles, even the present 135-mph Aerocar makes 250-mph airplanes ineffective.

"Don't tell me 'this is only two-place,' because that has nothing to do with the idea. If the idea is really successful, we can build them any size, any speed, to carry any number of people. And try not to be misled by what we have to do now, by hand, to attach the flight parts. There is no reason, except one of simple economics, that we haven't turned this into a single, automatic, push-button operation. Once the machine is tooled for production, it will go together or come apart as fast as you put the top up and down on your convertible."

Looking at the Aerocar through Taylor's enthusiastic eyes, one begins to see that what is really required is a physical adjustment of the dimensions of the machine to its two environments. It needs big dimensions to fly, and it needs small dimensions to fit on a highway. Why wouldn't it be possible to have the wings and tail telescope out from the body for flight, and retract for driving? No matter how tricky such a design might be, it surely would not require any higher level of engineering than is already extant.

A thin horizontal panel covers the ground instruments and is set within the otherwise aircraft instrument panel. Normal driving pedals, clutch, brake and accelerator and gear shift. Rudder pedals and a three-place retraction mechanism plus center throttle allow for speedy conversion. Note the key switch which has position for left/right/both magnetos.

Even in its present form, the Aerocar has several operational advantages. If the weather is bad ahead, the pilot lands, turns the wings into a trailer, and continues his trip on the ground. At home he can leave the trailer/wings in his garage or backyard and use the ground vehicle for local transportation. If he has no room at home, he can rent space at the local airport and hook up his wings there each time he flies.

How much would it cost to put the Aerocar into production, where would the money come from, and how long before anybody could buy one?

The cost of tooling and production facilities will be high—probably not less than $10,000,000. Completion of design and preparation of facilities will probably take at least five years. Nobody knows where the money is coming from yet, but there is something at least worth speculating about. In recent years the car makers have seen strong evidence that past marketing practices are probably not going to work in the future. The sharp increase in sales of small, low-priced cars, so far mostly imports, suggests that Detroit may be faced with selling the same number of cars each year but at only about half the price for each. It wouldn't take many flying automobiles to bring the dollar sales level back up, and for Detroit, an investment of $10,000,000—or even several times that—would raise no blood pressure.

THE ULTIMATE ENGINE

We fly. It is a source of some pride to us. We have learned to master an art that fascinated and puzzled men for centuries. We traffic with eagles. We are lords of the air.

At least until we run out of gas; then, like Cinderella at midnight, we find ourselves riding a pumpkin. The fact is, we do not really fly—we are flown. It is as if we had managed to carry out some antique scheme for harnessing several hundred larks to a chariot and flying to the moon. We are not worn out when we land because we have not remained aloft by our own exertions. In fact the impossibility of men flying under their own power was demonstrated persuasively by G. A. Borelli, nearly 300 years ago, and substantiated by a number of experimenters who attached various sorts of wings to their arms and flung themselves from windy bluffs, usually into oblivion.

The truth came out, however, in 1937, when two gliders powered by their pilots managed to remain aloft, once launched by a short tow, for better than half a mile. One was a German effort and the other Italian; the Italian, which was powered by two wing-mounted tractor propellers, made an unsubstantiated claim to have been the first airplane ever actually to take off under pilot-power alone.

The first properly documented case of genuine man-powered flight (a genuine flight must include a man-powered takeoff) dates to 1961, when, on a mild and calm day in November, one Derek Piggot, 39, pedaled very hard and rose into the air in SUMPAC (Southampton University Man-Powered Aircraft), a British project with a wingspan of 80 feet and an empty weight of 130 pounds. A week later, *Puffin,* a rival venture by a team from Hawker-Siddeley, also flew. *Puffin* was a little larger in span and lighter in weight than SUMPAC.

Since then, various man-powered aircraft have logged more than 150 flights—mostly in England, where development of the type has been going on for a long time. Numerous projects are currently under way, including autogyros, helicopters, ornithopters, and even a 38-pound inflatable flying (or, so far, nonflying) wing.

Perhaps, needless to say, the motivation behind much of the activity is money. There is a lot of prize money to be won—$36,000 in all. But the current spate of interest in man-powered flight antedates even the establishment of the prizes. It started in 1957 when 18 Englishmen variously concerned with aviation and sharing an elegant interest in "Art for Art's Sake" formed a committee to unify and encourage efforts toward man-powered flight, and obtained a small amount of money to attract and assist research. In 1959 a large-scale financial incentive, in the form of a prize of $12,000 for the first flight of a man-powered aircraft over a course a little more than a mile long, was offered by an industrialist named Henry Kremer. Only British Commonwealth entrants were eligible, and it is because of this stricture that England holds a lead. Only last year was the field opened to the rest of the world, with an additional $24,000 offered for the completion of a slightly different, more difficult flight. Neither prize has yet been won, but now Japanese and Canadian projects are under way and stand a chance of overtaking the English, whose climate makes opportunities for test flights few and far between.

One of the leading contenders is *Puffin II,* which was built in 1966 after *Puffin I* was badly damaged in landing. *Puffin I* had flown up to three quarters of a mile; *Puffin II* has done half a mile in the relatively short time it has been flying, and should eventually exceed the performance of its predecessor. With a wingspan of 93 feet and wing area of 400 square feet, *Puffin II* weighs 130 pounds empty; its nine-foot propeller drives it at a cruising speed of 16 mph, after takeoff speed has been attained by means of a bicycle-wheel landing gear. The structure is balsa, spruce, and Melinex, the last a transparent plastic .0035 inch thick; *Puffin*'s wing loading is .7 lb/sq ft, and its power loading about 700 lb/hp.

The technical problem of man-powered flight is one of efficiency. The man-powered aircraft is a *reductio ad absurdum* of orthodox aeronautical practice. Dr. D. R. Willkie, writing in *The New Scientist* in 1959, set forth

Puffin II, a British man-powered venture, has already flown more than half a mile. Plans are in hand for a two-man version with which it is hoped the $12,000 prize—on offer since 1959—will be won for completing the first flight of a man-powered aircraft over one mile. Total prize money to whomever achieves this feat should top $50,000.

the battle cry of the Kremer Contest: ". . . dogs and men are capable of flying . . . while horses are not." A hard blow for horses; but if there is hope for the .3 hp that a man is able to produce for fairly extended periods, then building a man-powered airplane is merely a matter of achieving low weight combined with a very high lift/drag ratio—which is precisely what *Puffin* and SUMPAC, to name only two, have done.

Unfortunately, the problems do not end with achieving a high degree of aerodynamic efficiency. Operating in ground effect, the man-powered craft encounter various modes of longitudinal and even directional instability (the latter due to the reduced drag of the low wing in a banked turn). The Japanese aircraft, *Linnet,* mounts the horizontal tail far above the wing to isolate it from downwash effects; *Puffin* uses wing-tip drag rudders in addition to differentially rigged ailerons to help overcome the yaw problem. But none of the man-powered aircraft is easy to fly; SUMPAC crashed in 1965 (a slow, majestic stall-spin sort of accident, from an altitude of 10 feet, injuring only SUMPAC) and is now a museum piece; and John Wimpenny, the Hawker-Siddeley engineer in charge of the Puffin Project, alone has flown *Puffin.*

Even instability would not be an insuperable problem—a man could learn a lot of tricks for $36,000—were it not that the power output of the pilot proves to drop, without his being conscious of it, when he is obliged to think as well as pedal. This phenomenon has encouraged several groups to develop two-seat designs, thus doubling power without doubling weight and reducing by half the percentage of power lost because of the necessity of thinking. Furthermore, one may use one's pick of crack oarsmen or bicyclists to complete the crew, once a pilot is aboard. One two-seater has flown—that of the British Southend Group; and the Canadian design, being built by a group from the Canadian Aeronautics and Space Institute, is a two-seater as well.

Only *Puffin,* SUMPAC, *Linnet,* and the Southend MPA have successfully flown so far, but a study of newspaper accounts on the subject reveals a number of reports, perhaps all apocryphal, of muscle-rotorcraft raising their two groaning pilots an inch above the ground, or bicycle-autogyros hopping along an empty pavement. A 1961 London *Evening Post* photograph shows something resembling a Ryan Aristocraft with flappable wings, rolling down a runway, trailing, for some reason, a small drag chute.

A man-powered aircraft in flight is a lovely thing to see. Light as a leaf, it responds to every breath of wind; resembling an immense dragonfly, it moves at a magically low speed, very stately and deliberate, while men run along below its wings tips, looking oddly frantic beside the delicate, vast, and slow airplane. The wings flex a great deal in flight, a turn is an adventure, and each landing a nightmare through which one holds one's breath with a sense of immense risk and infinite fragility. Through transparent skins, one sees sky, frame, and pedaling pilot, just as one sees the internal organs of some insects and tropical fish.

There are, of course, glorified sailplanes; and, though the Royal Aeronautical Society, which administers the Kremer Prizes, has given cash grants to some of the more promising projects, no one pretends that there is much practical application for the knowledge gained from the field of man-powered aircraft. Given the known limitations of lift/drag ratio available to fixed-wing aircraft, man-powered flight seems to be the domain solely of aircraft of very large size and impractically delicate construction, those which occupy only a small fringe of the flyability envelope of conventional aircraft. It is only by luck, in fact, that man can fly at all.

Yet there appears still to be some faint hope that people may one day pedal away into the air without risk of an early coronary. It was observed by Sir James Gray, a British zoologist known for his studies of animal locomotion, that, according to the accepted uses of fluid dynamics, birds ought not to be able to fly as well as they do either. Gray's Paradox remained mysterious for some time, and only recently has its explanation been glimpsed—in an unexpected kind of boundary layer control resulting from the motions of the trailing edges of birds' wings in the course of the flapping cycle.

A Farnborough aerodynamicist named J. S. Elliot, with a small group called the Farnborough Man-Powered Ornithopter Club, has for some time been investigating this phenomenon. The club is planning a flapping-wing aircraft powered by a single rowing man; but the theory of flapping wings would be applicable to powered aircraft in any flight regime, even the supersonic. Properly operated, a flapping wing can develop cruising lift coefficients on the order of 4.0 (*Puffin*'s is 0.8) without more drag than a conventional wing; lift/drag ratios in the hundreds are possible—as opposed to 30 or 40 for the best current sailplanes.

The problems involved in the realization of flapping-wing aircraft are immense. The structure of a flapping wing must be resonant, not resisting flutter as a rigid wing does, but in fact utilizing flutter as a source of energy for lift. No large machines in use today employ resonating structures; new materials and new techniques are required before efficient ornithopters can become a reality. But when and if they do, they will carry large loads to great heights and over long distances using little power and fuel—so little power, in fact, that a man could propel a small one without excessive effort.

CHAPTER 10

A Flight

UNTIL four o'clock he had been looking at his watch more and more often. Then the conference room to which they went for the last meeting mercifully had a clock on the wall, and he was able, while maintaining an air of attention, to take in the gradual waning of the day. The clock was on the verge of its jump to quarter of five when the men stood and with the customary halting progress, shaking hands and patting shoulders and turning from one to another on the way out, extracted themselves from the meeting. They collected again for what briefly threatened to become a protracted postscript in the elevator.

The chill of the Boston spring afternoon, with its sharp reflected light, and the feeling of sudden release from confinement and impatience seemed to wash him clean: ten of five on his watch seemed like a new chapter; he caught a cab as it unloaded another fare, tossed his small heavy valise on the seat, and, as he pulled the door shut with one hand, began to loosen his tie with the other.

"Logan Airport, the private plane terminal."

A thorough preflight is one thing you don't skimp—ever.

His blue-and-white airplane sat low to the ground, as if eager for the air. His pace was long and rapid as he pushed his crumpled charge receipt into his pocket and fished deeper for the airplane keys. He opened the door, tossed the bag into the back seat, and after a glance at the instrument panel—brake on, mag switch and master off—he stepped back down from the wing and began his preflight check. It took only three minutes—a dancelike

series of motions which, by many repetitions, he had made automatic. As always, everything was okay—the tanks full, the oil up, the landing gear struts and tires properly inflated, the prop smooth, the windshield and landing light covers clean, the airframe sound. In another moment he had removed his jacket and settled himself in the left seat. He shut the door and latched it, buckled his seat belt, and then for a moment before starting the engine he settled back and relaxed with a sigh, as he always did before

One of the last checks prior to takeoff: cycle the prop to make sure the oil is flowing properly. Cycling changes the pitch of the prop blades.

flying; though he could not have articulated his reasons, they were, more or less, that he liked to fly, and pausing this way seemed to clear the air and sharpen his appreciation of the ritual upon which he was embarked. For perhaps fifteen seconds he looked quietly and idly at the instruments, the slanted propeller, the wings, the airport outside, and the other parked airplanes; then with sudden and sharp motions, he switched on the master, pumped the throttle, turned the key. The engine turned once with a wheeze and then rumbled up and settled into an idle. Needles shivered and jumped into place. He turned on the radios and heard the tower voice come up: ". . . TWA 32 cleared to land. . . ."

Just 3,000 miles to go.

It had rained earlier in the afternoon, but the clouds were lifting when he took off. He had filed VFR to Cleveland, a flight of about three hours; the weather was clearing, it would be an easy trip, and the next day he would make San Francisco by evening. He was cleared for takeoff behind a jet airliner bound for New York, and as the jet curved away to the right, he climbed rapidly, turning to the left in the lightly loaded airplane past the first layer of fluffy clouds and then the second, bidding the tower "thanks and good day" and taking a heading to Chester. After five minutes he leveled off at 4,500 feet and watched his indicated speed creep up toward 170 mph. Formerly, he would now have gotten out his computer to check his true airspeed, but experience had made him casual about one or two miles per hour here and there. He knew that the vagaries of the winds would make more difference to his arrival time than would his true airspeed, and he also knew that through thick and thin, wet and dry, the airplane would cruise at about 180 miles per hour anyway.

A minute or two after six, he crossed Chester, and the setting sun before him glinted on what he guessed must be the Hudson; the sun fell below the horizon as he crossed the river, and the darkness which already enveloped the sky behind him crept forward overhead as he slid westward over the uncounted miles of gentle mountains and still-bare woods below. He had been running nav lights and rotating beacon from the start—he always did in the East from well before sunset—and now he turned on the instrument lights. As it grew darker, he dimmed the lights until the instruments were just comfortably visible; he liked to watch the lights of towns outside. He navigated by an IFR chart because it was easier to read at night and

Descending to 2,000 feet, and navigating on instruments with radio aids.

contained the necessary information for radio navigation and nothing much else. The omnis passed beneath in a monotonous line, De Lancey and Binghamton, Elmira, Wellsville, then a slight deviation to the south of Victor 270 Airway to Jefferson direct—he had always disliked the way airways would bifurcate about his desired route, leaving him to juggle omnis on either side until a more remote one cropped up in his path.

He was running late. "Wellsville Omni, Comanche 3636, Papa, over." "Three six Papa, this is Elmira Area Radio, go ahead." "Three six Pop, VFR flight plan from Boston to Cleveland Burke Airport, currently over Wellsville at 4,500 feet. Please correct my ETA to 0400 Greenwich. Say your winds aloft for three and six, please."

He had a headwind, as he expected; but he didn't mind because he was happier in the air than he would be in a motel in Cleveland anyway. The night was dark and clear, with a sugaring of stars losing themselves in the distorted ghost of his face as he leaned toward the windshield.

Lake Erie sneaked in on his right a half-hour later, with its string-of-pearls shore and its massive darkness pinpointed by the lights of ships. He thought he could see the glow of Detroit to the northwest and the brighter halo over Cleveland, a spreading haze of smoke and light stretching from Youngstown and Canton to Elyria. Following the coast of the lake, he began his letdown over Fairport after a call to Burke tower; there was no traffic, he was cleared for a straight-in approach. At nine o'clock, three and a half hours after takeoff, he touched down in Cleveland.

After tying down and ordering fuel, he had, as he always did, to debate with himself about going on. His plan had been to make one stage tonight, and then the rest of the way to San Francisco tomorrow; but if he went on now, he'd be in Denver before daybreak, filling the coffee thermos here and in Des Moines. Or just for the hell of it, if the winds weren't too bad, he could go straight from here to North Platte or Sidney and then make San Francisco nonstop; two six-hour hops, which was more than he was in the habit of doing, but then. . . .

"Will you be staying overnight, sir?"

Punt.

He was airborne at seven-thirty, winging west in gray blankness, IFR, expecting to break out west of Chicago. A warm front had moved in during the night, and his plan of being off by six-thirty had dissolved in filing IFR, waiting for clearance, and in the general bogging-down that comes with overcast and gusty rain.

He was hardly aware of the curious intimacy of the cockpit, with the instruments murmuring their unperturbed messages to him, the soft hum of the engine through the earplugs which he habitually wore when flying, the flickering transponder reply monitor. It was humid at 6,000 feet, and the fog outside was so thick and featureless that he seemed not to be moving at all. Nothing was moving; he looked about for something moving. Ah! the second hand of the clock. He occupied his mind with abortive games; he could never seem to get a good robust train of thought started. The hours were long. He imagined the terrain below him: flat country, brown and gray, wet, soggy, miserable. Lakes off to the right somewhere. He opened his thermos and poured himself a lidful of coffee, and was grateful when ATC called him to ask for an altitude change because of a traffic conflict; it gave him something to do.

More or less as anticipated, he broke out south of Rockford on Victor 8, first seeing sudden dark patches blur by in the grayness, then identifiable stretches of ground, and finally entering clear air between layers with a high, dense milky deck overhead and several broken layers beneath. Far off to the west, he could see the edge of the cloud banks and the sky of blanched blue. When he was once well established in visual flight conditions, he called center to cancel IFR; once out of it, he had no use for it.

He shifted in his seat and stretched himself; the Jepp charts went back into their brown case and the sectionals came out. Yesterday he had been crossing Indian country, with place-names that grunted like wild forest boar, honked like ducks, and burbled like streams. Now it was farmland, with sturdy Anglo-Saxon, Nordic, and Gallic family names, tribal names, names from the old country. A lot of French influence; a lot of names he didn't know how to say—Koszta, Ophiem, Des Plaines. Flatland, with mile-square patches that would be rich greens and browns in summer, but now were still muddy and bare. Winding rivers which, obliged like him to kill time, wound and meandered through the indifferent countryside—Iowa and Cedar, Des Moines and Wapsipinicon—with their indecisions and compromises, their tributaries and islands, and switchbacks and bridges in a thousand different styles that carried the two-lane highways, straight for miles and then jogging a few hundred feet and going straight again, from small town to small town: a yellow polyhedron, an airport circle, a stadium, an obstruction. Newton, Oskaloosa, Iowa City, What Cheer.

What cheer indeed? This part of the country was pleasant enough when you lived on the ground, but it bored you from up above. He longed to be out of it. The way out was past Des Moines, where he stopped at ten-thirty for refueling and a hamburger and a reheat of his thermos. It was a new time zone, and he spent the reprieve on a hamburger and a Coke and fries with lots of salt and catsup. After he took off again, he wondered why he didn't feel altogether well.

The plane, however, felt fine. He and his wife had called it—while in a mood for affectionate naming of inanimate things—*Carolina Day*, a name which seemed to reflect the breezy bright warmth of the paint job—white and blue—and a pert, coltish quality they imagined the airplane itself to have. *Carolina* loved to fly light; she climbed like "a homesick angel," as the hangar fliers always liked to say, and purred ever so smoothly and effortlessly in cruise, drinking up her 13 gallons an hour without a trace of sullenness or temper. She was soaring westward, homeward, now, where the bright lowland green of the sectionals gives place to a paler green, a premature hint of failing fertility, the beginning of the grand imperceptible rise of the land out of the wide basin of the Mississippi and the Missouri and the Arkansas up to the fortress wall of the Rockies. He was impatient to see the Rockies, and he could imagine that *Carolina* was too. The weather was clear now—though with a chance of thunderstorms developing later in the day—and he knew in his mind's eye how the mountains would be: the jagged edge like the edge of a saw just rising into view at the horizon, the ragged clouds and the drapery of snow on the whole thing, the blue vertical sky! They may be a thousand miles wide, but once you hit the Rockies, you were in the West, and home was always just over the next ridge.

That the land was rising he knew from the map, but below, on the surface itself, there was no sign of it; the smooth and imperturbable fields rolled on and on. Omaha, Grand Island, Hayes Center. Now matters began to change. There were unsectioned areas, uneven terrain, sandfields, and the roads lost their geometrical rigidity. Somewhere between Grand Island and Hayes Center, he began to fancy that he could see the line of the Rockies—an irregularity of smudges along the horizon. He drank a little coffee—his fourth cup that day—and he drank it with a feeling that soon he would have to cut out the coffee, since it was giving him a slightly jittery, speedy feeling.

The hourly weather gave thunderstorm build-ups west of Denver, and he had a little sensation of excitement thinking of picking his way across the mountains between the towering storms. In clear weather they were rarely more than a magnificent nuisance, since you could make your way around their bases in safety; it was the embedded ones, hidden within a larger cloud layer, that might tear you apart should you blunder into them. But it was clear now, and he had no qualms, though he heard the report with interest and primed himself for more.

Just beyond Hayes Center, over farmland and rangeland more rising and more bleak, he felt a roughness in his engine—a momentary hesitation and then a continuing bup-bup-brr-bur-rup undertone in the regular tapocketatapocketa. He loosened an earplug to listen, but now the noise level was, by comparison, so much higher that he could barely pick up the roughness. He ran through the cylinders with his EGT analyzer. Sure enough, a problem on number four: the exhaust gas temperature was running high, and it most probably meant a fouled plug. He checked mags: the left ran smoothly, but the right stumbled in a way that gave him a start.

He was disturbed; he disliked having the engine run roughly even though he was sure that the cause was minor. He tried changing power settings, increasing first manifold pressure and then rpm—to no avail. May-

Checking the ADF, the pilot announces his intentions to descend for landing.

be it was the trouble in the mag, not the plug. Akron-Washington was ahead of him, in sight; he decided to land.

He did it grudgingly, with a divided mind, because he knew that landing often involved more of a delay than one expected; nothing on the ground ever goes 180 miles per hour. Sure enough, the mechanic was away for a little while, his tools were locked up, but he would be back pretty soon if one didn't mind waiting a few minutes. He did wait, and after more than a few minutes the mechanic arrived. He was slow and gentle, with none of the sense of high pressure and time-is-money that you find at the big airports. He was friendly and chatty. A fellow had been through earlier who said that there was heavy turbulence over the mountains around Kremmling and a lot of thunderstorm activity starting. It was early in the day—and in the year, too—for that, the mechanic said, though a look at his watch made the pilot think that it was not so early at all.

He had a sandwich heated in a plastic bag in a small oven, a candy bar, and a bottle of fuchsia-colored soda, and soon his stomach was feeling a little heavy again—which he attributed to something he must have eaten back in Des Moines, or even in Cleveland. The mechanic emerged eventually from beneath the engine with a plug and a bright grin. "Sure as hell is fouled!" he said, and held up a plug with big tan globules of lead caught in the electrode gaps. He cleaned it with a big wire brush and compressed air and reinstalled it. The charge was $5, which was reasonable enough; but the whole stop had taken nearly two hours. On an impulse he called his wife to tell her he would be a little late, but the line was busy.

The mags checked out smooth now, but the weather didn't; unusually heavy thunderstorm activity west of Denver. As he neared the mountains, which now stood up before him in a neat wall, he could see the lines of thunderheads running across the peaks, straining up to 50,000 feet, with their dark and shapeless undersides mixing cloud and shadow and the wide, slanting shafts of rain. Very freakish weather, he thought in disbelief, but Denver radio gave him pessimistic pilot reports; moderate to severe turbulence, some passes obscured. He cursed his stars and headed on.

Denver is a mile above sea level; 30 miles further on, the peaks rise to nearly 15,000 feet in height. The wall is, in geologic terms, sheer; and an airplane which hitherto had raced unhindered across 2,000 miles of low and rolling land now would find itself picking its way, almost like a bird through a forest, among peaks and passes above which it would be impractical to climb without oxygen. He had a small bottle of supplemental oxygen for brief spells above 12,000 feet, but the Rockies were not a brief spell.

As he neared the mountains, he saw the magnitude of his problem: the clouds stood wide and intermingled among the peaks, indiscriminately blanketing passes with rain and grazing the ragged summits. Denver was still just before him when he made his decision to deviate south, and with a sudden steep bank he swung off 90 degrees to the left.

The wind was strong now, and almost on his tail; after 15 minutes he worked out an estimated groundspeed, and found it to be over 210 miles per hour. He crossed the Sangre de Cristo Mountains, still bleak and snowy from the storm he had met that morning, near Walsenburg, and picked up the Rio Grande a little north of Taos.

A touch of trim makes the work load light.

Keeping the storm line on his right, he swung down across northern New Mexico, leaving Taos far behind, picking up a light headwind again, marveling at the Indian names—Oraibi, Shongopovi, Kaiparowits—grazing the top end of the Painted Desert, picking up the Colorado below Lake Powell, and following it into the evening along the Grand Canyon which sunk in the long dusk, with an occasional flare of yellow sunset on the river below him. He was impatient now; night was falling, the Comanche was fast but not fast enough, as he crossed Lake Mead, picking up the brilliant jewel of Las Vegas, passing it, leaving it behind, hurtling through the dark all blinking lights and glowing needles, soft hum of the engine, Death Valley sliding by beneath, the remote lights of cars on highways, sometimes turning their beams past him so that they flared up briefly and brightly and then disappeared. Dark! He imagined the blackness below populated with immense cockroaches. The Sierra was ahead now, between him and San Francisco, and he crossed its south end near Bakersfield. San Joaquin Valley

Setting her up for the numbers . . .

all woven and strung with lights as though spiders had cast dewy webs about it, glows of towns, threads and glitter of highways. His fuel was low, however; he could go no farther, and he had known it for a long time. He had been airborne for almost six hours and traveled nearly 1,100 miles with unexpectedly fair winds, but there was no way to continue with safety. Throttling back, he set the nose for the green beacon of Meadows Field. He would refuel, have a bite to eat, call Sue, and be home by midnight. He shifted in his seat, ran his fingers through his hair, and folded up the map that had lain open for an hour on his lap. He knew the rest of the way by heart.

. . . And in for a perfect landing.

California was home, and from Bakersfield to SFO was a short enough hop to mean nothing to him. He had arrived. It was nice to get out in the balmy night and stretch his legs in the island of light by the gas truck. The line serviceman was filling the plane, one tank after another, working silently and methodically, while moths erratically orbited the overhead light. It was warm and humid, and he knew the hills were green. *Carolina Day*, squatting back on her haunches, seemed now not so much ready to leap into the air as resting back, settling down for a spell of relaxation before the last short hop home. The airplane reflected his moods in a way nothing else did; that was one reason he loved it.

Another reason he loved the aircraft was that it would do for him what it had just done: take him across the whole continent in a day and a half—or a day, for that matter, west to east, if he timed it right, 14 hours in fact with fair winds—and not only carry him bodily as an airliner might do, but also present him with all that land, make it his territory, give him the feel of the hills and valleys and streams and the great central sag and the buttressed west with its monster mountains and deserts, its vast reaches of tedium and blank remoteness. It gave him a sense not only of that geographical and geological reality, his homeland, but also of history in some mysterious way, of the old place-names and the sights the first settlers saw and the routes they followed and the troubles they faced, the sheer magnitude of their courage and accomplishment; it gave him a feeling of places and people, of time held still and of a panorama too vast for the eye to grasp: America, a continent brought within his reach, distance and time humbled before him, as the countryside is humbled to a hawk.

Impatient, he skipped his snack, paid the bill, and taxied off. From outside the office, the line man who had fueled the Comanche saw the blinking lights rise from the runway, heard the drop in rpm's as the power lowered to the climb setting, and idly watched as the lights rose, curved away to the north and, rising higher and higher into the sky, faded with the sound, grew faint, and vanished into the darkness.

CHAPTER 11

America Flying

THERE was a time shortly after World War II when everyone knew that the small airplane would replace the car as the swift and easy way to move about for business and pleasure. In retrospect, it seems foolish that so many knowledgeable people could have been convinced of this, but they were. In 1947 there were over 20 major manufacturers of light aircraft in the United States, producing two- and four-place single-engine airplanes. Airplane salesmen were eager and aggressive at most small airports in the country, with large manufacturers making enormous investments in new designs. A major airplane show in 1948 in New York City, much like the auto show or the boat show, drew people by the thousands. There were those who looked for 100,000 airplanes to be sold that year, and estimates of bigger sales to come were freely given and just as eagerly accepted.

By 1951 all but three strictly general aviation airplane manufacturers were out of business, and the few big military manufacturers who couldn't get out as fast as the smaller ones were frantically trying to sell off their tooling and convert the space allocated to building aircraft to something more profitable. One large manufacturer in Texas switched over to washing machines and pinball devices, both of which were in greater and more realistic demand than were small airplanes.

It wasn't that the nearly one million pilots who had been trained during the war didn't want to fly or didn't want an airplane of their own. Many of them longed for the freedom to fly as they chose to places that they had always wanted to visit. But, first, they wanted to get a job, raise a family, buy a house, and own a car. In the real world, then, buying an airplane or even taking an occasional flight in a rented airplane was far down the list of priorities. As it turned out, most of the military pilots who left the services never flew again. Even at the bargain prices of $3,000 to $5,000 for a first-rate single-engine machine, there were so few takers that hundreds of airplanes languished in the uncut weeds beside quiet runways.

Beside the matter of cost, another major deterrent to the casual buying of an airplane came to light. For all but the most determined flyers, the question of what to do with it after it had been bought cast a pall over the prospect of owning an airplane. Could one really take every other weekend off to go sightseeing? What about cutting the lawn and who would babysit with the children? And how about painting the back fence and fixing up the car? There was too a certain lack of enthusiasm on the part of many wives about flying, much less buying an airplane, to contend with. In the end many eager hopes were dashed when it became clear that it just wasn't feasible to think about buying an airplane for fun and an occasional trip to Grandmother's house.

The few airplanes that were sold in the late forties and early fifties

America is a flyer's country.

went to a smattering of the well-to-do and to businessmen who saw a way of combining their business traveling with an occasional pleasure trip. There was barely enough of this kind of business to keep the three surviving companies, Beech, Cessna, and Piper, afloat. Throughout the fifties, they husbanded their resources, introducing new models only when necessary and building airplanes largely when they were certain they could be sold.

With the introduction of small twin-engine aircraft, businessmen and a few wealthy pleasure seekers gained confidence in the ability of general aviation aircraft to take them almost anywhere, in almost any weather. Small twins too, along with higher performance, well-equipped single-engine aircraft, captured the attention of businessmen around the world and a small, though growing, export business began to flourish. Europe, particularly, seemed a fertile ground for sales of United States aircraft, as much of its production was in smaller sport planes.

As the world turned the corner of the sixties, general aviation found, somewhat to its surprise, that it had become a major transportation medium and its acceptance, while not universal, was growing rapidly. Statistics showed that almost as many people were carried in intercity travel in general aviation aircraft as were carried by the airlines. The number of student pilots grew to more than 100,000 per year. Many of these dropped out of flying as the press of other less demanding interests lured them to the ski slopes or the sports-car races or the quiet ways of boating; many went on to become private pilots. By the mid-sixties, there were over 150,000 such, and by 1970, there were 300,000. About half of this number didn't stop with the basic skills required for the private license, but went on to the more demanding proficiencies needed to add an instrument rating to their ticket.

The airplanes too grew in sophistication, speed, and utility. Most of the new models included all the equipment that would allow them to fly as safely and accurately as the airliners. The combination of high pilot skills

Modern technology brings added comfort and speed to the utility of private flying.

and modern equipment in general aviation aircraft brought a degree of utility that had not been anticipated by the airlines, the Federal Aviation Administration, and perhaps even by the owners of the aircraft themselves.

There are businessmen today who travel over 50,000 miles a year in their own airplanes. There are corporations who have their own fleets of airplanes, whose executives haven't been on an airliner in the last five years. There are families who explore the farthest reaches of Canada, Mexico, South America, and even Europe and Africa in their own airplanes. The story of the family flying to Alaska for a week's holiday of hunting and fishing is no longer unusual or even newsworthy. The sixty-five-year-old woman pilot who flies her single-engine airplane to Europe each year is admired, but not lionized.

More women than ever before are learning to fly. Some 35,000 already have licenses and, of the total number of student pilots, the proportion of women is increasing. To the surprise of many, their accident record is better than that of men. And they not only have fewer accidents in proportion to their numbers, they have far fewer serious accidents. The FAA is even wondering if they are not inherently more cautious, more methodical, more serious, and therefore better pilots than men. One statistical wag has even suggested that one way to reduce the number of general aviation accidents is to allow only women to fly.

The general aviation accident record is a source of concern to many. It needs to be improved, but it is not as awful as the unknowing think it is. In many statistical respects it is already improving; in the last several years it has dropped from 1.8 accidents per million miles flown to less than 1.4. Nonetheless, there were some 5,000 accidents in each of the last several years. About 10 percent of these involved a fatality, with most of these accidents the result not of engine failure or mechanical breakdown or poor pilot technique or radio or equipment failure, but of faulty judgment on the part of the pilot, just as most automobile accidents are the result of poor judgment by the driver.

Almost any transportation accident, be it bus, train, or car, is invariably staggering in its destruction, and it gives both the proponents of that form of transportation and observers pause. But today, unlike some years ago, the public seems ready to accept the point that general aviation airplanes are not the most dangerous form of transportation and, in fact, are inherently safer than cars. More important, a great many people are turning to the small airplane as a more pleasant way to travel than the automobile or even the airliner. For them, there are too many cars and too few airlines. A trip to almost anywhere reinforces their view of the former, and a look at the airline schedule and the reduced number of airports being served by the airlines supports the latter. Today there are fewer than 500 airports that see an airliner, whereas ten years ago the number was over 1,000. For the general aviation pilot there are more than 10,000 airports to choose from. It is the proliferation of cars and the scarcity of airliners, too, that seem to promote the constraint and lack of flexibility not experienced by general aviation partisans.

It would seem that many of the socioeconomic factors that doomed general aviation's boom in the forties have changed so markedly that today flying is on the threshold of the success it missed twenty years ago. The airplane is no longer an oddity to anyone. Over 1,000 high schools and 350

Fewer than 500 airports see a commercial airliner, but with a plane like this, the Cessna 210, some 12,000 are available in the continental United States alone.

colleges offer aviation courses. More than a third of the general aviation airplanes built in the United States today are exported to every country in the world. And in many remote lands the general aviation airplane is not only the best, but often the only way to travel from city to city. In many such places there are more airplanes in the country than there are paved roads.

The prospect of an airplane in every garage or of hordes of aircraft filling the sky is not comforting to most people, least of all to pilots. Pilots know that current talk of crowded skies is nonsense, since most of the origin of the talk was the result of too many airplanes arriving at the same place at the same time. They know, too, that there is plenty of room for more airplanes in the sky. What there may have to be more of are places to base them on the ground. The crunch comes when cities grow and find they have better uses for land than to have airplanes sit on it. The solution to this problem has so far escaped almost everyone, pilot and groundling alike.

The most frequently heard objection to learning to fly and owning an airplane is that it is too expensive. There is little disagreement on that point. There is small comfort, too, in the fact that almost everything today is too expensive. But pilots would be among the first to declare that if money is for spending, it might as well be spent in a way that offers a delight and joy and challenge unlike anything else in this world.

APPENDICES

APPENDIX A

THE FEDERAL AVIATION ADMINISTRATION

For a long, long time, the aviation pioneers worked alone, free of any kind of regulation. There were accidents and fatalities.

As powered flight became more likely, if not exactly reliable, the art of flight instruction was born. One of the articles of the Army contract with the Wright Brothers, in fact, required that they teach selected officers to fly. The fact that so many people survived the early years is simply amazing, but though the accident rate was unacceptable by modern standards—of all classes of flying, student instruction is near the top in safety—little was done about it. The problem was recognized early; in fact, the National Advisory Committee for Aeronautics (which has since metamorphosed into the National Aeronautics and Space Agency) drafted a regulatory bill which was submitted to Congress by President Wilson in 1919. Similar bills were offered annually for years afterward, and were ignored. By the middle 1920's matters were completely out of hand. One of aviation's great pioneers, the late Sigurd Varian, who helped develop the routes in Mexico and South America as a pilot for Pan American, described how serious the problem was:

"A few of us took lessons from the few who knew how to fly. Then those who had just learned taught the others to fly—but just barely. We carried pay passengers on about our second solo hop, squeezing them into the front seat two at a time, when our planes could hardly take off with one.

"At first our so-called 'airports' were scattered all around Los Angeles, later they gathered along Western Avenue and a few of the more important boulevards. Wild shows were put on to stop the motorists; we needed their business badly.

"There were long rides and short rides, straight rides and stunt rides. Every Jenny in the country clattered into the air as fast as it could get there. Green pilots who hardly knew how to fly sold stunt rides at whatever price they could get for them. As business came faster, we cut the rides shorter, began our stunt flights lower—quick spins from one thousand feet—lower yet, half rolls and loops at five hundred feet.

"A crazy kid from the next field attempted an ungainly Jenny roll, and he was much too low. His inverted engine starved and stopped, and some sticks and dust and a few clods of dirt fell out of the fuselage. The nose of the plane dove down and down and almost under, with the pilot sitting rigid, watching the end rush up at him, framed between the heads and shoulders of two high school kids in the front seat.

"Some of the pilots, realizing that reckless flying and spectacular accidents were destroying the future of aviation, promoted associations for the encouragement of safe flying. But to stabilize our wild gang of youngsters was almost impossible. . . ."

It was in fact completely impossible, and the troubles were not limited to flying standards and flight training. For every Wright and Curtiss, and all the others who scientifically approached aircraft design, there were several untrained inventors, who neither understood the unique structural requirements nor bothered to study the work of those who did. The matter of aircraft maintenance and repair was in an equally sorry state.

The most serious obstacle to congressional action on the previous aviation bills had been uncertainty about how to handle aviation in the military sense. General Mitchell's intransigence over the importance of air power finally forced the issue, and President Coolidge appointed a special board, under Dwight W. Morrow, to study the entire subject. The Morrow Board recommended separation of military and civilian aviation, as well as the appointment of three additional assistant secretaries, one each in the War, Navy, and Commerce departments, to take charge. For civil aviation the result was the Air Commerce Act of 1926.

This was a beginning, but it was not satisfactory, since aviation became a very small part of a very large government department. This was corrected by the Civil Aeronautics Act of 1938, which established the Civil Aeronautics Authority as an independent body, followed by the Federal Aviation Act of 1958, which changed the name to Federal Aviation Agency. The most recent change in status occurred in 1967, when the Department of Transportation was created. In one sense this completed the cycle: aviation is once again part of a large department of government. Another name change was made, fortunately keeping the same initials: FAA now stands for Federal Aviation Administration.

APPENDIX A

Through all the years and all the changes, the intent of the aviation laws has remained the same: the aviation agencies have been charged with two prime tasks on a nationwide basis. One is to foster and develop aviation; the other is to regulate it.

These seem to be opposed in principle, and are sometimes found to be so in practice. It has been suggested that things would go quicker and better if there were two agencies, one to foster and develop and the other to regulate. Such speculation is pointless, since there is nothing in the law to permit it; but the essential fact is that without regulation to end the chaos Sigurd Varian described, all of the fostering and developing in the world would be worthless.

The FAA sets standards for airmen, including pilots, mechanics, dispatchers, air traffic controllers, parachute riggers, flight and ground instructors, flight radio operators, flight navigators, and flight engineers. It describes the ways in which their competence is to be assured, and it issues their certificates.

It also sets airworthiness standards for aircraft, makes sure that the standards are met, and issues airworthiness certificates. It sets standards for inspections, which must be done by licensed mechanics (although there are a number of noncritical things an owner is permitted to do by himself) and approved by an aircraft inspector. It even keeps aircraft title records.

The FAA is also responsible for developing, equipping, and operating the air traffic control system. It maintains a research and development section.

Some states have their own aviation laws and regulations, most of which relate to registration of aircraft and airmen; but all of the basic standards and regulatory functions in all parts of aviation come under federal control. Considering the lack of physical limits in the air environment, federal control ensures that safety will be equally served everywhere in the country. Unfortunately, the federal system is weak in the area of enforcement. Unlike the county, city, and state systems, there are simply not enough FAA employees to get the job done; and one result is that aviation operates on more of an honor system than almost any other field of endeavor.

The accumulation of federal air regulations has proceeded steadily since the passage of the 1926 legislation. In several ways this is similar to the accumulation of religious laws, and for much the same reasons. In the beginning the rules seem simple and few. Matters which had not been perceived early, or which seemed to be of little consequence, were ignored, only to reappear later and then have to be dealt with. In spite of careful and commendable efforts at codification, the air regulations still are difficult to learn. It is often said that every pilot will some day violate at least one of them, if he hasn't done so already. This is probably true enough; but the same thing can be said about ordinary people and ordinary laws of the earth. By and large, men and women of good will manage to stay out of jail, no matter what their inadvertent transgressions.

Violations of the key regulations can often carry the death penalty, usually visited swiftly upon the sinner by the laws of aerodynamics. Fliers sometimes forget, when they get caught up in the labyrinths of the legal language of the aviation laws, that the function of the FAA is basically to keep them alive.

This is the negative side of "fostering and developing." There is an equally impressive body of accomplishment on the positive side.

The FAA has an incredible list of publications relating to every phase of aviation, some free, all others at modest prices. There are about 100 General Aviation District Offices throughout the United States, fully staffed with specialists, and ready to help the aviation and the general public alike. One of the unexpected assets of the FAA is that its people, with few exceptions, are both highly competent and deeply interested in aviation. Few large groups of any kind, especially government agencies, can have the same compliment paid to them.

One of the most unusual, and effective, tools the FAA uses in fostering and promoting aviation is the statutory authority it has to delegate many of its examining and inspecting tasks. There are specifically designated medical examiners, flight examiners, aircraft inspectors, engineering representatives, and even a design approval method called "delegation option authorization," by means of which manufacturers can approve their own new aircraft designs.

Naturally the FAA uses its delegation powers with care, and only people and companies with excellent records, well known to the FAA, are given these powers. The system works well; without it, aviation would simply not have been able to reach its present level.

For all of the years from the beginning to 1970, aviation was poor. Although there have been many men in Congress who were and are very well aware of the importance of civil aviation, they were a minority, and it was impossible to be sure of having the money needed for airports and airways expansion and improvement. In fact the most memorable rush of funds came after two airliners collided (in clear weather) above the Grand Canyon in 1956. This spurred the creation of the Airways Modernization Board and the passage of the Federal Aviation Act of 1958.

It was not many years later that money again became hard to come by. The modernization of the airways has not proceeded as rapidly as it could have, and the funds for airport development have been at what almost amounts to a poverty level.

Although it is fashionable to blame the problem on Congress, the aviation community must bear a share of the responsibility. For one thing, it never cohered very well in all its elements, and was thus never able to make a cogent case for all aviation's needs. A second important factor was reluctance to accept increased taxation, a characteristic universally shared by all taxpayers.

There is a good chance that the Airport-Airways Act of 1970 will prove to be the solution. It has a lot in common with the highway legislation which was responsible for the creation of the new Interstate Highway System: taxes are imposed and collected and deposited in a federal trust fund. Just as in the case of the highway fund, it is the users who pay the taxes. It will still take some years to do all the things needed, but at least a start in the right direction has been made.

Significant as this is for the future, it is important to remember that we have the world's best airport and airways system, in being and in operation now. In spite of money limitations in the past, the work of skilled and dedicated people at the federal, state, county, and local levels has slowed the rate of loss of airports, stopped it, and actually reversed it. The new trust fund simply helps to ensure the continued growth of aviation.

APPENDIX B

FLYING CLUBS AND ORGANIZATIONS

In aviation the word club has two meanings. The first refers to organizations of which there are many and a listing of some of the more prominent ones appears a little further on. The other meaning suggests multiple ownership of airplanes. The former are largely groupings of aviation people with common backgrounds and interests. The latter are generally the result of two or more pilots hoping to enjoy their flying less expensively than they would if each tried to own and maintain an airplane individually. What may be beyond the reach of any of them alone becomes possessable by all of them in concert. If there are ten of them, each can have a share for a tenth of the cost of sole ownership. If each of them flies the airplane for no more than 30 hours a year—an almost laughable figure, which works out to less than 40 minutes a week—the airplane will be used 300 hours a year, which is about the annual utilization required to make owning cheaper than renting.

The arithmetic is intoxicating: one-tenth of a $4,000 airplane is $400—maybe not quite pocket money, but manageable all the same. Cost of operation? Gas and oil come to about $2.75 an hour, including oil changes every 25 hours. Throw in $1.25 an hour for maintenance, and the total is $4. Tempting . . . tempting . . . $400 for a share of an airplane, and $4 an hour flight time! In most instances this kind of reasoning leads to disillusionment and disbanding of the club for the truth is that the only way to get a cost of $4 an hour is to leave out several items that can't really be left out. These include reserves for engine overhaul, accumulation of funds for inspection, and provision for repairs to instruments and radios. One small but irritating cost that is also almost never included is the labor charge for changing the oil.

All of these things are associated with the number of hours the airplane flies, but only fuel, oil, and oil changes are directly dependent on hours flown. An annual inspection, for example, is required to maintain the airplane's airworthiness certificate even if it doesn't fly at all. On the subtle side, both aircraft and engine maintenance, and engine overhaul, can easily cost more per hour (and perhaps even more altogether) for an airplane that is flown many hours a year, with long idle periods between flights, than for one that flies 100 hours a month.

In addition to the annual inspection, storage and insurance are both calendar items. They can be tied into the hourly cost, but it is unwise to do so; if the utilization of the airplane falls below the projected rate, the hourly charges won't accumulate enough money to pay the bills when they come due. The best way to deal with these is by way of monthly dues payments by each member. When the club is first established, insurance and storage for the first year should be added to the capital investment, and each share should include them.

We have seen that fuel and oil, including oil for changes every 25 hours, cost about $2.75. Normal maintenance on aircraft and engine is about $1.25 and 50 cents an hour will cover the labor of changing the oil. If the engine is factory remanufactured, and authorized for 2,000 hours between overhauls, 80 cents an hour should be enough, but it might not be, on low annual utilization. Anyway, the chances are that it has several hundred hours since new or overhaul, so better allow $2 an hour. If all goes well, this will produce more money than will be needed, but why take a chance? Inspections every 100 hours are not required unless the airplane is used commercially, but they are good insurance; so add $1.25 an hour for them. (The annual, which is the same as the 100-hour except for the paperwork, will be covered in the dues.) Finally, add $1 per hour per radio, which will probably cover any instrument repairs too.

This adds up to $8.75 an hour; let's round it off to $9. Now let's go back to the capital account and the monthly dues.

Storage and insurance will come to about $1,500 a year. For the first year, this is added to the cost of the airplane, which makes the total $5,500, and each member's share $550. The $150 assessment for insurance and storage is not part of the member's equity; that is, if he sells his membership to the club, he will only get his $400 back. (If he sells it to a new member, he can make whatever arrangement the market will allow, of course.)

Money for the next year's insurance and storage, and the annual inspection, should be accumulated through the monthly dues. In this example, $15 per month per member will be more than enough (it will produce a surplus of $175) without being a serious burden.

If each member flies his 30 hours a year, his total cost per hour, including pro-ration of the monthly dues, comes to $15.

Disappointed? You say you can rent an airplane for $17 an hour straight, $15.30 if you buy block time and get a 10 percent discount? That's true enough; but it's little more than a sad demonstration of the eternal fact that you can't get something for nothing.

Each member owns a tenth of an airplane and a tenth of the surplus, and a tenth of the engine overhaul reserve, and a tenth of any funds that haven't been spent for their intended purposes—and with this kind of conservative hourly rate-setting, that's quite likely to be a fair amount. He also owns a tenth of next year's storage and insurance fund. When the books are closed at the end of the year, each member's investment, or share of the book value of the project, will have shown a healthy increase. The chances are very good that there is enough in the surplus fund to buy any member out who has to resign for any reason.

If the club develops a tight professional-grade scheduling system, the chances are also very good that the airplane will be able to fly 600 hours a year, 60 hours per member. If this happens, the surpluses will be proportionately bigger, and the cost per flying hour to each member will drop to $12, which is $3.30 less than block-time renting.

As experience is gained, and actual costs become better known, the charges and monthly dues can be reduced; but it's really a much better practice to keep them high enough so that they can produce surpluses and annually transfer them to a capital account. In time, this can be used for adding equipment, or trading up to a bigger or faster airplane.

You might say that the choice is whether to be part of a going concern, soundly financed, or a member of a shaky operation that can be destroyed by a few weeks of bad weather and bad luck. Actually, the facts are even simpler: Any club that fails to provide for all the costs covered here is certain to fail. And fail they do, every year, in quantity. To be even more direct, if you and your friends cannot afford the cost levels, you have no business forming a flying club.

Much of the solution to successful operation of a flying club is good management and there is often a source of such management available for flying clubs at low cost which is overlooked. It is not available everywhere, and even where it exists, there are wide differences in quality. Where it does exist, and quality is high, it provides a very satisfactory solution. The source of this Instant Management is known as the Fixed Base Operator or FBO.

What is of great importance to a flying club in its search for management is the fact that the FBO already has all the necessary ingredients in place and working. He has a shop, a training department, and an accounting department. He knows how to schedule airplanes for both flight and maintenance. He can provide check pilots for the annual club member proficiency review. He is already doing all these things for his own business, so it follows that he could add an airplane or two (or more) without any major increase in his cost of doing business.

The agreement with the FBO must be clear and complete, and the club's first priority must be to make clear to the FBO that it will not compete with him. Usually, the most serious competition is in the business of flying training. Actually, it is almost always in the club's best interest to limit membership, at least in the early stages, to those who already have at least a private license. (The situation is different in Canada, where *ab initio* flight training is done in Aero Clubs, but there the clubs are really more like FBO's here.) In all but a few cases, FBO's can do a better training job than clubs can. The existence of a club in harmony with an FBO is good for all three: the club's management is in professional hands; the existence of the club helps attract students to the FBO's flight department; and the students can look forward to club membership as soon as they are licensed.

The FBO should be asked to take care of all the club's routine chores except one: scheduling flights, scheduling maintenance, reminding members of dates for renewals of medicals and annual flight checks, billing members for flight time and monthly dues, and keeping track of the maintenance and overhaul reserve accounts for the club airplanes.

The one thing which the club must not delegate is the collection of past due accounts from members. The club by-laws must make firm provision for dealing with this, including suspension of membership privileges, and it is up to the club to enforce its own rules.

One obvious way for the club to establish its bona fides with an FBO is to buy its airplanes from him. The idea of finding a great bargain independently and thus saving the middleman's profit is still a compelling dream; but dream it is most of the time. If airplanes are bought from the FBO who is going to handle the club affairs, the chances are very much better that there will be less trouble and cost, since the FBO is permanently available, and has a continuing interest in the club as a customer.

There is another important area of club and FBO cooperation, which also benefits both sides. In most clubs, airplanes fly mostly on weekends, while the flight time of FBO airplanes is fairly well distributed throughout the week. An agreement between the club and the FBO, under which the FBO can use the club's airplanes during the week while reserving the weekends for club members, reduces the fleet capital requirement for the FBO and increases annual utilization (thus lower cost per flight hour) for the club. The exact terms will differ in different cases, and must always be worked out with care. During his use of the club's airplanes, the FBO is responsible for paying the proper amounts into the maintenance accounts, as well as fuel and oil. If the cost of insurance is different because of this commercial operation, the FBO must be responsible for the difference in premium. As we have seen previously, initial insurance premiums are best paid in a lump sum, with an hourly charge made toward accruing the renewal premium.

The primary return to the club is a bookkeeping matter: with higher use, cost per hour drops. In most cases, this is enough return. The FBO should pay the club something for his use of their airplanes, and this might take the form of exchanging management services for airplane use, on an even exchange, hour for hour.

While the negotiations are going on, the club must be sure to preserve its own options, such as having the FBO understand that club members will be permitted to do all work allowed by the regulations, and to wash and wax their own airplanes. Most FBO's won't object to this, and can even be persuaded to allow members to work with his licensed mechanic during regular inspections.

This plan won't work unless there is a qualified, competent FBO at the airport the club plans to use, and those adjectives are important. If a local FBO is barely managing to keep afloat himself, he probably doesn't have enough management ability to be able to share it with a club, even if only one airplane is involved. But if there is an experienced and willing FBO available, he can help to make a club an outstanding success.

Flying Organizations

AIR FORCE ASSOCIATION
1750 Pennsylvania Ave., N.W.
Washington, D.C. 20006

AIRCRAFT OWNERS & PILOT ASSOCIATION (AOPA)
4650 East-West Hwy.
Bethesda, Md. 20014

AMERICAN BONANZA SOCIETY
Chemung County Airport
Horseheads, N.Y. 14845

THE AMERICAN HELICOPTER SOCIETY, INC.
30 E. 42nd Street
Suite 1408
New York, N.Y. 10017

AMERICAN NAVION SOCIETY
1585 Barbour St.
Municipal Airport
Banning, Calif. 92220

ANTIQUE AIRPLANE ASS'N
P.O. Box H
Ottumwa, Iowa 52501

ASSOCIATION OF AVIATION PSYCHOLOGISTS
5108 26th Ave., S.E.
Washington, D.C. 20031

AVIATION EXECUTIVES CLUB
500 Deer Run
Miami Springs Villas
Miami Springs, Fla. 33166

AVIATION/WRITERS ASS'N
c/o Ralph H. McClarren
101 Greenwood Ave.
Jenkentown, Pa. 19046

THE EARLY BIRDS OF AVIATION, INC.
524 S. 56th St.
Birmingham, Ala. 35212

EXPERIMENTAL AIRCRAFT ASS'N INC.
1131 W. Forest Homes Ave.
Franklin, Wis. 53130

FLYING ARCHITECTS ASSOCIATION, INC.
c/o H. B. Southern
571 E. Hazelwood Ave.
Rahway, N.J. 07065

FLYING CHIROPRACTORS ASSOCIATION
528 Franklin St.
Johnstown, Pa. 15905

FLYING DENTIST ASSOCIATION
N. Fifth St.
Sleepy Eye, Minn. 56086

APPENDIX B

FLYING FUNERAL DIRECTORS OF AMERICA
678 S. Snelling Ave.
St. Paul, Minn. 55116

FLYING PHYSICIANS ASS'N
801 Green Bay Rd.
Lake Bluff, Ill. 60044

FUTURE PILOTS OF AMERICA
707 RCA Bldg.
1725 K. St. N.W.
Washington, D.C. 20006

INTERNATIONAL FLYING BANKERS ASSOCIATION
Armour Ct.
801 Green Bay Rd.
Lake Bluff, Ill. 60044

INTERNATIONAL FLYING FARMERS
Municipal Airport
Wichita, Kans. 67209

LAWYER-PILOTS BAR ASS'N
Box 427
Alhambra, Calif. 91802

NATIONAL AERO CLUB
3861 Research Park Dr.
Research Park
Ann Arbor, Mich. 48104

NATIONAL AERONAUTIC ASS'N
Suite 610, Shoreham Bldg.
806 15th St., N.W.
Washington, D.C. 20005

NATIONAL ASSOCIATION OF FLIGHT INSTRUCTORS
Box N
Washington, D.C. 20014

NATIONAL BUSINESS AIRCRAFT ASSOCIATION, INC. (NBAA)
Suite 401
Pennsylvania Bldg.
423 13th St., N.W.
Washington, D.C. 20004

NATIONAL PILOT ASSOCIATION
806 15th St., N.W.
Washington, D.C. 20005

THE NINETY-NINES, INC.
Will Rogers World Airport
Oklahoma City, Okla. 73159

PILOTS INTERNATIONAL ASSOCIATION INC.
2649 Park Ave.
Minneapolis, Minn. 55407

POPULAR ROTORCRAFT ASSOCIATION
P.O. Box 2772
Raleigh, N.C. 27602

THE SOARING SOCIETY OF AMERICA, INC.
Box 66071
Los Angeles, Calif. 90066

THE SOCIETY OF EXPERIMENTAL TEST PILOTS

44814 N. Elm Ave.
(Mail: P.O. Box 9861)
Lancaster, Calif. 93534

UNITED STATES PARACHUTE ASSOCIATION
(Formerly the Parachute Club of America)
P.O. Box 109
Monterey, Calif. 93940

THE WHIRLY-GIRLS (Int'l Woman Helicopter Pilots)
Suite 700
1725 DeSales St., N.W.
Washington, D.C. 20036

WOMEN'S NATIONAL AERONAUTICAL ASSOCIATION OF THE UNITED STATES, INC.
Sherwood Rd.
Little Rock, Ark. 72207

APPENDIX C
AIRCRAFT DIRECTORY

From the $5,000 two-place Champ to a captain of industry's $5,000,000 DC-9, this directory covers most of the aircraft that are readily available today.

The format is designed to provide in capsule form all pertinent information about the aircraft listed. It works as follows:

GROUP A—DESIGNATION

This section gives the name of the manufacturer, the plane's model number and designation, the price (based on 1972 figures), number of seats, a side view and the overall length in feet and inches.

GROUP B—WEIGHTS

In this section are gross or takeoff (T/O) weight, empty weight, useful load, cabin load which represents the available payload with full fuel and average VFR or IFR equipment; in addition in the floatplane and amphibian floatplane sections the float weight and displacement are shown. The rotorcraft section also lists maximum external and sling loads and the ag plane section lists the hopper capacity.

GROUP C—PERFORMANCE

This group consists of two boxes, listing minimum field length over a 50-foot obstacle (MFL) for either takeoff or landing, whichever is longer, or the balanced field lengths (BFL) at full gross and as loaded for the average corporate flight, including 1,000 pounds cabin load, and fuel for 450 nm plus 30 minutes to an alternate plus 45-minute reserve, stall speed with gear and flaps down, sea-level rate of climb (SL R/C), single-engine rate of climb (SE R/C), the range at normal cruising speed with 45-minute reserve, cruise speed at 75-percent power, usable fuel in gallons, fuel consumption in gallons per hour, cabin altitude (CA) of pressurized aircraft and for rotorcraft the service ceiling (SC), the hovering-in-ground-effect ceiling (HIGE) and the hovering-out-of-ground-effect ceiling

(HOGE). In the sailplane section, the lift/drag ratio (L/D) is shown as is the minimum sink rate, the maximum allowable speed and the rough-air (R/A) speed.

GROUP D—ENGINE

The last section shows the engine make, model and horsepower, a front view of the aircraft and either the wing span or the rotor diameter in feet and inches.

Single Engine Sport & Training

DESIGNATION	PRICE	WEIGHT	PERFORMANCE		ENGINE
CHAMPION Champ * Seats 2 Length 21 ft 9.5 in	$4,995	Gross 1,220 Empty 730 Usefl 490 Cbn ld (V) 392	MFL 900 ft Stall 39 mph SL R/C 400 fpm	Range 227 sm Cruise 83 mph Fuel 13 gal Flow 3.7 gph	FR. 2A-120-B 60 hp Span 35 ft 1.5 in
CHAMPION Citabria 115 * Seats 2 Length 22 ft 7 in	$6,495	Gross 1,650 Empty 1,034 Usefl 616 Cbn ld (V) 425	MFL 890 ft Stall 51 mph SL R/C 725 fpm	Range 434 sm Cruise 112 mph Fuel 26 gal Flow 6 gph	L. O-235-C1 115 hp Span 33 ft 5 in
AMERICAN AVIATION AA-1 Yankee Seats 2 Length 19 ft 2.4 in	$8,750	Gross 1,500 Empty 975 Usefl 525 Cbn ld (V) 321	MFL 1,615 ft Stall 66 mph SL R/C 710 fpm	Range 363 sm Cruise 134 mph Fuel 22 gal Flow 6 gph	L. O-235-C2C 108 hp Span 24 ft 4.6 in
AMERICAN AVIATION AA-1A Trainer Seats 2 Length 19 ft 2.4 in	$8,950	Gross 1,500 Empty 980 Usefl 520 Cbn ld (V) 331	MFL 1,400 ft Stall 59 mph SL R/C 765 fpm	Range 346 sm Cruise 125 mph Fuel 22 gal Flow 6 gph	L. O-235-C2C 108 hp Span 24 ft 4.6 in
CESSNA 150 Standard Seats 2 Length 23 ft 8½ in	$ 9,425	Gross 1,600 Empty 1,000 Usefl 600 Cbn ld (V)* 424 *std fuel	MFL 1,385 ft Stall 48 mph SL R/C 670 fpm	Range 392/635 sm Cruise 117 mph Fuel 22.5/35 gal Flow 5.5 gph	C. O-200A 100 hp Span 33 ft 2 in
CHAMPION Citabria 150 * Seats 2 Length 22 ft 7 in	$9,995	Gross 1,650 Empty 1,118 Usefl 532 Cbn ld (V) 268	MFL 630 ft Stall 51 mph SL R/C 1,120 fpm	Range 521 sm Cruise 125 mph Fuel 39.5 gal Flow 8 gph	L. O-320-E2A 150 hp Span 33 ft 5 in
PIPER Cherokee 140E Seats 2-4 Length 23 ft 6 in	$10,990	Gross 2,150 Empty 1,237 Usefl 913 Cbn ld (V) 472	MFL 1,700 ft Stall 55 mph SL R/C 660 fpm	Range 634 sm Cruise 132 mph Fuel 50 gal Flow 9 gph	L. O-320 150 hp Span 30 ft 0 in
CESSNA 150 Trainer Seats 2 Length 23 ft 8½ in	$11,340	Gross 1,600 Empty 1,000 Usefl 600 Cbn ld (V)* 424 *std fuel	MFL 1,385 ft Stall 48 mph SL R/C 670 fpm	Range 392/635 sm Cruise 117 mph Fuel 22.5/35 gal Flow 5.5 gph	C. O-200A 100 hp Span 33 ft 2 in

*Please note: These aircraft are manufactured by the Bellanca Aircraft Corporation(Minnesota). There is a controversy as to the right to use the name Bellanca with regard to these aircraft between Bellanca Aircraft Corporation(Minnesota) and Bellanca Aircraft Corporation(Delaware).

Single Engine Sport & Training

DESIGNATION	PRICE	WEIGHT	PERFORMANCE		ENGINE
CESSNA Aerobat Seats 2 Length 23 ft 8½ in	$11,595	Gross 1,600 Empty 1,035 Usefl 565 Cbn ld (V)* 399 *std fuel	MFL 1,385 ft Stall 48 mph SL R/C 670 fpm	Range 385/625 sm Cruise 115 mph Fuel 22.5/35 gal Flow 5.5 gph	C. O-200A 100 hp Span 33 ft 2 in
CESSNA 150 Commuter Seats 2 Length 23 ft 8½ in	$12,550	Gross 1,600 Empty 1,000 Usefl 600 Cbn ld (V)* 424 *std fuel	MFL 1,385 ft Stall 48 mph SL R/C 670 fpm	Range 392/635 sm Cruise 117 mph Fuel 22.5/35 gal Flow 5.5 gph	C. O-200A 100 hp Span 33 ft 2 in
ME BOLKOW-BLOHM BO-209-125 Seats 2 Length 21 ft 6 in	$12,900	Gross 1,674 Empty 925 Usefl 749 Cbn ld (V) 553	MFL NA ft Stall 52 mph SL R/C 748 fpm	Range 581 sm Cruise 139 mph Fuel 38.8 gal Flow 6.4 gph	L. O-235 125 hp Span 27 ft 7 in
ME BOLKOW-BLOHM BO-209-150 Seats 2 Length 21 ft 6 in	$13,900	Gross 1,808 Empty 1,045 Usefl 763 Cbn ld (V) 567	MFL 1,079 ft Stall 57 mph SL R/C 1,040 fpm	Range 511 sm Cruise 149 mph Fuel 38.8 gal Flow 8.7 gph	L. O-320 150 hp Span 27 ft 7 in
CHAMPION Decathlon * Seats 2 Length 22 ft 9 in	$15,000	Gross 1,800 Empty 1,225 Usefl 575 Cbn ld (V) 305	MFL NA ft Stall 53 mph SL R/C 1,025 fpm	Range 496 sm Cruise 135 mph Fuel 40 gal Flow 9 gph	L. IO-320-E1A 150 hp Span 32 ft 0 in
BEECHCRAFT Sport Seats 2-4 Length 25 ft 8.5 in	$ 15,450	Gross 2,250 Empty 1,374 Usefl 876 Cbn ld (I) 556	MFL 1,320 ft Stall 56 mph SL R/C 700 fpm	Range 757 sm Cruise 131 mph Fuel 58.8 gal Flow 9 gph	Lyc. O-320-E2C 150 hp Span 32 ft 9 in
ME BOLKOW-BLOHM BO-209-160 Seats 2 Length 21 ft 6 in	$15,900	Gross 1,808 Empty 1,067 Usefl 741 Cbn ld (V) 545	MFL 794 ft Stall 57 mph SL R/C 1,180 fpm	Range 628 sm Cruise 158 mph Fuel 38.8 gal Flow 7.4 gph	L. IO-320 160 hp Span 27 ft 7 in
PITTS S-2A (Aerobatic) Seats 2 Length 17 ft 9 in	$24,395	Gross 1,500 Empty 1,000 Usefl 500 Cbn ld (V) 337	MFL 1,350 ft Stall 58 mph SL R/C 1,900 fpm	Range 228 sm Cruise 152 mph Fuel 24 gal Flow 10.8 gph	L. IO-360-A1A 200 hp Span 20 ft 0 in

* Mfrd. by Bellanca Aircraft/Minnesota

Single Engine, Fixed Gear

DESIGNATION	PRICE	WEIGHT	PERFORMANCE		ENGINE
COOK Challenger Seats 4 Length 22 ft 0 in	$9,700	Gross 2,150 Empty 1,130 Usefl 1,020 Cbn ld (I) 710	MFL 1,020 ft Stall 53 mph SL R/C 700 fpm	Range 575 sm Cruise 145 mph Fuel 40 gal Flow 8.7 gph	L. O-320 150 hp Span 27 ft 0 in
PIPER Cherokee 140E Cruiser Seats 2-4 Length 23 ft 6 in	$10,990	Gross 2,150 Empty 1,275 Usefl 875 Cbn ld (V) 510	MFL 1,700 ft Stall 55 mph SL R/C 660 fpm	Range 634 sm Cruise 132 mph Fuel 50 gal Flow 9 gph	L. O-320 150 hp Span 30 ft 0 in
PIPER Super Cub Seats 2 Length 22 ft 7 in	$12,195	Gross 1,750 Empty 930 Usefl 820 Cbn ld (V) 559	MFL 725 ft Stall 43 mph SL R/C 960 fpm	Range 374 sm Cruise 115 mph Fuel 36 gal Flow 9 gph	L. O-320 150 hp Span 35 ft 2.5 in
AMERICAN AVIATION AA-5 Traveler Seats 4 Length 22 ft 0.1 in	$13,595	Gross 2,200 Empty 1,200 Usefl 1,000 Cbn ld (I) 708	MFL 1,700 ft Stall 58 mph SL R/C 650 fpm	Range 464 sm Cruise 138 mph Fuel 37 gal Flow 9 gph	L. O-320 150 hp Span 31 ft 5.4 in
CESSNA 172 Seats 4 Length 26 ft 11 in	$14,050	Gross 2,300 Empty 1,265 Usefl 1,035 Cbn ld (I) 762	MFL 1,525 ft Stall 49 mph SL R/C 645 fpm	Range 524/670 sm Cruise 131 mph Fuel 38/48 gal Flow 8.1 gph	L. O-320-E2D 150 hp Span 35 ft 10 in
CESSNA Skyhawk Seats 4 Length 26 ft 11 in	$15,675	Gross 2,300 Empty 1,305 Usefl 995 Cbn ld (I) 722	MFL 1,525 ft Stall 49 mph SL R/C 645 fpm	Range 528/673 sm Cruise 132 mph Fuel 38/48 gal Flow 8.1 gph	L. O-320-E2D 150 hp Span 35 ft 10 in
PIPER Cherokee 180G Seats 4 Length 23 ft 7.6 in	$15,950	Gross 2,400 Empty 1,340 Usefl 1,060 Cbn ld (I) 690	MFL 1,625 ft Stall 57 mph SL R/C 750 fpm	Range 608 sm Cruise 143 mph Fuel 50 gal Flow 10 gph	L. O-360-A4A 180 hp Span 30 ft 0 in
THURSTON TSC-2 Explorer Seats 4 Length 23 ft 4 in	$17,500	Gross 2,200 Empty 1,340 Usefl 860 Cbn (I) 469	MFL 850 ft Stall 57 mph SL R/C 800 fpm	Range 450 sm Cruise 130 mph Fuel 41 gal Flow 10 gph	L. IO-320 200 hp Span 32 ft 0 in

Single Engine, Fixed Gear

DESIGNATION	PRICE	WEIGHT	PERFORMANCE		ENGINE
NO. AM. ROCKWELL Aero Commander 111 Seats 4 Length 24 ft 10 in	$ NA	Gross 2,500 Empty 1,362 Usefl 1,138 Cbn ld (l) 708	MFL 1,575 ft Stall 59 mph SL R/C 750 fpm	Range 746 sm Cruise 142 mph Fuel 60 gal Flow 10 gph	L. O-360-A4G 180 hp Span 32 ft 9 in
CESSNA 177 B Seats 4 Length 27 ft 3 in	$18,040	Gross 2,500 Empty 1,430 Usefl 1,070 Cbn ld (l) 706	MFL 1,400 ft Stall 53 mph SL R/C 840 fpm	Range 577 sm Cruise 139 mph Fuel 49 gal Flow 10.1 gph	L. 0-360-A1F6 180 hp Span 35 ft 6 in
BEECHCRAFT Sundowner Seats 4 Length 25 ft 8¾ in	$18,150	Gross 2,450 Empty 1,416 Usefl 1,034 Cbn ld (l) 636	MFL 1,380 ft Stall 60 mph SL R/C 820 fpm	Range 671 sm Cruise 143 mph Fuel 58.8 gal Flow 10.8 gph	L. O-360-A4G 180 hp Span 32 ft 9 in
CESSNA Cardinal Seats 4 Length 27 ft 3 in	$19,300	Gross 2,500 Empty 1,485 Usefl 1,015 Cbn ld (l) 676	MFL 1,400 ft Stall 53 mph SL R/C 840 fpm	Range 589 sm Cruise 142 mph Fuel 49 gal Flow 10.1 gph	L. 0-360-A1F6 180 hp Span 35 ft 6 in
CESSNA 180 Skywagon Seats 4-6 Length 25 ft 9 in	$20,500	Gross 2,800 Empty 1,545 Usefl 1,255 Cbn ld (l) 697	MFL 1,365 ft Stall 58 mph SL R/C 1,090 fpm	Range 781 sm Cruise 162 mph Fuel 79 gal Flow 14.1 gph	C. O-470-R 230 hp Span 35 ft 10 in
PIPER Cherokee 235E Seats 4 Length 23 ft 9.1 in	$20,670	Gross 2,900 Empty 1,493 Usefl 1,407 Cbn ld (l) 826	MFL 1,360 ft* Stall 60 mph SL R/C 825 fpm *fixed pitch prop	Range 819 sm Cruise 156 mph Fuel 84 gal Flow 14 gph	L- O-540-B4B5 235 hp Span 30 ft 0 in
CESSNA 182 Seats 4 Length 28 ft ½ in	$21,995	Gross 2,950 Empty 1,580 Usefl 1,370 Cbn ld (l) 812	MFL 1,350 ft Stall 57 mph SL R/C 890 fpm	Range 776 sm Cruise 160 mph Fuel 79 gal Flow 14.1 gph	C. O-470-R 230 hp Span 35 ft 10 in
CESSNA Skylane Seats 4 Length 28 ft ½ in	$23,040	Gross 2,950 Empty 1,640 Usefl 1,310 Cbn ld (l) 777	MFL 1,350 ft Stall 57 mph SL R/C 890 fpm	Range 776 sm Cruise 160 mph Fuel 79 gal Flow 14.1 gph	C. O-470-R 230 hp Span 35 ft 10 in

Single Engine, Fixed Gear

DESIGNATION	PRICE	WEIGHT	PERFORMANCE		ENGINE
CESSNA 185 Seats 1-6 Length 25 ft 9 in	$24,250	Gross 3,350 Empty 1,575 Usefl 1,775 Cbn ld (I) *1,217 * w. cargo int	MFL 1,400 ft Stall 59 mph SL R/C 1,010 fpm	Range 730 sm Cruise 169 mph Fuel 81 gal Flow 16.4 gph	C. IO-520-F 300 hp Span 35 ft 10 in
PIPER Cherokee Six 260 E Seats 6-7 Length 27 ft 8.6 in	$24,990	Gross 3,400 Empty 1,699 Usefl 1,701 Cbn ld (I) 1,120	MFL 1,360 ft Stall 63 mph SL R/C 750 fpm	Range 840 sm Cruise 160 mph Fuel 84 gal Flow 14 gph	L. O-540-E4B5 260 hp Span 32 ft 8.75 in
CESSNA 206 Skywagon Seats 1-6 Length 28 ft 0 in	$25,995	Gross 3,600 Empty 1,710* Usefl 1,890 Cbn ld (I) 1,301 * w. cargo int	MFL 1,780 ft Stall 61 mph SL R/C 920 fpm	Range 677 sm Cruise 164 mph Fuel 80 gal Flow 16.4 gph	C. IO-520-F 300 hp Span 35 ft 10 in
PIPER Cherokee Six 300 E Seats 6-7 Length 27 ft 8.6 in	$28,600	Gross 3,400 Empty 1,793 Usefl 1,607 Cbn ld (I) 1,026	MFL 1,140 ft Stall 63 mph SL R/C1,050 fpm	Range 756 sm Cruise 168 mph Fuel 84 gal Flow 16 gph	L. IO-540-K 300 hp Span 32 ft 8.75 in
CESSNA 207 Skywagon Seats 7 Length 31 ft 9 in	$29,750	Gross 3,800 Empty 1,880 Usefl 1,920 Cbn ld (I) 1307	MFL 1,970 ft Stall 67 mph SL R/C 810 fpm	Range 656 sm Cruise 159 mph Fuel 80 gal Flow 16.4 gph	C. IO-520-F 300 hp Span 35 ft 10 in
CESSNA Stationair Seats 6 Length 28 ft 0 in	$30,440	Gross 3,600 Empty 1,835 Usefl 1,765 Cbn ld (I) 1,176	MFL 1,780 ft Stall 61 mph SL R/C 920 fpm	Range 677 sm Cruise 164 mph Fuel 80 gal Flow 16.4 gph	C. IO-520-F 300 hp Span 35 ft 10 in

Single Engine, Retractable Gear

DESIGNATION	PRICE	WEIGHT	PERFORMANCE		ENGINE
THURSTON Teal TSC1A 2 seats Length 23 ft 7 in	$17,750	Gross 1,900 Empty 1,350 Usefl 550 Cbn ld (V) 355	MFL (l) 800 ft MFL (w) 1,300 ft Stall* 54 mph SL R/C 740 fpm	Range 218 sm Cruise 108 mph Fuel 25 gal Flow 9 gph	L.O-320-A3B 150 hp Span 32 ft 0 in

*gear and flaps down

Single Engine, Retractable Gear

DESIGNATION	PRICE	WEIGHT	PERFORMANCE		ENGINE
THURSTON Teal TSC 1A1 2-3 seats Length 23 ft 7 in	$18,790	Gross 2,200 Empty 1,360 Usefl 840 Cbn ld (V) 655	MFL (l) 980 ft MFL (w) 1,750 ft Stall* 57 mph SL R/C 600 fpm	Range 700 sm Cruise 105 mph Fuel 65 gal Flow 9 gph	L.O-320-A3B 150 hp Span 32 ft 0 in
ZLIN-526-L Seats 2 Length 25 ft 0 in	$21,000	Gross 2,175 Empty 1,489 Usefl 686 Cbn ld NA	MFL 1,050 ft Stall* 56 mph SL R/C1,380 fpm	Range 340 sm Cruise 140 mph Fuel 22/44 gal Flow 10.5 gph	L. AIO-360-B1B 200 hp Span 35 ft 0 in
LAKE Seaplane Seats 4 Length 25 ft 0 in	$21,500	Gross 2,400 Empty 1,345 Usefl 1,055 Cbn ld (V) 770	MFL 1,250 ft Stall* 45 mph SL R/C1,000 fpm	Range 455 sm Cruise 140 mph Fuel 40 gal Flow 10 gph	L. O-360-A1A 180 hp Span 38 ft 0 in
PIPER Arrow II Seats 4 Length 24 ft 7.4 in	$23,500	Gross 2,650 Empty 1,504 Usefl 1,146 Cbn ld (I) 770	MFL 1,600 ft Stall* 64 mph SL R/C 900 fpm	Range 683 sm Cruise 165 mph Fuel 50 gal Flow 10.2 gph	L. IO-360 200 hp Span 32 ft 2.3 in
BEECHCRAFT Sierra Seats 4-6 Length 25 ft 8.5 in	$24,950	Gross 2,750 Empty 1,610 Usefl 1,140 Cbn ld (I) 722	MFL 1,630 ft Stall* 66 mph SL R/C 862 fpm	Range 652 sm Cruise 162 mph Fuel 58.8 gal Flow 12.3 gph	L. IO-360-A1B 200 hp Span 32 ft 9 in
CESSNA Cardinal RG Seats 4 Length 27 ft 3 in	$25,995	Gross 2,800 Empty 1,630 Usefl 1,170 Cbn ld (I) 800	MFL 1,585 ft Stall* 57 mph SL R/C 860 fpm	Range 640 sm Cruise 165 mph Fuel 49 gal Flow 10.8 gph	L. IO-360 200 hp Span 35 ft 7½ in
Super Viking 300 Cont.* Seats 4 Length 23 ft 6 in	$27,700	Gross 3,325 Empty 1,900 Usefl 1,425 Cbn ld (I) 1,025	MFL 1,050 ft Stall* 62 mph SL R/C1,840 fpm	Range 940 sm Cruise 188 mph Fuel 72 gal Flow 13.5 gph	C. IO-520 300 hp Span 34 ft 2 in
NO. AM. ROCKWELL Aero Commander 112 Seats 4 Length 24 ft 10 in	$ NA	Gross 2,550 Empty 1,438 Usefl 1,112 Cbn ld (I) 682	MFL 1,640 ft Stall* 60 mph SL R/C 890 fpm	Range 830 sm Cruise 162 mph Fuel 60 gal Flow 10 gph	L. O-360-A1G6 180 hp Span 32 ft 9 in

* Mfrd. by Bellanca Aircraft/Minnesota

*gear and flaps down

Single Engine, Retractable Gear

DESIGNATION	PRICE	WEIGHT	PERFORMANCE		ENGINE
Super Viking 300 Lyc * Seats 4 Length 23 ft 6 in	$29,700	Gross 3,325 Empty 1,950 Usefl 1,375 Cbn ld (I) 975	MFL 1,100 ft Stall* 62 mph SL R/C 1,800 fpm	Range 890 sm Cruise 194 mph Fuel 72 gal Flow 14 gal	L. IO-540 300 hp Span 34 ft 2 in
LAKE LA 4 Seats 4 Length 25 ft 0 in	$29,950	Gross 2,400 Empty 1,545 Usefl 855 Cbn ld (I) 570	MFL (l) 1,275 ft MFL (w) 1,575 ft Stall* 45 mph SL R/C 800 fpm	Range 439 sm Cruise 135 mph Fuel 40 gal Flow 10 gph	L. O-360-A1A 180 hp Span 38 ft 0 in
PIPER Comanche C Seats 4-6 Length 25 ft 9.2 in	$31,800	Gross 3,200 Empty 1,773 Usefl 1,427 Cbn ld (I) 765	MFL 1,800 ft Stall* 67 mph SL R/C 1,320 fpm	Range 1,000 sm Cruise 185 mph Fuel 86 gal Flow 14 gph	L. IO-540-N1A5 260 hp Span 35 ft 11.75 in
LAKE Buccaneer Seats 4 Length 25 ft 0 in	$32,950	Gross 2,690 Empty 1,535 Usefl 1,155 Cbn ld (I) 780	MFL (l) 875 ft MFL (w) 1,125 ft Stall* 45 mph SL R/C 1,200 fpm	Range 674 sm Cruise 150 mph Fuel 55 gal Flow 10.5 gph	L. IO-360-A1B 200 hp Span 38 ft 0 in
CESSNA 210 Centurion Seats 6 Length 28 ft 3 in	$38,375	Gross 3,800 Empty 2,125 Usefl 1,675 Cbn ld (I) 1,039	MFL 1,900 ft Stall* 65 ph SL R/C 860 fpm	Range 879 sm Cruise 188 mph Fuel 89 gal Flow 16.4 gph	C. IO-520-L 300 hp Span 36 ft 9 in
BEECHCRAFT G33 Bonanza Seats 4-5 Length 25 ft 6 in	$41,450	Gross 3,300 Empty 1,935 Usefl 1,365 Cbn ld (I) 833	MFL 1,516 ft Stall* 56 mph SL R/C 1,060 fpm	Range 477/1,000 sm Cruise 193 mph Fuel 49/80 gal Flow 13.4 gph	C. IO-470-N 260 hp Span 33 ft 5.5 in
WINDECKER Eagle Seats 4 Length 28 ft 5 in	$41,500	Gross 3,400 Empty 2,150 Usefl 1,250 Cbn ld (I) 689	MFL 1,690 ft Stall* 66 mph SL R/C 1,220 fpm	Range 988 sm Cruise 207 mph Fuel 84 gal Flow 15.2 gph	C. IO-520-C 285 hp Span 32 ft 0 in
BEECHCRAFT F33A Bonanza Seats 4-6 Length 25 ft 6 in	$41,600	Gross 3,400 Empty 2,000 Usefl 1,400 Cbn ld (I) 865	MFL 1,320 ft Stall* 63 mph SL R/C 1,136 fpm	Range 496/892 sm Cruise 200 mph Fuel 49/80 gal Flow 15.3 gph	C. IO-520-BA 285 hp Span 32 ft 9.9 in

* Mfrd. by Bellanca Aircraft/Minnesota

*gear and flaps down

Single Engine, Retractable Gear

DESIGNATION	PRICE	WEIGHT	PERFORMANCE		ENGINE
BEECHCRAFT V35B Bonanza Seats 4-6 Length 26 ft 4.5 in	$41,600	Gross 3,400 Empty 1,985 Usefl 1,415 Cbn ld (l) 883	MFL 1,320 ft Stall* 63 mph SL R/C 1,136 fpm	Range 521/909 sm Cruise 203 mph Fuel 49/80 gal Flow 15.3 gph	C. IO-520-BA 285 hp Span 33 ft 5.5 in
CESSNA Centurion II Seats 6 Length 28 ft 3 in	$45,375	Gross 3,800 Empty 2,205 Usefl 1,595 Cbn ld (l) 1,024	MFL 1,900 ft Stall* 65 mph SL R/C 860 fpm	Range 879 sm Cruise 188 mph Fuel 89 gal Flow 16.4 gph	C. IO-520-L 300 hp Span 36 ft 9 in
BEECHCRAFT A 36 Bonanza Seats 4-6 Length 26 ft 8 in	$45,550	Gross 3,600 Empty 2,040 Usefl 1,560 Cbn ld (l) 998	MFL 1,525 ft Stall* 64 mph SL R/C 1,015 fpm	Range 485/861 sm Cruise 195 mph Fuel 49/80 gal Flow 15.3 gph	C. IO-520-BA 285 hp Span 33 ft 5.5 in

Single Engine Turbo-Charged

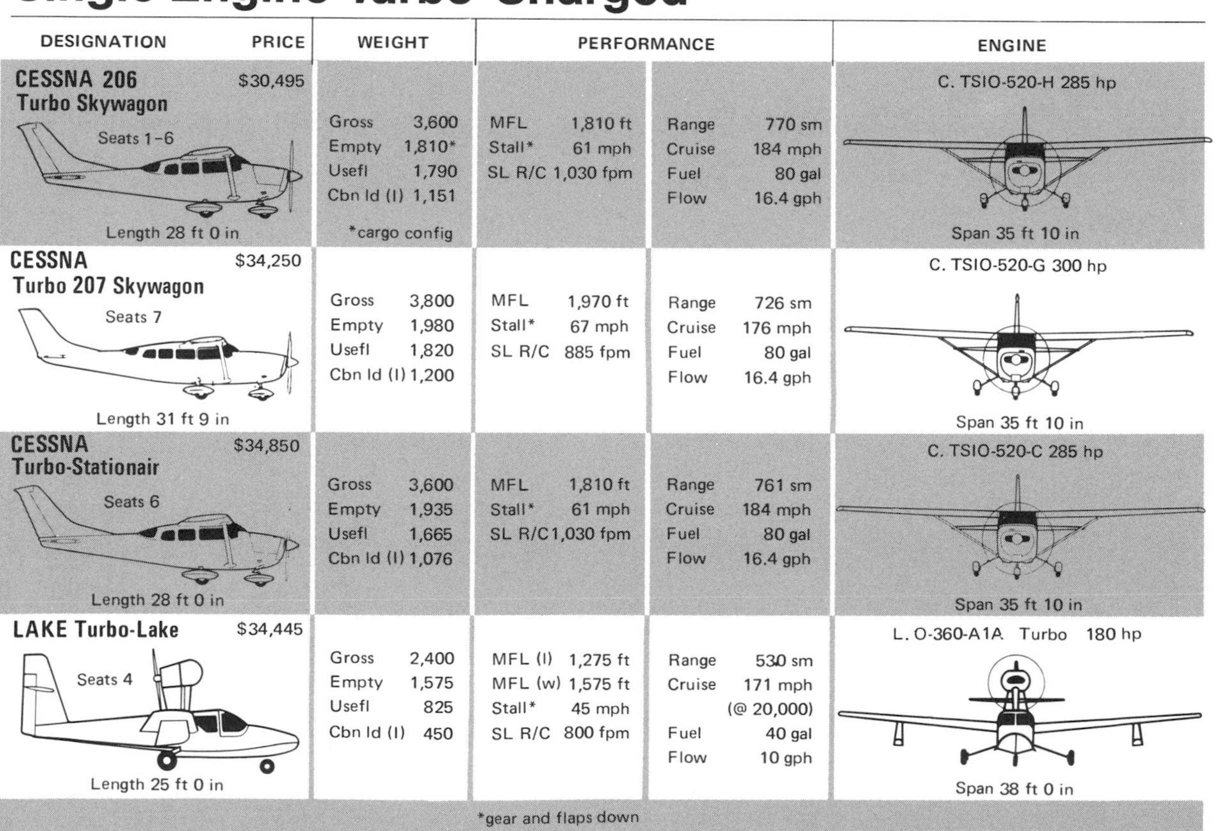

DESIGNATION	PRICE	WEIGHT	PERFORMANCE		ENGINE
CESSNA 206 Turbo Skywagon Seats 1–6 Length 28 ft 0 in	$30,495	Gross 3,600 Empty 1,810* Usefl 1,790 Cbn ld (l) 1,151 *cargo config	MFL 1,810 ft Stall* 61 mph SL R/C 1,030 fpm	Range 770 sm Cruise 184 mph Fuel 80 gal Flow 16.4 gph	C. TSIO-520-H 285 hp Span 35 ft 10 in
CESSNA Turbo 207 Skywagon Seats 7 Length 31 ft 9 in	$34,250	Gross 3,800 Empty 1,980 Usefl 1,820 Cbn ld (l) 1,200	MFL 1,970 ft Stall* 67 mph SL R/C 885 fpm	Range 726 sm Cruise 176 mph Fuel 80 gal Flow 16.4 gph	C. TSIO-520-G 300 hp Span 35 ft 10 in
CESSNA Turbo-Stationair Seats 6 Length 28 ft 0 in	$34,850	Gross 3,600 Empty 1,935 Usefl 1,665 Cbn ld (l) 1,076	MFL 1,810 ft Stall* 61 mph SL R/C 1,030 fpm	Range 761 sm Cruise 184 mph Fuel 80 gal Flow 16.4 gph	C. TSIO-520-C 285 hp Span 35 ft 10 in
LAKE Turbo-Lake Seats 4 Length 25 ft 0 in	$34,445	Gross 2,400 Empty 1,575 Usefl 825 Cbn ld (l) 450	MFL (l) 1,275 ft MFL (w) 1,575 ft Stall* 45 mph SL R/C 800 fpm	Range 530 sm Cruise 171 mph (@ 20,000) Fuel 40 gal Flow 10 gph	L. O-360-A1A Turbo 180 hp Span 38 ft 0 in

*gear and flaps down

Single Engine Turbo-Charged

DESIGNATION	PRICE	WEIGHT	PERFORMANCE		ENGINE
Turbo Viking*	$36,660	Gross 3,325 Empty 2,010 Usefl 1,315 Cbn ld (l) 657	MFL 1,100 ft Stall* 62 mph SL R/C 1,800 fpm	Range 1,379 sm Cruise 235 mph Fuel 92 gal Flow 14.5 gph	L. IO-540 Turbo 300 hp Span 34 ft 2 in
Length 23 ft 6 in					
PIPER Turbo Comanche C Seats 4-6	$37,530	Gross 3,200 Empty 1,894 Usefl 1,306 Cbn ld (l) 644	MFL 1,800 ft Stall* 67 mph SL R/C 1,320 fpm	Range 1,181 sm Cruise 228 mph Fuel 86 gal Flow 14.5 gph	L. IO-540 Turbo 260 hp Span 35 ft 11.75 in
Length 25 ft 9.2 in					
CESSNA 210 Turbo Centurion Seats 6	$43,075	Gross 3,800 Empty 2,240 Usefl 1,560 Cbn ld (l) 924	MFL 2,030 ft Stall* 65 mph SL R/C 930 fpm	Range 1,025 sm Cruise 219 mph Fuel 89 gal Flow 16.4 gph	C. TSIO-520-H 285 hp Span 36 ft 9 in
Length 28 ft 3 in					
CESSNA Turbo-Centurion II Seats 6	$50,065	Gross 3,800 Empty 2,320 Usefl 1,480 Cbn ld (l) 909	MFL 2,030 ft Stall* 65 mph SL R/C 930 fpm	Range 1,025 sm Cruise 219 mph Fuel 89 gal Flow 16.4 gph	C. TSIO-520-H 285 hp Span 36 ft 9 in
Length 28 ft 3 in					

Twin Engine Piston

DESIGNATION	PRICE	WEIGHT	PERFORMANCE		ENGINE
PIPER Twin Comanche C/R Seats 4-6	$46,640	Gross 3,600 Empty 2,270 Usefl 1,330 Cbn ld (l) 659	MFL 1,870 ft Stall* 70 mph SL R/C 1,460 fpm SE R/C 260 fpm	Range 842 sm Cruise 198 mph Fuel 86 gal Flow 17.2 gph	L. IO-320-B1A (2) 160 hp Span 36 ft 0 in
Length 25 ft 2 in					
PIPER Seneca Seats 6-7	$49,900	Gross 4,000 Empty 2,479 Usefl 1,521 Cbn ld (l) 821	MFL 1,335 ft Stall* 67 mph SL R/C 1,460 fpm SE R/C 230 fpm	Range 861 sm Cruise 187 mph Fuel 95 gal Flow 20.6 gph	L. IO-360 (2) 200 hp Span 38 ft 10.75 in
Length 28 ft 6 in					
CESSNA Super Skymaster Seats 6	$53,775	Gross 4,630 Empty 2,695 Usefl 1,935 Cbn ld (l) 925	MFL 1,675 ft Stall* 70 mph SL R/C 1,100 fpm SE R/C 235 fpm	Range 920 sm Cruise 190 mph Fuel 128 gal Flow 22.9 gph	C. IO-360-C (2) 210 hp Span 38 ft 4 in
Length 29 ft 9 in					

* Mfrd. by Bellanca Aircraft/Minnesota

*gear and flaps down

Twin Engine Piston

DESIGNATION	PRICE	WEIGHT		PERFORMANCE				ENGINE
BURNS BA-42 Seats 6, Length 32 ft 4 in	$59,950	Gross Empty Usefl Cbn ld (l)	4,500 2,700 1,800 952	MFL Stall* SL R/C SE R/C	1,795 ft 74 mph 1,650 fpm 400 fpm	Range Cruise Fuel Flow	956 sm 225 mph 100 gal 20 gph	C. IO-360-D (2) 210 hp Span 34 ft 5 in
BEECHCRAFT Baron B55 Seats 4-6, Length 27 ft 3.4 in	$67,950	Gross Empty Usefl Cbn ld (l)	5,100 3,080 2,020 1,043	MFL Stall* SL R/C SE R/C	1,370 ft 78 mph 1,670 fpm 320 fpm	Range Cruise Fuel Flow	980 sm 225 mph 142 gal 27.6 gph	C. IO-470-L (2) 260 hp Span 37 ft 9.8 in
PIPER Aztec E Seats 6, Length 31 ft 2.6 in	$69,990	Gross Empty Usefl Cbn ld (l)	5,200 3,042 2,158 1,168	MFL Stall* SL R/C SE R/C	1,620 ft 68 mph 1,490 fpm 240 fpm	Range Cruise Fuel Flow	924 sm 208 mph 140 gal 27 gph	L. IO-540-C4B5 (2) 250 hp Span 37 ft 1.75 in
CESSNA 310 Seats 6, Length 29 ft 3 in	$73,175	Gross Empty Usefl Cbn ld (l)	5,300 3,190 2,110 1,090	MFL Stall* SL R/C SE R/C	1,795 ft 72 mph 1,495 fpm 327 fpm	Range Cruise Fuel Flow	930 sm 221 mph 140 gal 28.2 gph	C. IO-470-VO (2) 260 hp Span 36 ft 11 in
BEECHCRAFT Baron E55 Seats 4-6, Length 29 ft 0 in	$86,750	Gross Empty Usefl Cbn ld (l)	5,300 3,115 2,185 1,216	MFL Stall* SL R/C SE R/C	1,414 ft 77 mph 1,670 fpm 335 fpm	Range Cruise Fuel Flow	910 sm 230 mph 142 gal 30.6 gph	C. IO-520-C (2) 285 hp Span 37 ft 9.8 in
BEECHCRAFT Baron 58 Seats 4-6, Length 29 ft 10 in	$98,500	Gross Empty Usefl Cbn ld (l)	5,400 3,215 2,185 895	MFL Stall* SL R/C SE R/C	1,469 ft 83 mph 1,694 fpm 382 fpm	Range Cruise Fuel Flow	1,100 sm 230 mph 168 gal 30.6 gph	C. IO-520-C (2) 285 hp Span 37 ft 10 in
NO. AM. ROCKWELL Shrike Commander Seats 4-7, Length 36 ft 7 in	$109,250	Gross Empty Usefl Cbn ld (l)	6,750 4,608 2,146 865	MFL Stall* SL R/C SE R/C	2,235 ft 68 mph 1,340 fpm 266 fpm	Range Cruise Fuel Flow	797 sm 205 mph 156 gal 34 gph	L. IO-540-E (2) 290 hp Span 49 ft 0.5 in
BEECHCRAFT Queen Air B80 Seats 7-11, Length 35 ft 6 in	$192, 500	Gross Empty Usefl Cbn ld (l)	8,800 5,075 3,725 1,993	MFL Stall* SL R/C SE R/C	2,311 ft 82 mph 1,275 fpm 265 fpm	Range Cruise Fuel Flow	1,155 sm 224 mph 264 gal 42.7 gph	L. IGSO-540-A1D (2) 380 hp Span 49 ft 0.5 in

*gear and flaps down

Twin Engine Turbo-Charged

DESIGNATION	PRICE	WEIGHT	PERFORMANCE		ENGINE
PIPER Turbo Twin Comanche C/R Seats 4-6 Length 25 ft 2 in	$57,490	Gross 3,725 Empty 2,416 Usefl 1,309 Cbn ld (l) 470	MFL 1,900 ft Stall* 70 mph SL R/C 1,290 fpm SE R/C 225 fpm	Range 1,338 sm Cruise 228 mph Fuel 114 gal Flow 17.2 gph	L. IO-320 Turbo (2) 160 hp Span 36 ft 0 in
PIPER Turbo Aztec E Seats 6 Length 31 ft 2.6 in	$80,115	Gross 5,200 Empty 3,229 Usefl 1,971 Cbn ld (l) 981	MFL 1,620 ft Stall* 68 mph SL R/C 1,530 fpm SE R/C 265 fpm	Range 951 sm Cruise 233 mph Fuel 140 gal Flow 29 gph	L. TIO-540-C1A (2) 250 hp Span 37 ft 1.75 in
CESSNA Turbo 310 Seats 6 Length 29 ft 3 in	$93,900	Grass 5,500 Empty 3,292 Usefl 2,208 Cbn ld (l) 1,188	MFL 1,790 ft Stall* 78 mph SL R/C 1,790 fpm SE R/C 408 fpm	Range 984 sm Cruise 259 mph Fuel 140 gal Flow 30.8 gph	C. TSIO-520-B (2) 285 hp Span 36 ft 11 in
CESSNA Turbo 401 B Seats 6-8 Length 33 ft 8.9 in	$111,750	Gross 6,300 Empty 3,665 Usefl 2,635 Cbn ld (l) 1,342	MFL 2,220 ft Stall* 79 mph SL R/C 1,610 fpm SE R/C 255 fpm	Range 809 sm Cruise 240 mph Fuel 140 gal Flow 34 gph	C. TSIO-520-E (2) 300 hp Span 39 ft 10.3 in
PIPER Turbo Navajo B Seats 6-9 Length 34 ft 6 in	$115,570	Gross 6,500 Empty 3,849 Usefl 2,651 Cbn ld (l) 1,053	MFL 2,270 ft Stall* 71 mph SL R/C 1,395 fpm SE R/C 245 fpm	Range 1,119 sm Cruise 247 mph Fuel 190 gal Flow 36 gph	L. TIO-540-A (2) 310 hp Span 40 ft 8 in

Pressurized Piston Engine

DESIGNATION	PRICE	WEIGHT	PERFORMANCE		ENGINE
CESSNA Pressurized Skymaster Seats 4-5 Length 29 ft 9 in	$78,500	Gross 4,700 Empty 2,900 Usefl NA Cbn ld NA	MFL 1,675 ft Stall* 71 mph SL R/C 1,250 fpm SE R/C 375 fpm	Range 1,070 sm Cruise 230 mph Fuel 120 gal Flow NA gph CA 7,000 @ 16,000	C. NA (2) 225 hp Span 38 ft 4 in
CESSNA 340 Seats 6 Length 34 ft 4 in	$127,500	Gross 5,975 Empty 3,697 Usefl 2,278 Cbn ld (l) 840	MFL 2,430 ft Stall* 82 mph SL R/C 1,500 fpm SE R/C 250 fpm	Range 540/1,180 sm Cruise 236 mph Fuel 102/184 gal Flow 34 gph CA 8,000 @20,000	C. TSIO-520-K (2) 285 hp Span 38 ft 1 in

*gear and flaps down

Pressurized Piston Engine

DESIGNATION	PRICE	WEIGHT	PERFORMANCE		ENGINE
CESSNA 414 Seats 6-7 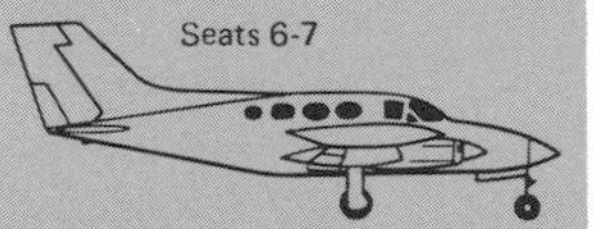	$153,500	Gross 6,350 Empty 4,039 Usefl 2,311 Cbn ld (I) 1,018	MFL 2,350 ft Stall* 81 mph SL R/C1,580 fpm SE R/C 240 fpm	Range 849 sm Cruise 252 mph Fuel 140 gal Flow 34 gph CA 8,000@ 20,100	C. TSIO-520-J (2) 310 hp 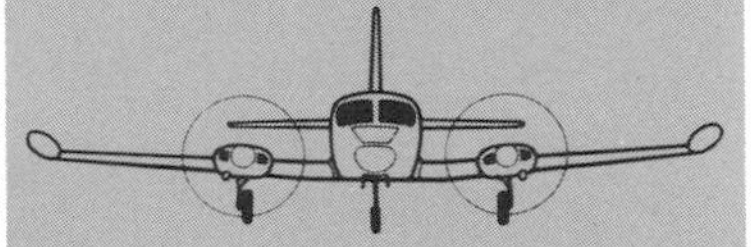
BEECHCRAFT Duke Seats 4-6 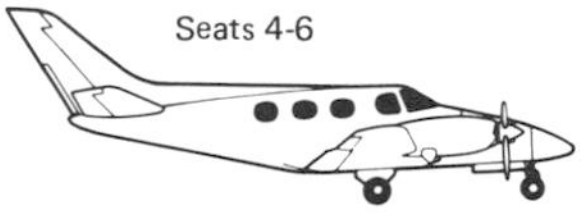 Length 33 ft 10 in	$179,500	Gross 6,775 Empty 4,195 Useful 2,580 Cbn ld (I) 1,028	MFL 2,380 ft Stall* 87 mph SL R/C1,601 fpm SE R/C 307 fpm	Range 973 sm Cruise 271 mph Fuel 204 gal Flow 43.6 gph CA 10,000@ 25,000	L. TIO-541-E1A4 (2) 380 hp  Span 39 ft 3¼ in
PIPER Pressurized Navajo Seats 6-8 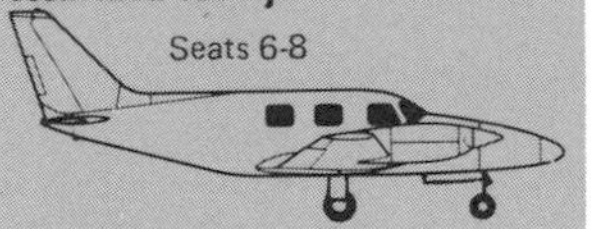 Length 34 ft 6 in	$197,000	Gross 7,800 Empty 4,842 Usefl 2,958 Cbn ld (I) 1,065	MFL 2,960 ft Stall* 83 mph SL R/C1,740 fpm SE R/C 240 fpm	Range 963 sm Cruise 266 mph Fuel 236 gal Flow 54 gph CA 8000@24,500 ft	L. TIGO-541-E1A (2) 425 hp 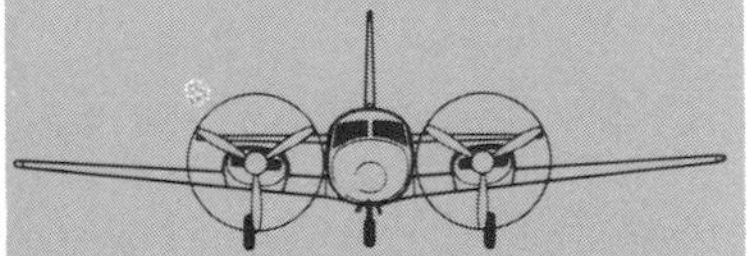 Span 40 ft 8 in
CESSNA 421 B Seats 6-8 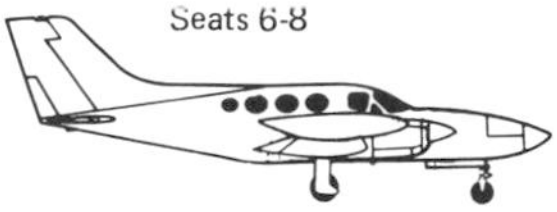 Length 36 ft 1 in	$197,900	Gross 7,250 Empty 4,359 Usefl 2,891 Cbn ld (I) 1,217	MFL 2,325 ft Stall* 86 mph SL R/C1,950 fpm SE R/C 345 fpm	Range 1,029 sm Cruise 270 mph Fuel 196 gal Flow 43 gph CA 8,000@ 20,100	C. GTSIO-520-H (2) 375 hp  Span 41 ft 10.3 in

Turbo-Prop

DESIGNATION	PRICE	WEIGHT	PERFORMANCE		ENGINE
INTERCEPTOR 400 Seats 4 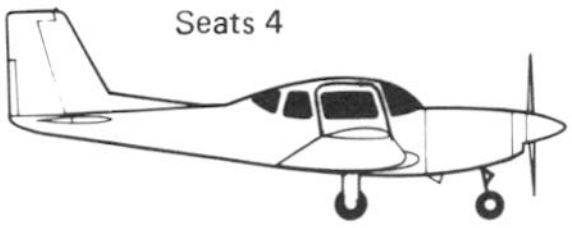 Length 25 ft 2 in	$108,000	Gross 4,030 Empty 2,400 Usefl 1,630 Cbn ld (I) 424	MFL NA ft Stall* 68 mph SL R/C1,500 fpm	Range 1,100 sm Cruise 275 mph Fuel 146 gal Flow 32 gph CA 9,500@ 18,000	G. TPE-331-1-101 (1) 400 shp  Span 30 ft 6 in
MITSUBISHI MU-2F Seats 7-9 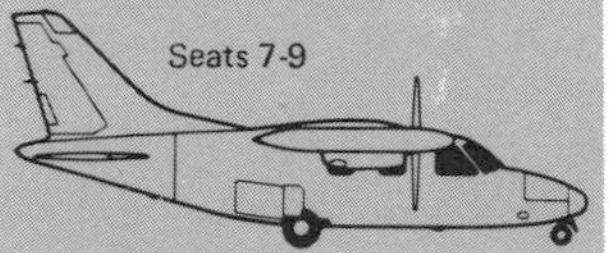 Length 33 ft 3 in	$379,950	T/O 9,920 Empty 5,790 Usefl 4,130 Cbn ld (I) 1,155	MFL 1,320 ft Stall* 82 mph SL R/C 2,875 fpm SE R/C 920 fpm	Range 1,560 sm Cruise 340 mph Fuel 366 gal Flow 75 gph CA 3,500@ 16,000	G. TPE-331 (2) 665 shp 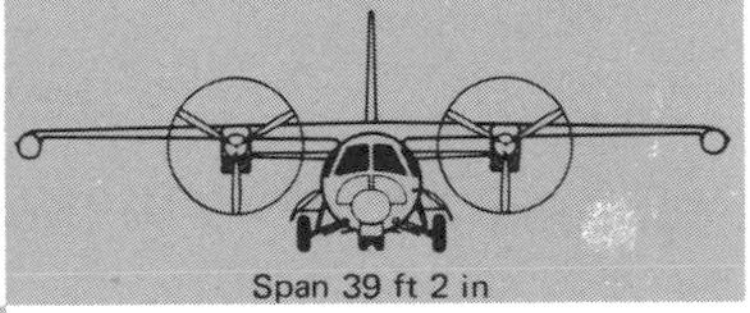 Span 39 ft 2 in
BEECHCRAFT King Air C90 6-10 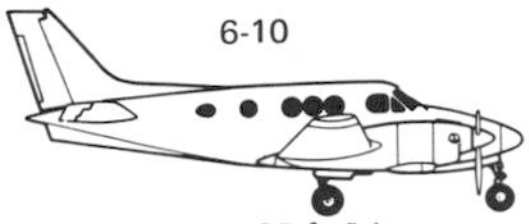 Length 35 ft 6 in	$434,500	T/O 9,650 Empty 5,600 Usefl 4,050 Cbn ld (I) 1,404	MFL 1,340 ft Stall* 85 mph SL R/C2,000 fpm SE R/C 555 fpm	Range 1,321 sm Cruise 250 mph Fuel 384 gal Flow 62.4 gph CA 8,000@ 21,200	P&W PT6A-20 (2) 550 shp  Span 50 ft 2.94 in

*gear and flaps down

Turbo-Prop

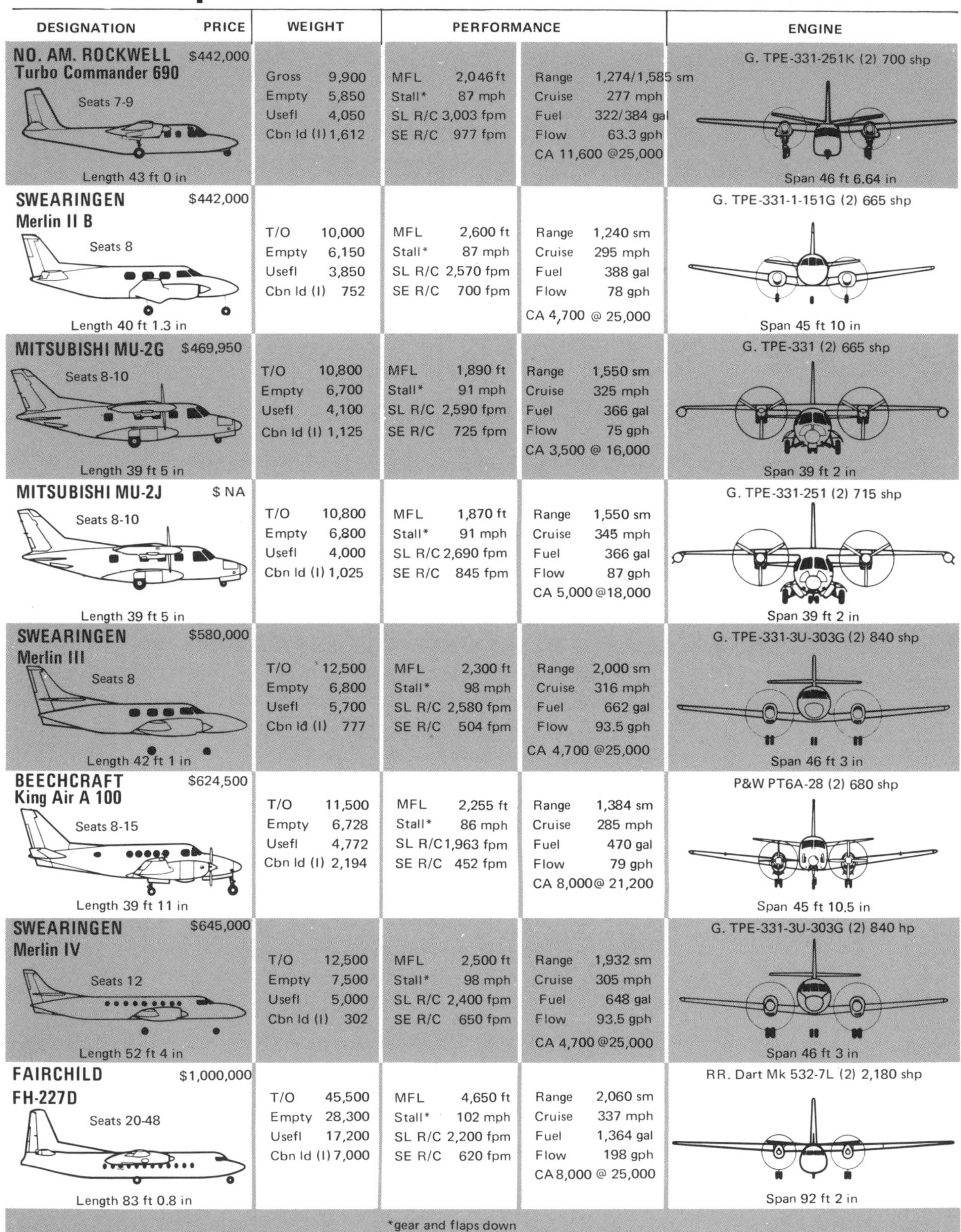

DESIGNATION	PRICE	WEIGHT	PERFORMANCE		ENGINE
NO. AM. ROCKWELL Turbo Commander 690 Seats 7-9 Length 43 ft 0 in	$442,000	Gross 9,900 Empty 5,850 Usefl 4,050 Cbn ld (I) 1,612	MFL 2,046 ft Stall* 87 mph SL R/C 3,003 fpm SE R/C 977 fpm	Range 1,274/1,585 sm Cruise 277 mph Fuel 322/384 gal Flow 63.3 gph CA 11,600 @25,000	G. TPE-331-251K (2) 700 shp Span 46 ft 6.64 in
SWEARINGEN Merlin II B Seats 8 Length 40 ft 1.3 in	$442,000	T/O 10,000 Empty 6,150 Usefl 3,850 Cbn ld (I) 752	MFL 2,600 ft Stall* 87 mph SL R/C 2,570 fpm SE R/C 700 fpm	Range 1,240 sm Cruise 295 mph Fuel 388 gal Flow 78 gph CA 4,700 @ 25,000	G. TPE-331-1-151G (2) 665 shp Span 45 ft 10 in
MITSUBISHI MU-2G Seats 8-10 Length 39 ft 5 in	$469,950	T/O 10,800 Empty 6,700 Usefl 4,100 Cbn ld (I) 1,125	MFL 1,890 ft Stall* 91 mph SL R/C 2,590 fpm SE R/C 725 fpm	Range 1,550 sm Cruise 325 mph Fuel 366 gal Flow 75 gph CA 3,500 @ 16,000	G. TPE-331 (2) 665 shp Span 39 ft 2 in
MITSUBISHI MU-2J Seats 8-10 Length 39 ft 5 in	$ NA	T/O 10,800 Empty 6,800 Usefl 4,000 Cbn ld (I) 1,025	MFL 1,870 ft Stall* 91 mph SL R/C 2,690 fpm SE R/C 845 fpm	Range 1,550 sm Cruise 345 mph Fuel 366 gal Flow 87 gph CA 5,000 @18,000	G. TPE-331-251 (2) 715 shp Span 39 ft 2 in
SWEARINGEN Merlin III Seats 8 Length 42 ft 1 in	$580,000	T/O 12,500 Empty 6,800 Usefl 5,700 Cbn ld (I) 777	MFL 2,300 ft Stall* 98 mph SL R/C 2,580 fpm SE R/C 504 fpm	Range 2,000 sm Cruise 316 mph Fuel 662 gal Flow 93.5 gph CA 4,700 @25,000	G. TPE-331-3U-303G (2) 840 shp Span 46 ft 3 in
BEECHCRAFT King Air A 100 Seats 8-15 Length 39 ft 11 in	$624,500	T/O 11,500 Empty 6,728 Usefl 4,772 Cbn ld (I) 2,194	MFL 2,255 ft Stall* 86 mph SL R/C 1,963 fpm SE R/C 452 fpm	Range 1,384 sm Cruise 285 mph Fuel 470 gal Flow 79 gph CA 8,000 @ 21,200	P&W PT6A-28 (2) 680 shp Span 45 ft 10.5 in
SWEARINGEN Merlin IV Seats 12 Length 52 ft 4 in	$645,000	T/O 12,500 Empty 7,500 Usefl 5,000 Cbn ld (I) 302	MFL 2,500 ft Stall* 98 mph SL R/C 2,400 fpm SE R/C 650 fpm	Range 1,932 sm Cruise 305 mph Fuel 648 gal Flow 93.5 gph CA 4,700 @25,000	G. TPE-331-3U-303G (2) 840 hp Span 46 ft 3 in
FAIRCHILD FH-227D Seats 20-48 Length 83 ft 0.8 in	$1,000,000	T/O 45,500 Empty 28,300 Usefl 17,200 Cbn ld (I) 7,000	MFL 4,650 ft Stall* 102 mph SL R/C 2,200 fpm SE R/C 620 fpm	Range 2,060 sm Cruise 337 mph Fuel 1,364 gal Flow 198 gph CA 8,000 @ 25,000	RR. Dart Mk 532-7L (2) 2,180 shp Span 92 ft 2 in

*gear and flaps down

Turbojet

DESIGNATION	WEIGHT	PERFORMANCE		ENGINE
CESSNA Citation $695,000 incl equpmt & crew tng Seats 7-8 Length 43 ft 6 in	T/O 10,850 Empty 6,350 Usefl 4,650 Cbn ld (I) 1,201	BFL (1) 3,100 ft BFL (2) 2,500 ft Stall* 97 mph SL R/C NA fpm SE R/C 820 fpm	Range 1,322 sm Cruise 400 mph Fuel 536 gal Flow 145 gph	UAC JT15D-1 (2) 2,200 lbs Span 43 ft 9 in
GATES LEARJET 24 D $839,000 Seats 8 Length 43 ft 3 in	T/O 13,500 Empty 6,875 Usefl 6,625 Cbn ld (I) 997	BFL (1) 3,917 ft BFL (2) NA ft Stall* 114 mph SL R/C 6,800 fpm SE R/C 2,100 fpm	Range 1,780 sm Cruise 507 mph Fuel 840 gal Flow 192 gph	GE CJ610-6 (2) 2,950 lbs Span 35 ft 7 in
GATES LEARJET 25 B $959,000 fully equipped Seats 10 Length 47 ft 7 in	T/O 15,000 Empty 7,277 Usefl 7,723 Cbn ld (I) 1,625	BFL (1) 5,186 ft BFL (2) NA ft Stall* 124 mph SL R/C 6,050 fpm SE R/C 1,750 fpm	Range 1,863 sm Cruise 507 mph Fuel 910 gal Flow 220 gph	GE CJ610-6 (2) 2,950 lbs Span 35 ft 7 in
NO. AM. ROCKWELL Sabre Commander $995,000 Seats 9 Length 43 ft 9 in	T/O 18,650 Empty 10,050 Usefl 8,600 Cbn ld (I) 1,650	BFL (1) 4,500 ft BFL (2) 3,150 ft Stall* 92 mph SL R/C 4,600 fpm SE R/C 1,200 fpm	Range 1,780 sm Cruise 563 mph Fuel 1,063 gal Flow 228.3 gph	P&W JT12-A-8 (2) 3,300 lbs Span 44 ft 5 in
COMMODORE JET Eleven 23 $995,000 Seats 12 Length 52 ft 3 in	T/O 20,500 Empty 11,300 Usefl 9,200 Cbn ld (I) 289	BFL (1) 5,450 ft BFL (2) 3,000 ft Stall* 120 mph SL R/C 4,100 fpm SE R/C 1,135 fpm	Range 1,900 sm Cruise 497 mph Fuel 1,330 gal Flow 179 gph	GE CJ-610-9 (2) 3,100 lbs Span 44 ft 9½ in
AEROSPATIALE SN-600 Corvette $ NA Seats 6-13 Length 44ft 8 in	T/O 13,450 Empty 7,700 Usefl 5,750 Cbn ld (I) 2,320	BFL (1) 4,070 ft BFL (2) 3,100 ft Stall* 93 mph SL R/C 3,400 fpm SE R/C NA fpm	Range 1,150 sm Cruise 480 mph Fuel 570 gal Flow 105 gph	P&W JT15D-4 (2) 2,300 lbs Span 42 ft 0 in
GATES LEARJET 25 C $1,005,000 equipped Seats 6 Length 47 ft 7 in	T/O 15,000 Empty 7,167 Usefl 7,833 Cbn ld (I) 339	BFL (1) 5,186 ft BFL (2) NA ft Stall* 124 mph SL R/C 6,050 fpm SE R/C 1,750 fpm	Range 2,139 sm Cruise 507 mph Fuel 1,103 gal Flow 220 gph	GE CJ610-6 (2) 2,950 lbs Span 35 ft 7 in
DASSAULT/PAN AM Falcon 10 $1,150,000 Seats 4-7 Length 45 ft 0 in	T/O 18,300 Empty 10,175 Usefl 8,125 Cbn ld (I) 2,726	BFL (1) 5,050 ft BFL (2) 3,000 ft Stall* 90 mph SL R/C 6,000 fpm SE R/C NA fpm	Range 2,400 sm Cruise 570 mph Fuel 890 gal Flow NA gph	G. TFE 731 (2) 3,250 lbs Span 43 ft 0 in

*gear and flaps down

Turbojet

DESIGNATION		WEIGHT	PERFORMANCE		ENGINE
HANSA JET 9 Seats 7-8 Length 54ft 6 in	$1,150,000	T/O 20,280 Empty 11,875 Usefl 8,405 Cbn ld (I) 1,325	BFL (1) 4,800 ft BFL (2) NA ft Stall* 108 mph SL R/C 4,000 fpm SE R/C 1,100 fpm	Range 1,390 sm Cruise 530 mph Fuel 1,090 gal Flow 340 gph	GE CJ-610-9 (2) 3,100 lbs Span 47 ft 6½ in
BEECHCRAFT-HAWKER BH 125-400 Seats 6-11 Length 47 ft 5 in	$1,245,000	T/O 23,300 EMPTY 11,905 Usefl 11,395 Cbn ld (I) 1,930	BFL (1) 5,450 ft BFL (2) 3,350 ft Stall* 88 mph SL R/C 4,800 fpm SE R/C 1,330 fpm	Range 1,770 sm Cruise 508 mph Fuel 1,365 gal Flow 254 gph	BS Viper 522 (2) 3,360 lbs Span 47 ft 0 in
DASSAULT/PAN AM Falcon D Seats 12 Length 56 ft 3 in	$1,440,000	T/O 27,337 Empty 16,400 Usefl 10,937 Cbn ld (I) 2,800	BFL (1) 6,000 ft BFL (2) 4,150 ft Stall* 110 mph SL R/C3,500 fpm SE R/C1,500 fpm	Range 1,900 sm Cruise 535 mph Fuel 1,340 gal Flow 285 gph	GE CF 700-2D (2) 4,250 lbs Span 53 ft 6 in
NO. AM. ROCKWELL Sabre 75 Seats 12 Length 47 ft 0 in	$1,600,000	T/O 20,603 Empty 11,600 Usefl 9,600 Cbn ld (I) 2,256	BFL (1) NA ft BFL (2) 3,850 ft Stall* 99 mph SL R/C 3,950 fpm SE R/C 980 fpm	Range 1,740 sm Cruise 563 mph Fuel 1,100 gal Flow 257.5 gph	P&W JT12-A-8 3,300 lbs Span 44 ft 4 in
DASSAULT/PAN AM Falcon F Seats 12 Length 56 ft 3 in	$1,650,000	T/O 28,660 Empty 17,100 Usefl 11,560 Cbn ld (I) 1,700	BFL (1) 5,120 ft BFL (2) 3,500 ft Stall* 105 mph SL R/C3,500 fpm SE R/C1,500 fpm	Range 2,042 sm Cruise 535 mph Fuel 1,380 gal Flow 285 gph	GE CF 700-2D2 (2) 4,315 lbs Span 53 ft 6 in
LOCKHEED Dash-8 Jetstar Seats 12 Length 60 ft 4 in	$1,750,000	T/O 42,000 Empty 21,337 Usefl 21,163 Cbn ld (I) 3,617	BFL (1) 6,000 ft BFL (2) 3,700 ft Stall* 123 mph SL R/C 5,200 fpm SE R/C 2,800 fpm	Range 2,283 sm Cruise 507 mph Fuel 2,660 gal Flow 522 gph	P&W JT12A-8 (4) 3,300 lbs Span 54 ft 4 in
DASSAULT/PAN AM Falcon D Cargo Payload 6,650 lbs Length 56 ft 3 in	$1,900,000	T/O 28,660 Empty 15,350 Usefl 13,310 Cbn ld NA	BFL (1) 6,000 ft BFL (2) 4,150 ft Stall* 110 mph SL R/C3,500 fpm SE R/C1,500 fpm	Range 1,640 sm Cruise 525 mph Fuel 1,340 gal Flow 285 gph	GE CF-700-2D (2) 4,250 lbs Span 53 ft 6 in
GRUMMAN Gulfstream II, 1159 Seats 12-19 Length 59 ft 11 in	$3,100,000	T/O 62,000 Empty 35,600 Usefl 26,400 Cbn ld (I) 4,072	BFL (1) 5,000 ft BFL (2) 3,000 ft Stall* 133 mph SL R/C4,350 fpm SE R/C1,525 fpm	Range 3,750 sm Cruise 530 mph Fuel 3,883 gal Flow 533 gph	RR Spey Mk 511-8 (2) 11,400 lbs Span 68 ft 10 in

*gear & flaps down

Turbojet

DESIGNATION		WEIGHT	PERFORMANCE		ENGINE
McDONNELL DOUGLAS DC-9-10 Seats 20-90 Length 104 ft 4 in	$3,200,000	T/O 90,700 Empty 51,390 Usefl 39,310 Cbn ld (I) 18,300	BFL (1) 7,000 ft BFL (2) 3,775 ft Stall* 102 mph SL R/C 3,690 fpm SE R/C 890 fpm	Range 3,615 sm Cruise 531 mph Fuel 6,111.5 gal Flow 723.3 gph	P & W JT8D-7 (2) 14,000 lbs Span 89 ft 4 in
FOKKER F 28 Seats 20-65 Length 80 ft 6.5 in	$3,450,000	T/O 65,000 Empty 36,500 Usefl 28,500 Cbn ld (I) 3,419	BFL (1) 5,500 ft BFL (2) 4,000 ft Stall* 105 mph SL R/C 3,450 fpm	Range 2,530 sm Cruise 479 mph Fuel 3445 gal Flow 750 gph	RR. Spey Mk 555 (2) 9850 lbs Span 89 ft 10.7 in
BOEING 737 Business Jet Seats 20-130 Length 100 ft 0 in	$5,000,000	T/O 114,500 Empty 62,500 Usefl 52,000 Cbn ld (I)20,175	BFL (1) 7,950 ft BFL (2) NA ft Stall* 94 mph SL R/C 3,765 fpm SE R/C 775 fpm	Range 4,850 sm Cruise 575 mph Fuel 4,783 gal Flow 650 gph	P&W JT8D-9/15 (2) 14,500 lbs Span 93 ft 0 in
McDONNELL DOUGLAS DC-9-20 Seats 20-90 Length 104 ft 4 in	$5,100,000	T/O 100,000 Empty 55,042 Usefl 44,958 Cbn ld (I) 20,609	BFL (1) 5,750 ft BFL (2) 3,075 ft Stall* 93 mph SL R/C 3,350 fpm SE R/C 730 fpm	Range 4,070 sm Cruise 531 mph Fuel 6,743.5 gal Flow 735 gph	P & W JT8D-9 (2) 14,500 lbs Span 93 ft 4 in
McDONNELL-DOUGLAS DC-9-30 Seats 25-115 Length 104 ft 4 in	$5,300,000	T/O 108,000 Empty 59,247 Usefl 48,753 Cbn ld (I) 23,600	BFL (1) 6,940 ft BFL (2) 3,475 ft Stall* 97 mph SL R/C 2,960 fpm SE R/C 670 fpm	Range 3,640 sm Cruise 531 mph Fuel 6,621 gal Flow 785 gph	P & W JT8D-9 (2) 14,500 lbs Span 93 ft 4 in
BOEING 727 Business Jet Seats 20-130 Length 133 ft 2 in	$6,500,000	T/O 170,000 Empty 92,000 Usefl 78,000 Cbn ld (I)46,175	BFL (1) 7,800 ft BFL (2) 2,750 ft Stall* 91 mph SL R/C 3,950 fpm SE R/C 2,270 fpm	Range 5,050 sm Cruise 619 mph Fuel 10,900 gal Flow 1,050 gal	P&W JT8D-9/15 (3) 14,500 lbs Span 108 ft 0 in

Commuter Airliners

DESIGNATION	PRICE	WEIGHT	PERFORMANCE		ENGINE
BRITTEN-NORMAN Islander BN-2A 8 Pass Length 35 ft 8 in	$89,970	Gross 6,200† Empty 3,560 Usefl 2,640 Cbn ld (I) 1,243 † 6,300 outside U.S.	MFL 1,090 ft Stall* 48 mph SL R/C 1,050 fpm SE R/C 190 fpm	Range 1,061 sm Cruise 160 mph Fuel 192 gal Flow 26 gph	L. O-540-E4C5 (2) 260 hp Span 53 ft 0 in

*gear & flaps down

Commuter Airliners

DESIGNATION		WEIGHT		PERFORMANCE				ENGINE
BRITTEN-NORMAN Turbo Islander 8 Pass, Length 35 ft 8 in	$99,970	Gross 6,300 Empty 3,620 Usefl 2,680 Cbn ld (l) 1,283		MFL 1,090 ft Stall* 48 mph SL R/C 1,370 fpm SE R/C 250 fpm		Range 1,221 sm Cruise 186 mph Fuel 192 gal Flow 26 gph		L. TIO-540-H (2) 270 hp, Span 53 ft 0 in
BRITTEN-NORMAN Islander-300 8 Pass, Length 35 ft 8 in	$100,688	Gross 6,300 Empty 3,620 Usefl 2,680 Cbn ld (l) 1,283		MFL 990 ft Stall* 49 mph SL R/C 1,370 fpm SE R/C 250 fpm		Range 1,221 sm Cruise 180 mph Fuel 192 gal Flow 26 gph		L. IO-540-K (2) 300 hp, Span 53 ft 0 in
CESSNA 402 B 8 Pass, Length 36 ft 0.9 in	$117,425	Gross 6,300 Empty 3,719 Usefl 2,581 Cbn ld (l) 1,393		MFL 2,220 ft Stall* 79 mph SL R/C 1,610 fpm SE R/C 255 fpm		Range 809 sm Cruise 240 mph Fuel 140 gal Flow 34 gph		C. TSIO-520-E (2) 300 hp, Span 39 ft 10.3 in
BRITTEN-NORMAN Trislander Mark III 16 Pass, Length 43 ft 9 in	$250,000*	Gross 9,350 Empty 5,638 Usefl 3,712 Cbn ld (l) 2,028		MFL 1,800 ft Stall* 49 mph SL R/C 1,120 fpm SE R/C 400 fpm		Range 772 sm Cruise 180 mph Fuel 192 gal Flow 39 gph		L. O-540 (3) 260 hp, Span 53 ft 0 in
VOLPAR Turboliner II 17 Pass, Length 44 ft 25 in	$325,000	Gross 11,500 Empty 6,500 Usefl 5,000 Cbn ld (l) 1,796		MFL 2,800 ft Stall* 92 mph SL R/C 1,500 fpm SE R/C 225 fpm		Range 825/1,960 sm Cruise 253 mph Fuel 300/630 gal Flow 75 gph		G TPE 331-101B (2) 665 shp, Span 46 ft 0 in
BEECHCRAFT 99 Airliner 15 Pass, Length 44 ft 6.81 in	$405,000	Gross 10,400 Empty 5,800 Usefl 4,600 Cbn (l) 2,081		BFL 3,900 ft Stall* 73 mph SL R/C 1,700 fpm SE R/C 335 fpm		Range 1,135 sm Cruise 254 mph Fuel 376 gal Flow 72 gph		P & W PT6-20 (2) 550 shp, Span 45 ft 10.5 in
BEECHCRAFT 99A Airliner 15 Pass, Length 44 ft 6.81 in	$430,000	Gross 10,900 Empty 6,000 Usefl 4,900 Cbn ld (l) 3,198		BFL 3,600 ft Stall* 73 mph SL R/C 2,090 fpm SE R/C 505 fpm		Range 590 sm Cruise 285 mph Fuel 376 gal Flow 90 gph		P&W PT6A-27 (2) 680 shp, Span 45 ft 10.5 in
SWEARINGEN Metro (pressurized) 19-22 Pass, Length 52 ft 4 in	$540,000	T/O 12,500 Empty 7,646 Usefl 4,854 Cbn ld (l) 419		MFL 3,880 ft Stall* 98 mph SL R/C 2,400 fpm SE R/C 650 fpm		Range 1,931 sm Cruise 305 mph Fuel 648 gal Flow 93.5 gph CA 4,000 @24,000		G. TPE-331-311-303G (2) 940 shp, Span 46 ft 3 in

*gear and flaps down

Conversions

DESIGNATION	WEIGHT	PERFORMANCE		ENGINE
AVCON 150 & Aerobat (Cessna) $12,895 Kit $4,000 Seats 2 Length 23 ft 10 in	Gross 1,600 Empty 1,005 Usefl 595 Cbn ld (V) 419	MFL 350 ft Stall 47 mph SL R/C 1,100 fpm	Range 255 sm Cruise 145 mph Fuel 22.5 gal Flow 9 gph	L. O-320 150 hp Span 33 ft 2 in
AVCON 172 (Cessna 172) $18,425 Kit $5,000 Seats 4 Length 27 ft 0 in	Gross 2,300 Empty 1,289 Usefl 1,011 Cbn ld (V) 738	MFL 500 ft Stall 48 mph SL R/C 1,100 fpm	Range 445 sm Cruise 155 mph Fuel 38 gal Flow 10.5 gph	L. O-360 180 hp Span 35 ft 10 in
AVCON Cherokee 140/180 (Piper Cherokee 140) Kit $3,877 Seats 4	Gross 2,200 Empty 1,367 Usefl 833 Cbn ld (V) 657	MFL 550 ft Stall NA mph SL R/C 950 fpm	Range 630 sm Cruise 150 mph Fuel 50 gal Flow 10 gph	L. O-360 180 hp
SEGUIN-Geronimo (Apache) $35,000 Seats 5-6 Length 29 ft 11 in	Gross 4,000 Empty 2,450 Usefl 1,550 Cbn ld (I) 852	MFL 800 ft Stall* 56 mph SL R/C 1,900 fpm SE R/C 600 fpm	Range 1,000/1,650 sm Cruise 200 mph Fuel 108/156 gal Flow 21 gph	L. O-360-A1D 180 hp Span 35 ft 3 in
MILLER JET PROFILE Custom Apache $38,608 Seats 5	Gross 4,000 Empty 2,400 Usefl 1,600 Cbn ld (I) 434	MFL 1,100 ft Stall* 57 mph SL R/C 2,000 fpm SE R/C 500 fpm	Range 1,450 sm Cruise 200 mph Fuel 153 gal Flow 19.5 gph	L. IO-360-C1C (2) 200 hp
MILLER JET PROFILE Twin Comanche 200 $44,995 Kit $23,385 Seats 6	Gross 3,780 Empty 2,366 Usefl 1,414 Cbn ld (I) 296	MFL 1,875 ft Stall* 69 mph SL R/C 1,900 fpm SE R/C 500 fpm	Range 1,278 sm Cruise 220 mph Fuel 128 gal Flow 19.5 gph	L. IO-360-C1C (2) 200 hp
COLEMILL Super 300 (Aero Commander 500A) $14,950* Seats 7 *exchange	Gross 6,530 Empty 4,200 Usefl 2,130 Cbn ld (I) 849	MFL 2,195 ft Stall* 70.3 mph SL R/C1,265 fpm SE R/C 290 fpm	Range 1,022 sm Cruise 208 mph* Fuel 156 gal Flow 28 gph *at 65%	C. 10-520-E (2) 300hp
MILLER JET PROFILE Turbo Twin Com 200 $53,145 Kit $31,635 Seats 6	Gross 3,780 Empty 2,406 Usefl 1,374 Cbn ld (I) 256	MFL 1,875 ft Stall* 69 mph SL R/C 1,900 fpm SE R/C 500 fpm	Range 1,220/1,475 sm Cruise 260 mph * Fuel 128/158 gal Flow 23 gph *at 20,000 ft	L. IO-360-C1C (2) (Rajay Turbo) 200 hp

*gear and flaps down

Conversions

DESIGNATION	PRICE	WEIGHT	PERFORMANCE		ENGINE
McKINNON G-44 Super Widgeon Seats 5-6	$65,000	Gross 5,000 Empty 4,000 Usefl 1,000 Cbn ld (l) 272	MFL 1,200 ft Stall* 62.9 mph SL R/C 1,500 fpm SE R/C NA fpm	Range 530/860 sm Cruise 165 mph Fuel 108/180 gal Flow 28 gph	
EXCALIBUR 800 (Twin Bonanza) Seats 6	$80,000 (Mod. $45,100)	Gross 7,600 Empty 5,100 Usefl 2,500 Cbn ld (l) 1,072	MFL 2,175 ft Stall* 84 mph SL R/C 1,680 fpm SE R/C NA fpm	Range 1,150 sm Cruise 245 mph Fuel 230 gal Flow 37 gph	L. IO-720 (2) 400 hp
COLEMILL Pres. 600 (Beech Baron 55, A, B) Seats 6	$14,950 exchange	Gross 5,100 Empty 3,200 Usefl 1,900 Cbn ld (l) 903	MFL NA ft Stall* 76 mph SL R/C NA fpm SE R/C 450 fpm	Range 1,068 sm Cruise 234 mph* Fuel 142 gph Flow 28 gph *at 65%	C. IO-520 (2) 300 hp
COLEMILL Exec. 300 (Cessna 310G-P) Seats 6	$14,950 exchange	Gross 5,200 Empty 3,125 Usefl 2,075 Cbn ld (l) 1,055	MFL NA ft Stall* 74 mph SL R/C NA fpm SE R/C 420 fpm	Range 1,040 sm Cruise 230 mph* Fuel 140 gal Flow 28 gph *at 65%	C. IO-520 (2) 300 hp
EXCALIBUR (Twin Bonanza) Seats 6	$88,000 (Mod. $52,900)	Gross 7,300 Empty 5,100 Usefl 2,200 Cbn ld (l) 772	MFL 2,600 ft Stall* 82 mph SL R/C 1,900 fpm SE R/C 400 fpm	Range 1,320 sm Cruise 260 mph Fuel 230 gal Flow 55 gph	L. IGSO-540 (2) 340 hp
RILEY Turbo Stream Seats 6	$96,950	Gross 5,400 Empty 3,600 Usefl 1,800 Cbn ld (l) 780	MFL 1,790 ft Stall* 78 mph SL R/C 2,200 fpm SE R/C 520 fpm	Range 1,060 sm Cruise 315 mph Fuel 140 gal Flow 34 gph	L. TIO-540-A2B (2) 310 hp
EXCALIBUR Queenaire 800 (Queen Air) Seats 8-10	$100,000 (Mod. $41,640)	Gross 7,900 Empty 5,300 Usefl 2,600 Cbn ld (l) 1,172	MFL 2,175 ft Stall* 79 mph SL R/C 1,375 fpm SE R/C NA fpm	Range 1,290 sm Cruise 231 mph Fuel 230 gal Flow 37 gph	L. IO-720 (2) 400 hp
VOLPAR Turbo 18 (Beech 18) Seats 7-11	$178,000 Kit $125,000	Gross 10,286 Empty 6,200 Usefl 4,086 Cbn ld (l) 2,077	MFL 2,200 ft Stall* 88 mph SL R/C 1,720 fpm SE R/C 420 fpm	Range 860/2,060 sm Cruise 266 mph Fuel 300/630 gal Flow 74 gph	G. TPE 331-47 605 eshp

*gear and flaps down

Conversions

DESIGNATION	PRICE	WEIGHT	PERFORMANCE		ENGINE
TURBO-THREE (DC-3) Seats 34	$295,000	Gross 31,900 Empty 18,400 Usefl 13,500 Cbn Id (I) 4,248	MFL 2,500 ft Stall* 65 mph SL R/C 1,200 fpm SE R/C 420 fpm	Range 1,500 sm Cruise 225 mph Fuel 1,542 gal Flow 207 gph	RR Dart (2) 1,740 tehp
McKINNON G-21E Turbinc Goose Seats 13	$464,000	Gross 10,500 Empty 6,635 Usefl 3,865 Cbn Id (I) 2,268	MFL 1,500 ft Stall* 79 mph SL R/C 2,000 fpm SE R/C NA fpm	Range 1,600 sm Cruise 240 mph Fuel 586 gal Flow 90 gph	P&W PT6-27 (2) 715 eshp
McKINNON G-21G Turbine Goose Seats 13	$484,000	Gross 12,500 Empty 6,635 Usefl 5,865 Cbn Id (I) 4,268	MFL 1,500 ft Stall* 84 mph SL R/C 2,000 fpm SE R/C NA fpm	Range 1,600 sm Cruise 240 mph Fuel 586 gal Flow 90 gph	P&W PT6-27 (2) 715 eshp

STOL

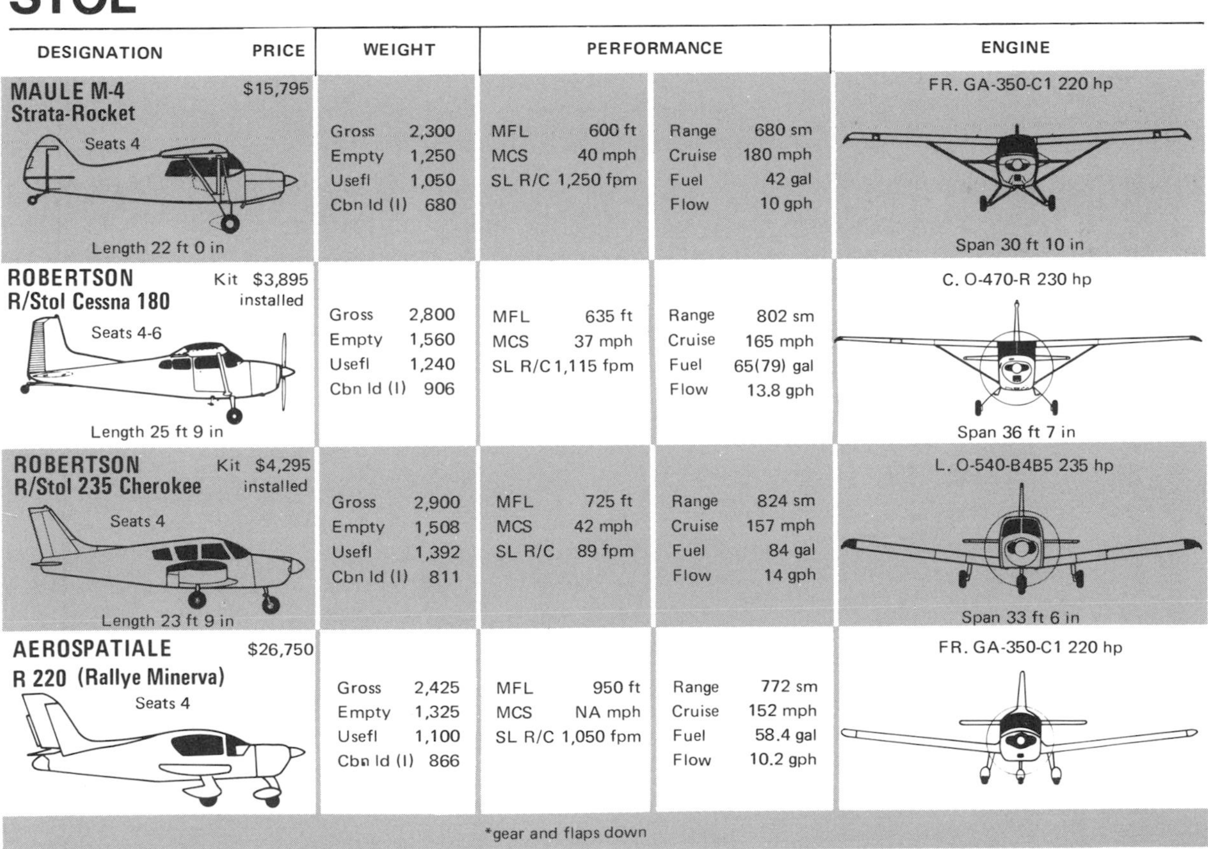

DESIGNATION	PRICE	WEIGHT	PERFORMANCE		ENGINE
MAULE M-4 Strata-Rocket Seats 4 Length 22 ft 0 in	$15,795	Gross 2,300 Empty 1,250 Usefl 1,050 Cbn Id (I) 680	MFL 600 ft MCS 40 mph SL R/C 1,250 fpm	Range 680 sm Cruise 180 mph Fuel 42 gal Flow 10 gph	FR. GA-350-C1 220 hp Span 30 ft 10 in
ROBERTSON R/Stol Cessna 180 Seats 4-6 Length 25 ft 9 in	Kit $3,895 installed	Gross 2,800 Empty 1,560 Usefl 1,240 Cbn Id (I) 906	MFL 635 ft MCS 37 mph SL R/C 1,115 fpm	Range 802 sm Cruise 165 mph Fuel 65(79) gal Flow 13.8 gph	C. O-470-R 230 hp Span 36 ft 7 in
ROBERTSON R/Stol 235 Cherokee Seats 4 Length 23 ft 9 in	Kit $4,295 installed	Gross 2,900 Empty 1,508 Usefl 1,392 Cbn Id (I) 811	MFL 725 ft MCS 42 mph SL R/C 89 fpm	Range 824 sm Cruise 157 mph Fuel 84 gal Flow 14 gph	L. O-540-B4B5 235 hp Span 33 ft 6 in
AEROSPATIALE R 220 (Rallye Minerva) Seats 4	$26,750	Gross 2,425 Empty 1,325 Usefl 1,100 Cbn Id (I) 866	MFL 950 ft MCS NA mph SL R/C 1,050 fpm	Range 772 sm Cruise 152 mph Fuel 58.4 gal Flow 10.2 gph	FR. GA-350-C1 220 hp

*gear and flaps down

STOL

DESIGNATION	PRICE	WEIGHT	PERFORMANCE		ENGINE
ROBERTSON R/Stol Cherokee Six 300 Seats 6-7 Length 27 ft 8 in	Kit $4,295 installed	Gross 3,400 Empty 1,810 Usefl 1,590 Cbn ld (l) 1,009	MFL 835 ft MCS 43 mph SL R/C1,110 fpm	Range 756 sm Cruise 168 mph Fuel 84 gal Flow 16 gph	L. IO-540-K 300 hp Span 35 ft 1 in
HELIO H-250 Courier Seats 6 Length 31 ft 5 in	$38,400	Gross 3,400 Empty 1,960 Usefl 1,440 Cbn ld (l) 612	MFL 750 ft MCS 31 mph SL R/C 830 fpm	Range 1,186 sm Cruise 152 mph Fuel 120 gal Flow 14 gph	L. O-540-A1A5 250 hp Span 39 ft 0 in
ROBERTSON R/Stol Turbo Comanche Seats 4-6 Length 25 ft 4 in	Kit $4,295 installed	Gross 3,200 Empty 1,909 Usefl 1,291 Cbn ld (l) 629	MFL 860 ft MCS 45 mph SL R/C1,345 fpm	Range 1,181 sm Cruise 228 mph Fuel 86 gal Flow 14.5 gph	L. IO-540 Turbo 260 hp Span 36 ft 10 in
HELIO H-295 Super Courier Seats 6 Length 31 ft 5 in	$44,400	Gross 3,400 Empty 2,080 Usefl 1,320 Cbn ld (l) 858	MFL 610 ft MCS 30 mph SL R/C 1,150 fpm	Range 1,176 sm Cruise 165 mph Fuel 120 gal Flow 15.2 gph	L. GO-480-G1D6 295 hp Span 39 ft 0 in
ROBERTSON R/S Twin Comanche C/R Seats 4-6 Length 25 ft 2 in	Kit $4,995 installed	Gross 3,800 Empty 2,285 Usefl 1,515 Cbn ld (l) 820	MFL 985 ft MCS 75 mph SL R/C1,385 fpm SE R/C 310 fpm	Range 1,175 sm Cruise 198 mph Fuel 114 gal Flow 17.2 gph	L. IO-320 (2) 160 hp Span 36 ft 10.95 in
ROBERTSON R/Stol Super Skymaster Seats 4-6 Length 29 ft 9 in	Kit $6,500 installed	Gross 4,630 Empty 2,718 Usefl 1,912 Cbn ld (!) 1,112	MFL 731 ft MCS 45 mph SL R/C 1,210 fpm SE R/C 270 fpm	Range 940 sm Cruise 194 mph Fuel 128 gal Flow 22.9 gph	C. IO-360-C (2) 210 hp Span 39 ft 10 in
EVANGEL 4500-300 Seats 9 Length 31 ft 6 in	$70,500	Gross 5,500 Empty 3,460 Usefl 2,040 Cbn ld (l) 1,241	MFL 1,140 ft MCS 79 mph SL R/C1,500 fpm SE R/C 225 fpm	Range 540 sm Cruise 182 mph Fuel 110 gal Flow 32 gph	L. IO-540-K1B5 (2) 300 hp Span 41 ft 3 in
ROBERTSON R/S Turbo Aztec E Seats 6 Length 31 ft 2.6 in	Kit $5,995 installed	Gross 5,200 Empty 3,244 Usefl 1,956 Cbn ld (l) 966	MFL 975 ft Stall 59 mph SL R/C1,530 fpm SE R/C 305 fpm	Range 1,210 sm Cruise 233 mph Fuel 170 gal Flow 29 gph	L. TIO-540-C1A (2) 250 hp Span 38 ft 7.75 in

STOL

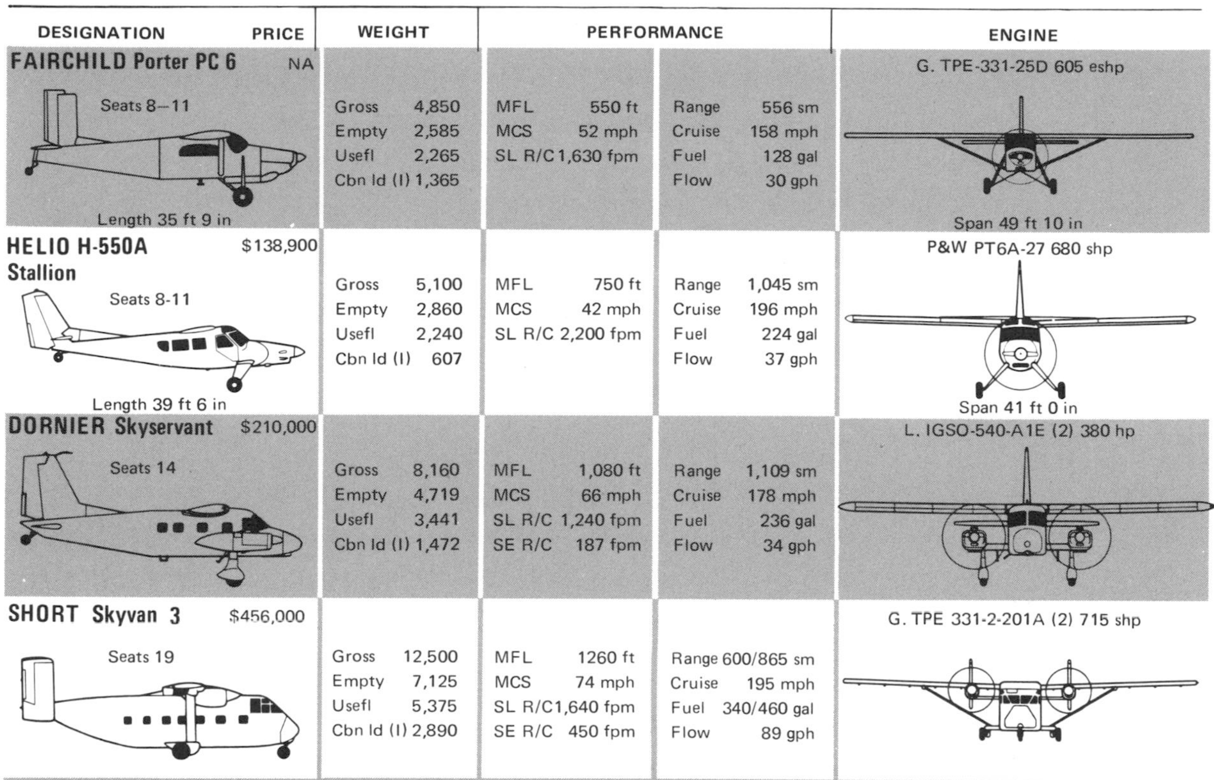

DESIGNATION	PRICE	WEIGHT	PERFORMANCE		ENGINE
FAIRCHILD Porter PC 6 Seats 8–11 Length 35 ft 9 in	NA	Gross 4,850 Empty 2,585 Usefl 2,265 Cbn ld (l) 1,365	MFL 550 ft MCS 52 mph SL R/C 1,630 fpm	Range 556 sm Cruise 158 mph Fuel 128 gal Flow 30 gph	G. TPE-331-25D 605 eshp Span 49 ft 10 in
HELIO H-550A Stallion Seats 8-11 Length 39 ft 6 in	$138,900	Gross 5,100 Empty 2,860 Usefl 2,240 Cbn ld (l) 607	MFL 750 ft MCS 42 mph SL R/C 2,200 fpm	Range 1,045 sm Cruise 196 mph Fuel 224 gal Flow 37 gph	P&W PT6A-27 680 shp Span 41 ft 0 in
DORNIER Skyservant Seats 14	$210,000	Gross 8,160 Empty 4,719 Usefl 3,441 Cbn ld (l) 1,472	MFL 1,080 ft MCS 66 mph SL R/C 1,240 fpm SE R/C 187 fpm	Range 1,109 sm Cruise 178 mph Fuel 236 gal Flow 34 gph	L. IGSO-540-A1E (2) 380 hp
SHORT Skyvan 3 Seats 19	$456,000	Gross 12,500 Empty 7,125 Usefl 5,375 Cbn ld (l) 2,890	MFL 1260 ft MCS 74 mph SL R/C 1,640 fpm SE R/C 450 fpm	Range 600/865 sm Cruise 195 mph Fuel 340/460 gal Flow 89 gph	G. TPE 331-2-201A (2) 715 shp

Rotary Wing

DESIGNATION	PRICE	WEIGHT	PERFORMANCE		ENGINE
BENSON B-8 Gyrocopter Seats 1	$1,195	Gross 500 Empty 247 Usefl 253	S/C 12,500 ft HIGE NA ft HOGE NA in SL R/C 1,000 fpm MFL 300 ft	Range 150 sm Cruise 60 mph	McC 4319G 90 hp
McCULLOCH J2 Gyroplane Seats 2 Length 16 ft 0 in	$19,950	Gross 1,550 Empty 1,000 Usefl 550 Cbn ld 395	S/C 11,000 ft SL R/C 700 fpm	Range 200 sm Cruise 100 mph Vne 110 mph Fuel 24 gal Flow 12 gph	L. O-360-A 180 hp Blade Diam 26 ft 0 in
ROTORWAY Scorpion Too Seats 2 Length 23 ft 3 in	$ NA (Kits for assembly)	Gross 1,135 Empty 690 Usefl 445 Sling 200	S/C 7,200 ft HIGE 5,500 ft HOGE 3,500 ft SL R/C 1,000 fpm	Range 140 sm Cruise 75 mph Vne 85 mph Fuel 10 gal Flow 6 gph	VULCAN V4 Blade Diam. 24 ft 0 in

Rotary Wing

DESIGNATION	PRICE	WEIGHT	PERFORMANCE		ENGINE
SCHEUTZOW B Seats 2 Length 24 ft 1 in	$ NA	Gross 1,685 Empty 1,135 Usefl 550 Cbn ld 858	S/C 14,000 ft HIGE 7,300 ft HOGE 4,500 ft SL R/C1,000 fpm	Range 175 sm Cruise 85 mph Vne 93 mph Fuel 22 gal	L. IVO-360 180 hp Blade Diam 27 ft 0 in
CONTINENTAL Mk V A El Tomcat Seats 1	$ 29,000	Gross 2,650 Empty 1,420 Usefl 1,230 Cbn ld 1,034 Sling 844	S/C NA ft HIGE NA ft HOGE NA ft SL R/C 850 fpm	Range 157 sm Cruise 75 mph Vne 100 mph Fuel 29 gal Flow 14.6 gph	L. VO-435-A1 220 hp
CONTINENTAL Mk VI Seats 1	$34,500	Gross 2,950 Empty 1,590 Usefl 1,360 Cbn ld 1,164 Sling 1,049	S/C 11,000 ft HIGE 6,300 ft HOGE 1,500 ft SL R/C 900 fpm	Range 168 sm Cruise 80 mph Vne 105 mph Fuel 29 gal Flow 13.8 gph	L. TVO-435-B1A 265 hp
HUGHES 300 Seats 3 Length 22 ft 10 in	$38,500	Gross 1,670 Empty 972 Usefl 698 Cbn ld 473	S/C 13,000 ft HIGE 7,700 ft HOGE 5,800 ft SL R/C 1,150 fpm	Range 220 sm Cruise 80 mph Vne 87 mph Fuel 30 gal Flow 12 gph	L. HIO-360-A1A 180 hp Blade Diam 25 ft 3.5 in
ENSTROM F-28A Seats 3 Length 27 ft 7 in	$39,750	Gross 2,150 Empty 1,450 Usefl 700 MEL 500	S/C 12,000 ft HIGE 5,600 ft HOGE 3,400 ft SL R/C 950 fpm	Range 237 sm Cruise 100 mph Vne 112 mph Fuel 30 gal Flow 13 gph	L. HIO-360-C1A 205 hp Blade Diam. 32 ft 0 in
HUGHES 300C Seats 3 Length 22 ft 2¼ in	$42,000	Gross 1,900 Empty 1,039 Usefl 861 Cbn ld 634	S/C 12,000 ft HIGE 6,900 ft HOGE 4,250 ft SL R/C 990 fpm	Range 233/380 sm Cruise 100 mph Vne 105 mph Fuel 30/49 gal Flow 13 gph	L. HIO-360-D1A (Derated) 190 hp Blade Diam 27 ft 0 in
BELL 47G-5 Seats 3 Length 31 ft 7 in	$49,500	Gross 2,850 Empty 1,712 Usefl 1,138 Cbn ld 744 Sling 1,000	S/C 10,500 ft HIGE 5,900 ft HOGE 1,350 ft SL R/C 860 fpm	Range 238 sm Cruise 81 mph Vne 105 mph Fuel 57 gal Flow 19 gph	L. VO-435-B1A 265 hp Blade Diam 37 ft 2 in
BELL 47G-4A Seats 3 Length 31 ft 7 in	$58,000	Gross 2,950 Empty 1,880 Usefl 1,070 Cbn ld 676 Sling 1,000	S/C 11,200 ft HIGE 7,700 ft HOGE 3,900 ft SL R/C 800 fpm	Range 244 sm Cruise 85 mph Vne 105 mph Fuel 57 gal Flow 19 gph	L. VO-540-B1B3 280 hp Blade Diam 37 ft 2 in

Rotary Wing

DESIGNATION	PRICE	WEIGHT	PERFORMANCE		ENGINE
BELL 47G-3B-2 Seats 3 Length 31 ft 7 in	$60,000	Gross 2,950 Empty 1,937 Usefl 1,013 Cbn ld 619 Sling 1,000	S/C 18,400 ft HIGE 16,600 ft HOGE 12,300 ft SL R/C 990 fpm	Range 239 sm Cruise 81 mph Vne 105 mph Fuel 57 gal Flow 20 gph	L. TVO-435-G1A 280 hp Blade Diam 37 ft 2 in
HUGHES 500 (w. 250 C20) Seats 5-7 Length 23 ft 0 in	$110,000	Gross 2,550 Empty 1,127 Usefl 1,423 MEL 1,800 Cbn ld 1,004	S/C 14,425 ft HIGE 13,200 ft HOGE 7,500 ft SL R/C 1,700 fpm	Range 376 sm Cruise 150 mph Vne 150 mph Fuel 64 gal Flow 25.5 gph	AL. 250-C20 (Derated) 278 hp Blade Diam 26 ft 4 in
HUGHES 500 (w. 250 CBA) Seats 5-7 Length 23 ft 0 in	$110,000	Gross 2,550 Empty 1,110 Usefl 1,440 MEL 1,800 Cbn ld 1,017	S/C 14,425 ft HIGE 8,200 ft HOGE 5,500 ft SL R/C 1,700 fpm	Range 376 sm Cruise 150 mph Vne 150 mph Fuel 64 gal Flow 25.5 gph	AL.250-CBA (Derated) 278 hp Blade Diam 26 ft 4 in
FAIRCHILD FH 1100 Seats 5 Length 28 ft 4.5 in	$112,500	Gross 2,750 Empty 1,415 Usefl 1,335 Cbn ld (I) 879	S/C 14,100 ft HIGE 13,000 ft HOGE 8400 ft SL R/C 1,600 fpm	Range 420 sm Cruise 133 mph Vne 127 mph Fuel 66.9 gal Flow NA	AL. 250-C18 317 shp Blade diam. 35 ft 3 in
BELL 206A Jet Ranger Length 28 ft 8.2 in	$112,500	Gross 3,000 Empty 1,480 Usefl 1,520 Cbn ld 1,022 Sling 1,200	S/C 17,000 ft HIGE 7,900 ft HOGE 3,500 ft SL R/C 1,430 fpm	Range 351 sm Cruise 131 mph Vne 150 mph Fuel 76 gal Flow 30 gph	AL. 250-C18 317 shp Blade Diam 33 ft 4 in
BELL 206 Jet Ranger II Seats 5 Length 28 ft 8.2 in	$125,000	Gross 3,000 Empty 1,475 Usefl 1,525 MEL 1,200 Cbn ld 1,017	S/C 20,000+ ft HIGE 13,200 ft HOGE 8,700 ft SL R/C 1,540 fpm	Range 360 sm Cruise 136 mph Vne 150 mph Fuel 76 gal Flow 35 gph	AL. 250-C20 400 shp Blade Diam 33 ft 4 in
VOUGHT SA 318C Alouette II Seats 5 Length 31 ft 6 in	$125,500	Gross 3,650 Empty 1,990 Usefl 1,660 Cbn ld 621 Sling 1,322	S/C 14,800 ft HIGE 13,600 ft HOGE 11,200 ft SL R/C 1,820 fpm	Range 444 sm Cruise 112 mph Vne 127 mph Fuel 149 gal Flow 37.4 gph	Turbomeca Astazou II A 523 shp Blade Diam 33 ft 6 in
VOUGHT SA 341 Gazelle Seats 5 Length 30 ft 1 in	$178,600	Gross 3,748 Empty 1,905 Usefl 1,843 MEL 1,322 Cbn ld 1,339	S/C 19,685 ft HIGE 19,685 ft HOGE 19,685 ft SL R/C 2,060 fpm	Range 376 sm Cruise 158 mph Vne 192 mph Fuel 120 gal Flow NA	Turbomeca Astazou IIIB 592 shp Blade Diam 34 ft 6 in

Rotary Wing

DESIGNATION	PRICE	WEIGHT	PERFORMANCE		ENGINE
VOUGHT SA 316B Alouette III Seats 7 Length 42 ft 1 in	$208,900	Gross 4,850 Empty 2,467 Usefl 2,383 MEL 2,000 Cbn ld 1,369	S/C 21,300 ft HIGE 18,900 ft HOGE 17,100 ft SL R/C 1,720 fpm	Range 292 sm Cruise 115 mph Vne 130 mph Fuel 146 gal Flow 57 gph	Turbomeca Arouste III B 858 shp Blade Diam 36 ft 2 in
BELL 205A-1 Seats 15 Length 44 ft 10 in	$425,000	Gross 9,500 Empty 5,197 Usefl 4,303 Cbn ld 2,802 Sling 5,000	S/C 14,700 ft HIGE 10,400 ft HOGE 6,000 ft SL R/C 1,680 fpm	Range 311 sm Cruise 127 mph Vne 127 mph Fuel 215 gal Flow 87 gph	L. T-5313A 1400 shp Blade Diam 48 ft 0 in
SIKORSKY S-58 T (Turbine Conversion) Seats 15 Length 46 ft 3 in	$485,000	Gross 13,000 Empty 7,400 Usefl 5,600 MEL 5,000 Cbn ld 4,254	S/C 12,000 ft HIGE 8,000 ft HOGE 7,700 ft SL R/C 1,320 fpm	Range 300 sm Cruise 118 mph Vne 126 mph Fuel 274 gal Flow 108 gph	P&W Twin Pac PT6T-3 1,800 shp Blade Diam 56 ft 0 in
BELL Twin Two-Twelve Seats 15 Length 45 ft 10.6 in	$575,000	Gross 10,000 Empty 5,800 Usefl 4,200 MEL 4,501 Cbn ld 2,693	S/C 17,300 ft HIGE 13,900 ft HOGE 9,300 ft SL R/C 1,745 fpm	Range 286 sm Cruise 127 mph Vne 127 mph Fuel 217 gal Flow 97 gph	P &W Twin Pac PT6T-3 1800 shp Blade Diam 48 ft 0 in
VOUGHT SA 330F Puma Seats 20 Length 48 ft 7 in	$950,000	Gross 14,110 Empty 7,720 Usefl 6,390 MEL 4,960 Cbn ld 3,587	S/C 19,685 ft HIGE 18,685 ft HOGE 15,500 ft SL R/C 2,210 fpm	Range 384 sm Cruise 171 mph Vne 192 mph Fuel 410 gal Flow 190 gph	Turbomeca Turma IV A (2) 1,415 hp Blade Diam 49 ft 3 in
SIKORSKY S-61L Mk II Airliner Seats 30 Length 58 ft 11 in	$1,225,000	Gross 19,000 Empty 11,792 Usefl 7,208 Cbn ld 4,401	S/C 12,500 ft HIGE 8,700 ft HOGE 3,800 ft SL R/C 1,300 fpm	Range 282 sm Cruise 138 mph Vne 146 mph Fuel 410 gal Flow 199 gph	GE CT58-140 (2) 1,500 shp Blade Diam 62 ft 0 in
SIKORSKY S 61N Mk II Amphibian Seats 26 Length 61 ft 5 in	$1,225,000	Gross 19,000 Empty 12,336 Usefl 6,664 Cbn ld 3,857	S/C 12,500 ft HIGE 8,700 ft HOGE 3,800 ft SL R/C 1,300 fpm	Range 282/495 sm Cruise 139 mph Vne 151 mph Fuel 410/654 gal Flow 200 gph	GE CT 58-140 (2) 1,500 shp Blade Diam 62 ft 0 in
SIKORSKY S-64E Seats 3 Length 88 ft 6 in	$2,146,750	Gross 42,000 Empty 19,234 Usefl 22,766 MEL 20,000 Cbn ld 9,852	S/C 9,000 ft HIGE 6,400 ft HOGE 2,400 ft SL R/C 1,330 fpm	Range 230 sm Cruise 109 mph Vne 132 mph Fuel 1,345 gal Flow 551 gph	P&W JFTD12A-4A (2) 4,500 shp Blade Diam 72 ft 0 in

Floatplanes

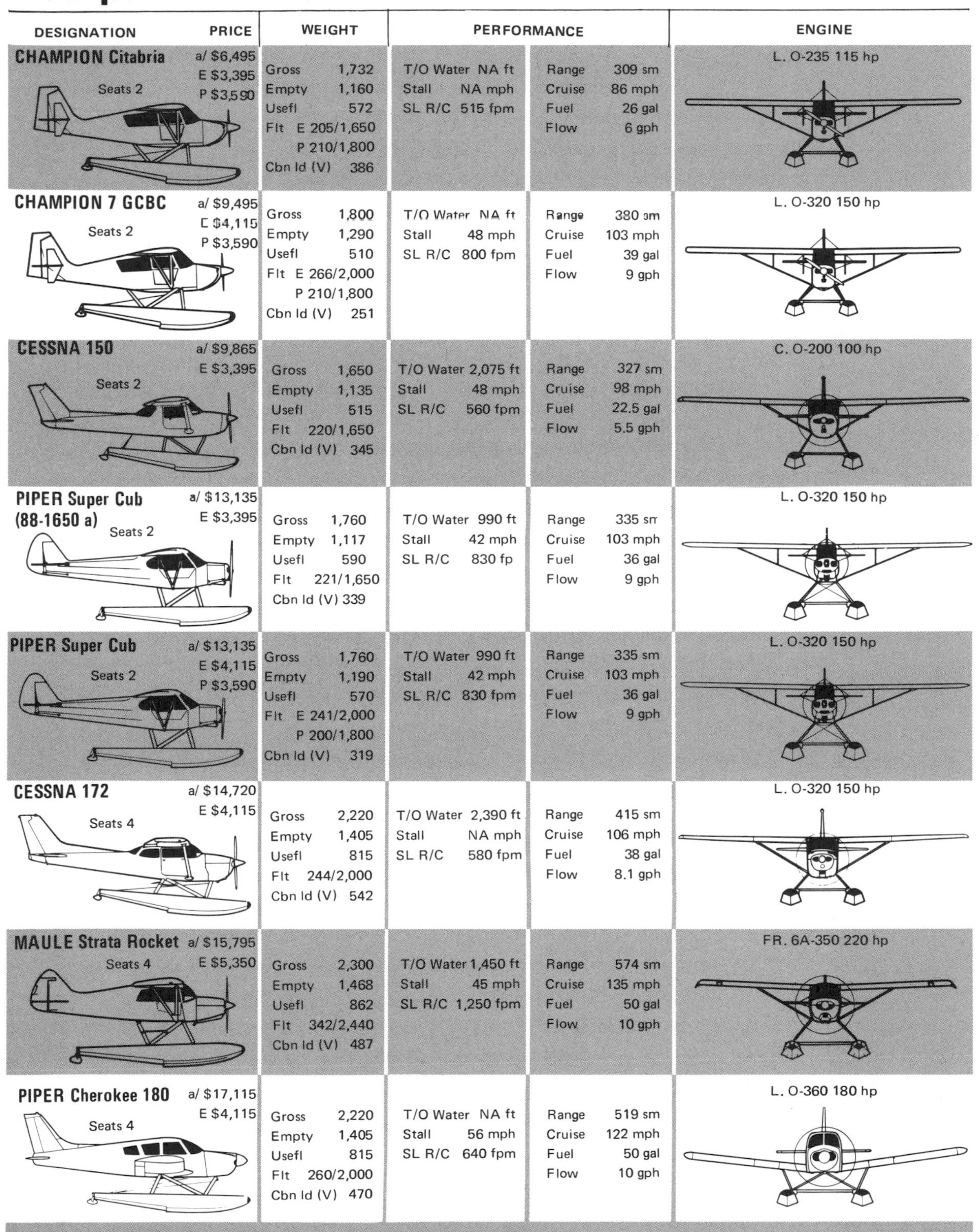

DESIGNATION	Seats	PRICE	WEIGHT: Gross	Empty	Usefl	Flt	Cbn ld (V)	PERFORMANCE: T/O Water	Stall	SL R/C	Range	Cruise	Fuel	Flow	ENGINE
CHAMPION Citabria	2	a/ $6,495 E $3,395 P $3,590	1,732	1,160	572	E 205/1,650 P 210/1,800	386	NA ft	NA mph	515 fpm	309 sm	86 mph	26 gal	6 gph	L. O-235 115 hp
CHAMPION 7 GCBC	2	a/ $9,495 E $4,115 P $3,590	1,800	1,290	510	E 266/2,000 P 210/1,800	251	NA ft	48 mph	800 fpm	380 sm	103 mph	39 gal	9 gph	L. O-320 150 hp
CESSNA 150	2	a/ $9,865 E $3,395	1,650	1,135	515	220/1,650	345	2,075 ft	48 mph	560 fpm	327 sm	98 mph	22.5 gal	5.5 gph	C. O-200 100 hp
PIPER Super Cub (88-1650 a)	2	a/ $13,135 E $3,395	1,760	1,117	590	221/1,650	339	990 ft	42 mph	830 fp	335 sm	103 mph	36 gal	9 gph	L. O-320 150 hp
PIPER Super Cub	2	a/ $13,135 E $4,115 P $3,590	1,760	1,190	570	E 241/2,000 P 200/1,800	319	990 ft	42 mph	830 fpm	335 sm	103 mph	36 gal	9 gph	L. O-320 150 hp
CESSNA 172	4	a/ $14,720 E $4,115	2,220	1,405	815	244/2,000	542	2,390 ft	NA mph	580 fpm	415 sm	106 mph	38 gal	8.1 gph	L. O-320 150 hp
MAULE Strata Rocket	4	a/ $15,795 E $5,350	2,300	1,468	862	342/2,440	487	1,450 ft	45 mph	1,250 fpm	574 sm	135 mph	50 gal	10 gph	FR. 6A-350 220 hp
PIPER Cherokee 180	4	a/ $17,115 E $4,115	2,220	1,405	815	260/2,000	470	NA ft	56 mph	640 fpm	519 sm	122 mph	50 gal	10 gph	L. O-360 180 hp

Floatplanes

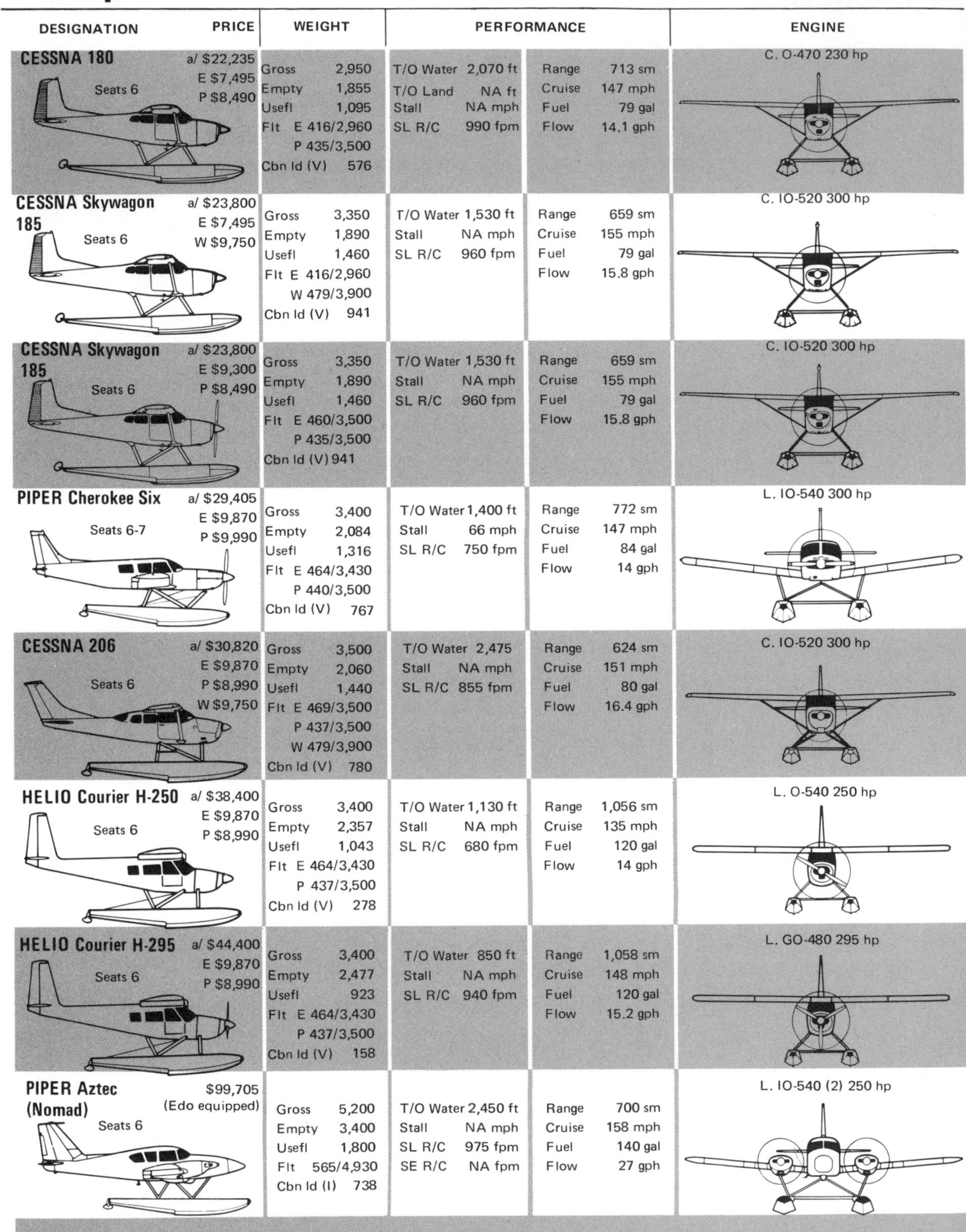

DESIGNATION	PRICE	WEIGHT	PERFORMANCE		ENGINE
CESSNA 180 Seats 6	a/ $22,235 E $7,495 P $8,490	Gross 2,950 Empty 1,855 Usefl 1,095 Flt E 416/2,960 P 435/3,500 Cbn Id (V) 576	T/O Water 2,070 ft T/O Land NA ft Stall NA mph SL R/C 990 fpm	Range 713 sm Cruise 147 mph Fuel 79 gal Flow 14.1 gph	C. O-470 230 hp
CESSNA Skywagon 185 Seats 6	a/ $23,800 E $7,495 W $9,750	Gross 3,350 Empty 1,890 Usefl 1,460 Flt E 416/2,960 W 479/3,900 Cbn Id (V) 941	T/O Water 1,530 ft Stall NA mph SL R/C 960 fpm	Range 659 sm Cruise 155 mph Fuel 79 gal Flow 15.8 gph	C. IO-520 300 hp
CESSNA Skywagon 185 Seats 6	a/ $23,800 E $9,300 P $8,490	Gross 3,350 Empty 1,890 Usefl 1,460 Flt E 460/3,500 P 435/3,500 Cbn Id (V) 941	T/O Water 1,530 ft Stall NA mph SL R/C 960 fpm	Range 659 sm Cruise 155 mph Fuel 79 gal Flow 15.8 gph	C. IO-520 300 hp
PIPER Cherokee Six Seats 6-7	a/ $29,405 E $9,870 P $9,990	Gross 3,400 Empty 2,084 Usefl 1,316 Flt E 464/3,430 P 440/3,500 Cbn Id (V) 767	T/O Water 1,400 ft Stall 66 mph SL R/C 750 fpm	Range 772 sm Cruise 147 mph Fuel 84 gal Flow 14 gph	L. IO-540 300 hp
CESSNA 206 Seats 6	a/ $30,820 E $9,870 P $8,990 W $9,750	Gross 3,500 Empty 2,060 Usefl 1,440 Flt E 469/3,500 P 437/3,500 W 479/3,900 Cbn Id (V) 780	T/O Water 2,475 Stall NA mph SL R/C 855 fpm	Range 624 sm Cruise 151 mph Fuel 80 gal Flow 16.4 gph	C. IO-520 300 hp
HELIO Courier H-250 Seats 6	a/ $38,400 E $9,870 P $8,990	Gross 3,400 Empty 2,357 Usefl 1,043 Flt E 464/3,430 P 437/3,500 Cbn Id (V) 278	T/O Water 1,130 ft Stall NA mph SL R/C 680 fpm	Range 1,056 sm Cruise 135 mph Fuel 120 gal Flow 14 gph	L. O-540 250 hp
HELIO Courier H-295 Seats 6	a/ $44,400 E $9,870 P $8,990	Gross 3,400 Empty 2,477 Usefl 923 Flt E 464/3,430 P 437/3,500 Cbn Id (V) 158	T/O Water 850 ft Stall NA mph SL R/C 940 fpm	Range 1,058 sm Cruise 148 mph Fuel 120 gal Flow 15.2 gph	L. GO-480 295 hp
PIPER Aztec (Nomad) Seats 6	$99,705 (Edo equipped)	Gross 5,200 Empty 3,400 Usefl 1,800 Flt 565/4,930 Cbn Id (I) 738	T/O Water 2,450 ft Stall NA mph SL R/C 975 fpm SE R/C NA fpm	Range 700 sm Cruise 158 mph Fuel 140 gal Flow 27 gph	L. IO-540 (2) 250 hp

Amphibian Floatplanes

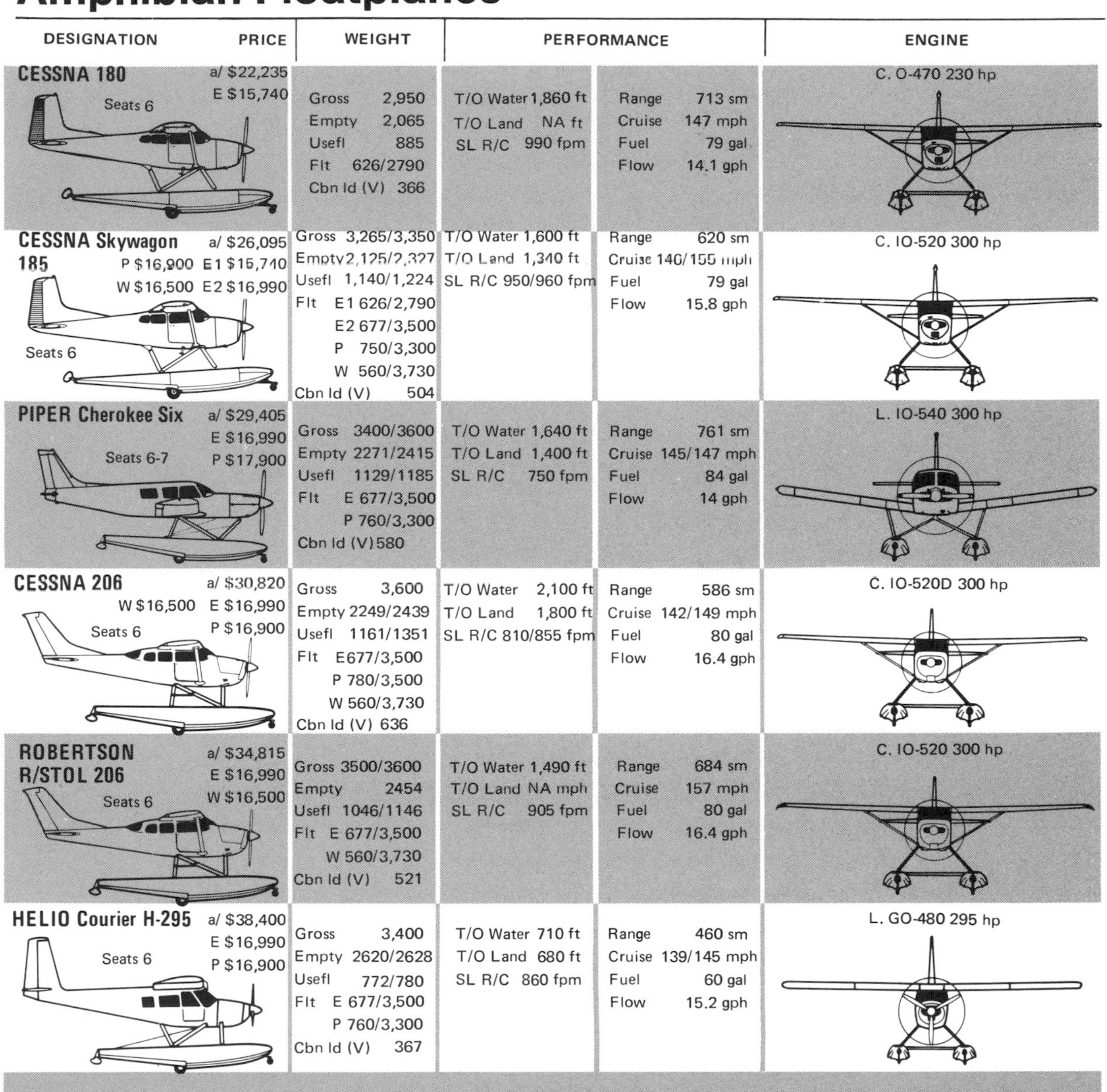

DESIGNATION	PRICE	WEIGHT	PERFORMANCE		ENGINE
CESSNA 180 Seats 6	a/ $22,235 E $15,740	Gross 2,950 Empty 2,065 Usefl 885 Flt 626/2790 Cbn ld (V) 366	T/O Water 1,860 ft T/O Land NA ft SL R/C 990 fpm	Range 713 sm Cruise 147 mph Fuel 79 gal Flow 14.1 gph	C. O-470 230 hp
CESSNA Skywagon 185 Seats 6	a/ $26,095 P $16,900 E1 $15,740 W $16,500 E2 $16,990	Gross 3,265/3,350 Empty 2,125/2,327 Usefl 1,140/1,224 Flt E1 626/2,790 E2 677/3,500 P 750/3,300 W 560/3,730 Cbn ld (V) 504	T/O Water 1,600 ft T/O Land 1,340 ft SL R/C 950/960 fpm	Range 620 sm Cruise 140/155 mph Fuel 79 gal Flow 15.8 gph	C. IO-520 300 hp
PIPER Cherokee Six Seats 6-7	a/ $29,405 E $16,990 P $17,900	Gross 3400/3600 Empty 2271/2415 Usefl 1129/1185 Flt E 677/3,500 P 760/3,300 Cbn ld (V) 580	T/O Water 1,640 ft T/O Land 1,400 ft SL R/C 750 fpm	Range 761 sm Cruise 145/147 mph Fuel 84 gal Flow 14 gph	L. IO-540 300 hp
CESSNA 206 Seats 6	a/ $30,820 W $16,500 E $16,990 P $16,900	Gross 3,600 Empty 2249/2439 Usefl 1161/1351 Flt E677/3,500 P 780/3,500 W 560/3,730 Cbn ld (V) 636	T/O Water 2,100 ft T/O Land 1,800 ft SL R/C 810/855 fpm	Range 586 sm Cruise 142/149 mph Fuel 80 gal Flow 16.4 gph	C. IO-520D 300 hp
ROBERTSON R/STOL 206 Seats 6	a/ $34,815 E $16,990 W $16,500	Gross 3500/3600 Empty 2454 Usefl 1046/1146 Flt E 677/3,500 W 560/3,730 Cbn ld (V) 521	T/O Water 1,490 ft T/O Land NA mph SL R/C 905 fpm	Range 684 sm Cruise 157 mph Fuel 80 gal Flow 16.4 gph	C. IO-520 300 hp
HELIO Courier H-295 Seats 6	a/ $38,400 E $16,990 P $16,900	Gross 3,400 Empty 2620/2628 Usefl 772/780 Flt E 677/3,500 P 760/3,300 Cbn ld (V) 367	T/O Water 710 ft T/O Land 680 ft SL R/C 860 fpm	Range 460 sm Cruise 139/145 mph Fuel 60 gal Flow 15.2 gph	L. GO-480 295 hp

Agricultural Aircraft

DESIGNATION	PRICE	WEIGHT	PERFORMANCE		ENGINE
CHAMPION Scout * Length 22 ft 7 in	$10,750	Gross 2,325 Empty 1,150 Usefl 1,175 Hopper Cpcty 90 gal	MFL NA ft Stall 60 mph SL R/C 350 fpm	Working Endur 4 hrs Fuel 39.5 gal Flow 9.8 gph	L. IO-320-A2B 150 hp Span 34 ft 5 in

* Mfrd. by Bellanca Aircraft/Minnesota

Agricultural Aircraft

DESIGNATION	PRICE	WEIGHT		PERFORMANCE				ENGINE
PIPER Pawnee C 235 (Length 24 ft 8.5 in)	$19,925	Gross	2,900	MFL	1,370 ft	Working		L. O-540 235 hp
		Empty	1,420	Stall	61 mph	Endur	2.7 hrs	Span 36 ft 2 in
		Usefl	1,480	SL R/C	630 fpm	Fuel	38 gal	
		Hopper				Flow	14 gph	
		Cpcty	1,000					
PIPER Pawnee C260 (Length 24 ft 8.5 in)	$20,425	Gross	2,900	MFL	1,270 ft	Working		L. O-540 260 hp
		Empty	1,472	Stall	61 mph	Endur	2.7 hrs	Span 36 ft 2 in
		Usefl	1,428	SL R/C	685 fpm	Fuel	38 gal	
		Hopper				Flow	14.1 gph	
		Cpcty	940					
CESSNA Agwagon 230B (Length 26 ft 3 in)	$20,995	Gross	3,800	MFL	1,365 ft	Working		C. O-470-R 230 hp
		Empty	1,815	Stall	58 mph	Endur	2.8 hrs	Span 41 ft 2 in
		Usefl	2,185	SL R/C	710 fpm	Fuel	37 gal	
		Hopper				Flow	13.1 gph	
		Cpcty	200 gal					
CESSNA Agwagon B300 (Length 26 ft 3 in)	$23,995	Gross	4,000	MFL	1,265 ft	Working		C. IO-520-D 300 hp
		Empty	1,845	Stall	58 mph	Endur	2.4 hrs	Span 41 ft 2 in
		Usefl	2,155	SL R/C	940 fpm	Fuel	37 gal	
		Hopper				Flow	15.1 gph	
		Cpcty	200 gal					
WEATHERLY 201A (Length 26 ft 7½ in)	$24,460	Gross	4,800	MFL	1,800 ft	Working		P&W R 985 450 hp
		Empty	2,550	Stall	69 mph	Endur	2.6 hrs	Span 39 ft 0 in
		Usefl	2,250	SL R/C	960 fpm	Fuel	50 gal	
		Hopper				Flow	20 gph	
		Cpcty	260 gal					
GRUMMAN Ag Cat (Length 23 ft 4 in)	$35,000	Gross	5,650	MFL	750 ft	Working		P&W R-985 450 hp
		Empty	2,690	Stall	67 mph	Endur	2.4 hrs	Span 35 ft 11 in
		Usefl	2,960	SL R/C	1,080 fpm	Fuel	46 gal	
		Hopper				Flow	22 gph	
		Cpcty	2,474					
GRUMMAN Super Ag Cat (Length 23 ft 4 in)	$35,000	Gross	5,650	MFL	395 ft	Working		P&W R-1340 600 hp
		Empty	3,160	Stall	67 mph	Endur	1.6 hrs	Span 35 ft 11 in
		Usefl	2,490	ST R/C	1,600 fpm	Fuel	46 gal	
		Hopper				Flow	28 gph	
		Cpcty	2,004					
NO. AM. ROCKWELL Thrush Commander (Length 29 ft 4.5 in)	$42,650	Gross	6,900	MFL	775 ft	Working		P&W R-1340-AN-1 600 hp
		Empty	3,700	Stall	57 mph	Endur	3.8 hrs	Span 44 ft 5 in
		Usefl	3,200	SL R/C	900 fpm	Fuel	106 gal	
		Hopper				Flow	27 gph	
		Cpcty	400 gal					

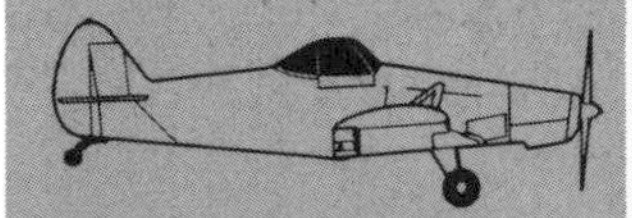

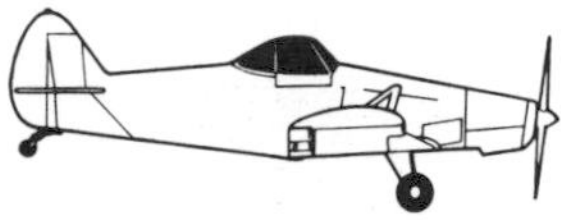

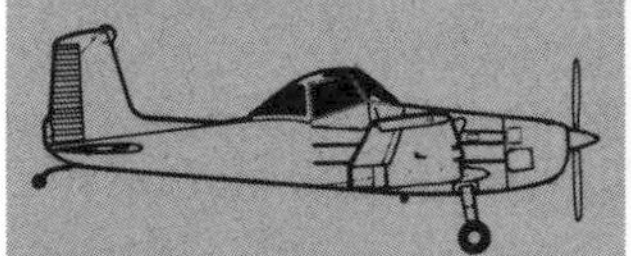

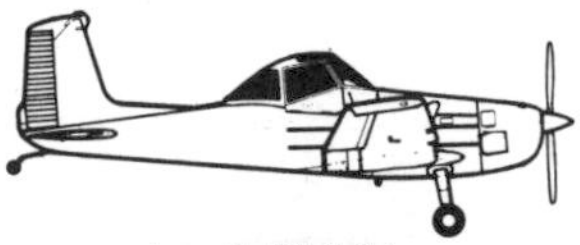

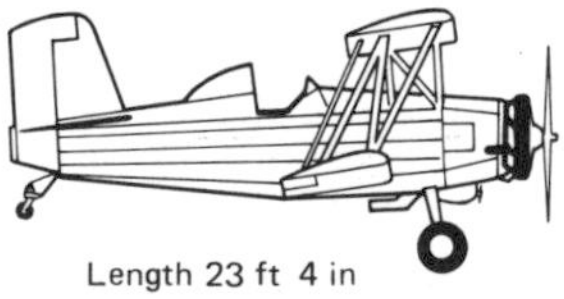

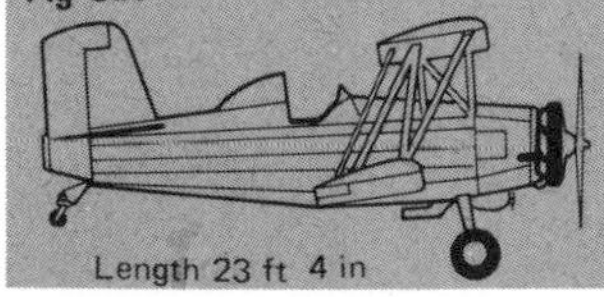

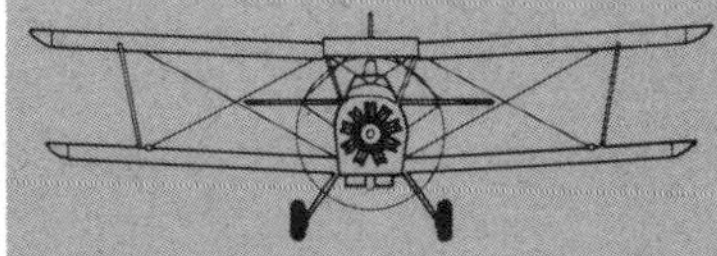

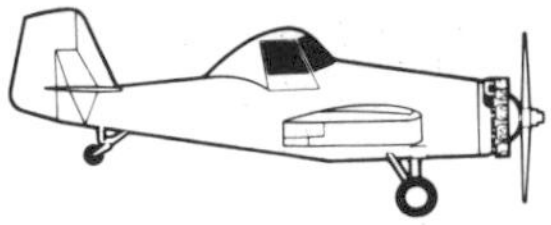

Sailplanes

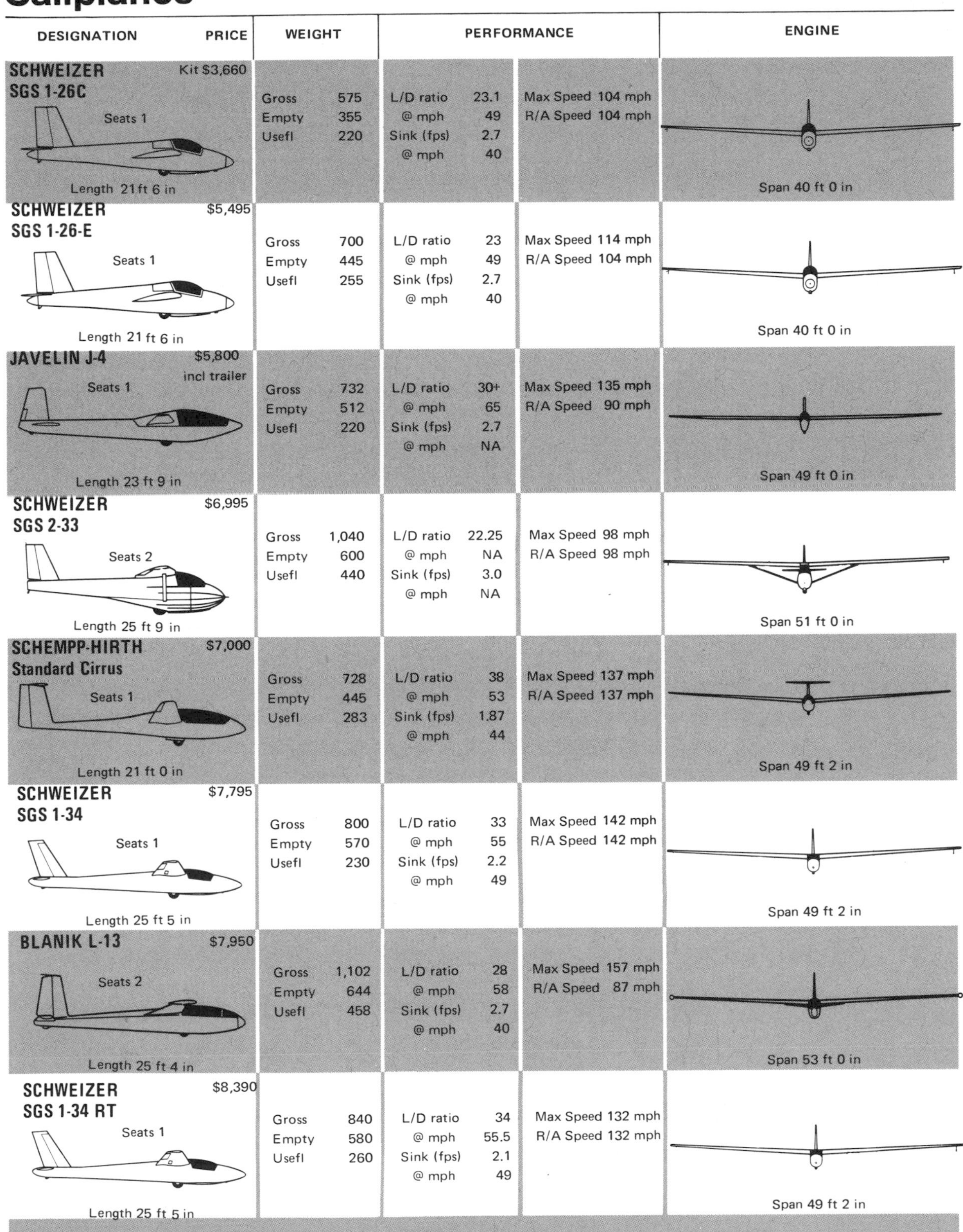

DESIGNATION	PRICE	Seats	Length	WEIGHT Gross	Empty	Usefl	PERFORMANCE L/D ratio	@ mph	Sink (fps)	@ mph	Max Speed	R/A Speed	ENGINE Span
SCHWEIZER SGS 1-26C	Kit $3,660	1	21 ft 6 in	575	355	220	23.1	49	2.7	40	104 mph	104 mph	40 ft 0 in
SCHWEIZER SGS 1-26-E	$5,495	1	21 ft 6 in	700	445	255	23	49	2.7	40	114 mph	104 mph	40 ft 0 in
JAVELIN J-4	$5,800 incl trailer	1	23 ft 9 in	732	512	220	30+	65	2.7	NA	135 mph	90 mph	49 ft 0 in
SCHWEIZER SGS 2-33	$6,995	2	25 ft 9 in	1,040	600	440	22.25	NA	3.0	NA	98 mph	98 mph	51 ft 0 in
SCHEMPP-HIRTH Standard Cirrus	$7,000	1	21 ft 0 in	728	445	283	38	53	1.87	44	137 mph	137 mph	49 ft 2 in
SCHWEIZER SGS 1-34	$7,795	1	25 ft 5 in	800	570	230	33	55	2.2	49	142 mph	142 mph	49 ft 2 in
BLANIK L-13	$7,950	2	25 ft 4 in	1,102	644	458	28	58	2.7	40	157 mph	87 mph	53 ft 0 in
SCHWEIZER SGS 1-34 RT	$8,390	1	25 ft 5 in	840	580	260	34	55.5	2.1	49	132 mph	132 mph	49 ft 2 in

Sailplanes

DESIGNATION	PRICE	WEIGHT		PERFORMANCE			ENGINE
SCHLEICHER AS-W15 Seats 1 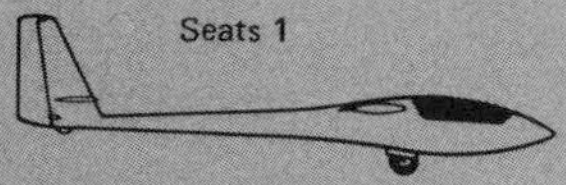 Length 21 ft 6 in	$8,735	Gross 700 Empty 450 Usefl 250		L/D ratio 38 @ mph 55 Sink (fps) 1.8 @ mph 42		Max Speed 135 mph R/A Speed 135 mph	 Span 49 ft 2 in
GLASFLUGEL Libelle Seats 1 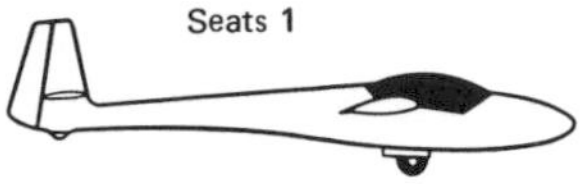 Length 20 ft 4 in	$9,350	Gross 639 Empty 408 Usefl 231		L/D ratio 38 @ mph 53 Sink (fps) 1.8 @ mph 47		Max Speed 137 mph R/A Speed 137 mph	 Span 49 ft 2.5 in
SCHLEICHER AS-K14 (powered) 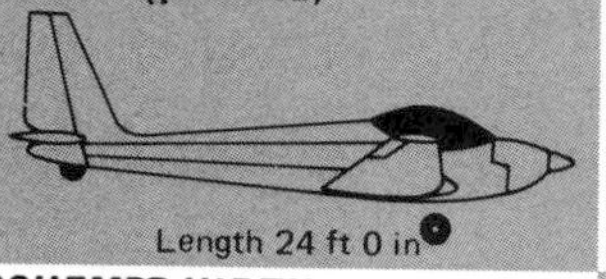 Length 24 ft 0 in	$10,432	Gross 715 Empty 530 Usefl 265		L/D ratio 29 @ mph 51.5 Sink (fps) 2.46 @ mph 44.8		Max Speed 124 mph R/A Speed 92 mph	Hirth 4 cyl. 2 cyc. 28 hp  Span 47 ft 2 in
SCHEMPP HIRTH Nimbus II Seats 1 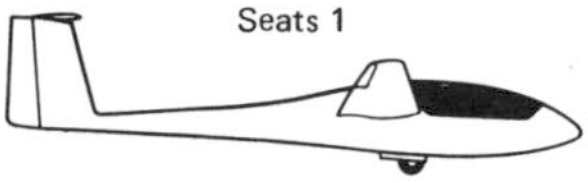 Length 22 ft 0 in	$12,000	Gross 1,040 Empty 750 Usefl 290		L/D ratio 49 @ mph 56 Sink (fps) 1.58 @ mph 47		Max Speed 138 mph R/A Speed 138 mph	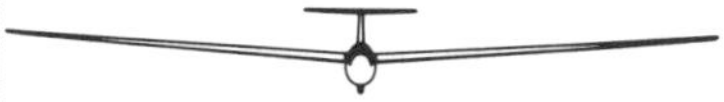 Span 67 ft 0 in
SCHLEICHER AS-W17 Seats 1 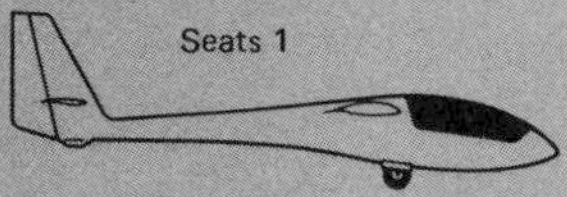 Length 24 ft 9 in	$13,292	Gross 1,035 Empty 770 Usefl 265		L/D ratio 49 @ mph 65 Sink (fps) 1.64 @ mph 53		Max Speed 155 mph R/A Speed 155 mph	 Span 65 ft 7 in
SCHLEICHER AS-K16 (powered) Seats 2 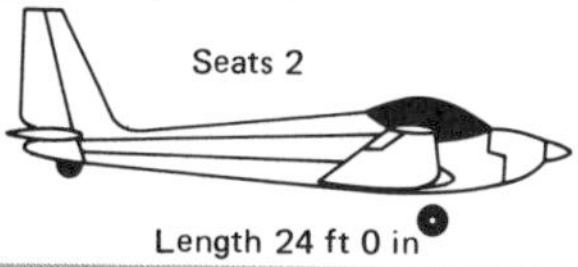 Length 24 ft 0 in	$14,850	Gross 1,320 Empty 880 Usefl 440		L/D ratio 25 @ mph 55 Sink (fps) 2.78 @ mph 45		Max Speed 125 mph R/A Speed 125 mph	VW. 75 hp/C. 110 hp  Span 52 ft 6 in
SCHWEIZER SGS 2-32 Seats 2½ 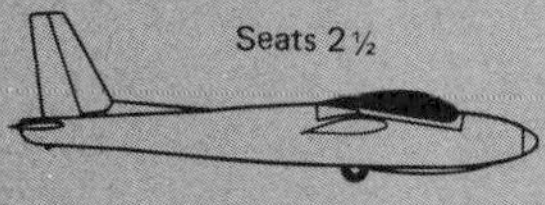 Length 26 ft 9 in	$14,995	Gross 1,340 Empty 850 Usefl 490		L/D ratio 34 @ mph 59 Sink (fps) 2.1 @ mph 52		Max Speed 158 mph R/A Speed 150 mph	 Span 57 ft 0 in
CAPRONI-Aviamerica A-21J (jet powered) Seats 2 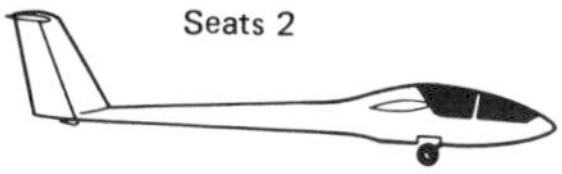 Length 24 ft 9 in	$27,500	Gross 1,580 Empty 990 Usefl 580		L/D ratio 42 @ mph 67 Sink (fps) 2 @ mph 56		Max Speed 208 mph R/A Speed NA mph	 Span 66 ft 9 in

BIBLIOGRAPHY

GENERAL

Bach, Richard. *Biplane.* Harper & Row. Flight from North Carolina to California in a 1929 Detroit-Ryan Speedster.

Bach, Richard. *Stranger to the Ground.* Harper & Row. The thoughts and deeds of a United States jet fighter pilot in peacetime Europe.

Bergman, Jules. *Anyone Can Fly.* Doubleday & Co. Introduction to learning to fly.

Caidin, Martin. *Let's Go Flying.* E. P. Dutton & Co. An introduction to flying for the would-be or student pilot.

Collins, Richard. *The Subject Is Safety.* Air Facts. Fifteen articles on general aviation safety.

Dwiggins, Don. *Hollywood Pilot.* Doubleday & Co. Story of Paul Mantz, who flew so many of those spectacular movie scenes.

Gann, Ernest K. *Fate Is the Hunter.* Simon & Schuster, Fawcett, paperback. The experiences of one of aviation's most articulate pilots.

Gardner, Erle Stanley. *Hovering Over Baja.* William Morrow & Company. The late creator of the Perry Mason series had a lifetime love affair with Baja, California, and this book is the story of his collaboration with Hiller Aircraft and Bob Boughton in exploring areas which are otherwise inaccessible.

BIBLIOGRAPHY

Garnett, David. *A Rabbit in the Air.* Chatto and Windus. Notes from the diary Garnett kept while learning to fly.

Lindbergh, Anne Morrow. *North to the Orient.* Harcourt, Brace & World, paperback. The story of a flight Mrs. Lindbergh made with her famous husband to Japan and China.

Penrose, Harold. *Airymouse.* Vernon and Yates. "A prose poem dedicated to the intoxications of open cockpit flight," says James Gilbert, senior editor of *Flying* Magazine.

Rickenbacker, Edward V. *Rickenbacker.* Prentice-Hall. Autobiography of one of America's most famous pilots, who was a World War I ace and later head of Eastern Airlines.

Saint-Exupéry, Antoine de. *A Sense of Life.* Funk & Wagnalls. A chronological collection of Saint-Exupéry's shorter writings, including "The Aviator," an excerpt from an early novella, and "Nobleman . . . Bondsman," the preface in Grandeur et Servitude de l'Aviation.

Saint-Exupéry, Antoine de. *Southern Mail.* Quinn and Boden. A story of early French air mail flights.

Saint-Exupéry, Antoine de. *Wind, Sand and Stars.* Harcourt, Brace & World, paperback. Flying with Air France's predecessor, Latecoere Company.

Saint-Exupéry, Antoine de. *Wisdom of the Sands.* Harcourt, Brace & World.

Scharff, Robert. *Who, Me Fly?* Tower Publications, paperback. What it takes to learn to fly, including costs, techniques, and aircraft uses.

Schiff, Barry. *All About Flying.* Aero Products Research. Encyclopedic introduction to private flying.

Scott, Robert L. *God Is My Copilot.* Ballantine Books, paperback. Autobiography of a pilot who first "flew" at age twelve and went on to become a World War II pilot.

Serling, Robert J. *The Probable Cause.* Ballantine Books, paperback. Generally good reporting of various accidents, and the ways in which accidents are studied to find the probable cause.

Smith, Frank Kingston. *Flights of Fancy.* Random House. Flying for fun in a "Fancy Comanche."

Smith, Frank Kingston. *I'd Rather Be Flying.* Random House. The weekend pilot tackles instrument and twin-engine flying.

Smith, Frank Kingston. *Weekend Pilot.* Random House. How our favorite ex-Philadelphia lawyer learned the joys of flying for fun.

Traylor, Captain W. L. *Pilot's Guide to an Airline Career.* Aviation Book Company. A very good review of an airline pilot's job conditions and prospects, and how to look for employment.

Trigg, James R. *Used Plane Buying Guide.* Sports Car Press. The book to get when you're ready for your first used plane.

1972 Flying Annual & Pilots' Guide. Aviation Division of Ziff-Davis Publishing Company; order from Ziff-Davis Service Division, 595 Broadway, New York, N. Y. 10012.

1972 Invitation to Flying. Aviation Division of Ziff-Davis Publishing Company; order from Ziff-Davis Service Division, 595 Broadway, New York, N.Y. 10012.

FICTION

Gann, Ernest K. *The High and the Mighty.* William Sloan Associates, Harper & Row, paperback. A crisis develops on an airline flight across the Pacific.

Gann, Ernest K. *In the Company of Eagles.* Simon & Schuster, Dell, paperback. French World War I pilot tries to revenge a friend shot down by a German.

BIBLIOGRAPHY

Gann, Ernest K. *Island in the Sky*. Simon & Schuster. The story of the professional pilots who flew for the Army Air Transport Command during World War II.

Hunter, Jack D. *The Blue Max*. Bantam Books, paperback. World War I German pilots and their exploits.

Miller, Ed Mack. *Exile to the Stars*. Doubleday & Co. Struggle for command of an Air National Guard unit.

Saint-Exupéry, Antoine de. *Airman's Odyssey*. Harcourt, Brace & World. A collection of his earlier works.

Saint-Exupéry, Antoine de. *Night Flight*. New American Library, paperback. A classic story of the early night air mail flights in South America.

Serling, Robert J. *The Left Seat*. Doubleday & Co. The life of an airline captain, from training to left seat.

Serling, Robert J. *The President's Plane Is Missing*. Doubleday & Co. Suspenseful account of disappearance of presidential plane and the President.

Shute, Nevil. *The Rainbow and the Rose*. William Morrow & Company. Ballantine Books, paperback. An aging airline pilot crashes on the Tasmanian coast, and one of his former students attempts to rescue him.

Shute, Nevil. *Round the Bend*. Ballantine Books, paperback. An Englishman starts an air transport service on the Persian Gulf.

HISTORY

Baker, Ralph. *Great Mysteries of the Air*. The Macmillan Co. The stories of aviators, and some not so famous, whose adventures have not been completely explained.

BIBLIOGRAPHY

Borden, Jr., Norman E. *Air Mail Emergency: 1934.* The Bond Wheelwright Company, Freeport, Maine. This is a highly readable study of the domestic air mail contracts with the air lines.

Caidin, Martin. *Barnstorming.* Duell, Sloan & Pearce. Adventures of the early barnstormers.

Dwiggins, Don. *The Air Devils.* J. B. Lippincott Co. Story of the early pioneers in ballooning, stunt flying, and aerobatics.

Dwiggins, Don. *They Flew the Bendix Race.* J. B. Lippincott Co. The contributions made to aviation progress in the race for the Bendix Trophy.

Gablehouse, Charles. *Helicopters and Autogiros.* J. B. Lippincott Co. The development of rotary-wing aircraft.

Gibbs-Smith, C. H. *Sir George Cayley's Aeronautics 1786–1855.* Soaring International. The contributions of one of the pioneers of human flight.

Gilbert, James. *The Great Planes.* Grosset & Dunlap. From the Wright Flyer to the Boeing 707, a collection of truly great airplanes in outstanding photographs and well-written, well-researched prose.

Glines, Carroll V., Col. USAF. *The Saga of the Air Mail.* D. Van Nostrand Co. The story of the beginnings of the air mail.

Goerner, Fred. *Search for Amelia Earhart.* Doubleday & Co. Theories as to what might have happened to the world's most famous woman pilot.

Helmericks, Harmon. *Last of the Bush Pilots.* Alfred A. Knopf. An affectionate and engaging history of the Alaska bush pilots, written by one of the last of them.

Joy, William. *The Aviators.* Shakespeare Head Press. History of aviation in Australia.

BIBLIOGRAPHY

Kelly, Fred. *The Wright Brothers.* Ballantine Books, paperback. Biography of the two brothers who put man into the air.

Kelly, Lloyd L., as told to Robert B. Parke. *The Pilot Maker.* Grosset & Dunlap. The fascinating story of simulation, from the Pioneer Link Trainer, "The Plane That Flew on the Ground," to its use for space and undersea exploration.

Lindbergh, Charles A. *The Spirit of St. Louis.* Charles Scribner's Sons, paperback. The detailed story of Lindbergh's solo nonstop flight across the Atlantic, including the log of his famous plane.

Lindbergh, Charles A. *We.* G. P. Putnam's Sons. A short account of Lindbergh's life, including that famous trans-Atlantic flight.

Mason, Jr., Herbert Molloy. *Bold Men, Far Horizons.* J. B. Lippincott Co. The story of the great pioneer flights.

Randolph, Stella. *Before the Wrights Flew.* G. P. Putnam's Sons. The attempts and theories of powered flight before the Wrights' success.

Roseberry, C. R. *The Challenging Skies.* Doubleday & Co. Aviation history from 1918 to 1939, with emphasis on exploration.

Shamburger, Page, and Christy, Joe. *Command the Horizon.* A. S. Barnes & Co. Flyers who made aviation history.

Townsend, Peter. *Duel of Eagles.* Simon & Schuster. A truly remarkable work showing the development of the philosophies of the British and German Air Forces beginning in the First World War.

Whitehouse, Arch. *The Early Birds.* Doubleday & Co. Pioneers in the early days of aircraft production.

Woodmansee, Keith. *A Short History of Aviation.* Aero Publishers, Inc., paperback. An amusing glance at aviation history.

Wright, Orville. *How We Invented the Airplane.* David McKay Company, out of print. A tiny gem that was actually taken from Orville Wright's testimony in a lawsuit. Perhaps your library or secondhand bookstore has a copy.

American Heritage. *History of Flight.* A handsome volume of aviation's heritage.

BASIC INSTRUCTION

Airguide Manual. Airguide Publications. Flight training for pilots, from student to commercial and instrument. Includes techniques, regulations, tips—mostly gathered from FAA publications.

Airman's Information and Services. Aviation Book Co. Explains services and information available to the pilot.

Campbell's Pilot Rating Guides. Aviation Book Co. Private pilot guide.

Cockpit Navigation. Sports Car Press. Private pilot's guide to navigation.

Federal Aviation Regulations. Aero Products Research, Inc. Contains FAR's and other information necessary to pass written exams.

Federal Aviation Regulations and Flight Standards for Pilots. Aero Publishers, Inc. Includes regulations applying to general aviation, maneuvers, procedures, sample private exam.

Flight Maneuvers. Aero Products Research, Inc. Programmed guide to basic maneuvers.

Ground School Workbook, by Betty Hicks. Iowa State University Press. Practice for private and commercial written exams.

The Human Factor in Aircraft Accidents, by David Beaty. Tower Books, paperback. One of the few attempts to focus attention on the human factor involved in aviation. Primarily aimed at airline flying, but still valuable in personal flying.

BIBLIOGRAPHY

The Joy of Soaring, by Carle Conway. The Soaring Society of America. Excellent instruction manual on gliding and soaring, with many fine photographs and sketches.

Modern Airmanship (Third Edition), by Neil D. Van Sickle, USAF, ed. D. Van Nostrand. Instructional handbook covering the whole spectrum of aviation.

Practical Air Navigation, by Thoburn C. Lyon. Jeppesen & Co. Revised version of government publication that explains the art of navigation.

Private Pilot. Aero Products Research. Programmed course for private pilot's written exam; contains sample test with answers to check your progress.

Private Pilot Course. Jeppesen & Co. A programmed guide for the private written, includes FAR's and sample exam.

Private Pilot Exam Kit. Kane Aero Co. Course for those preparing for FAA written.

Stick and Rudder, by Wolfgang Langewiesche. McGraw-Hill Book Co. A classic book on the art of flying. Somewhat dated, but you won't be unsure of theory after reading this.

The Student Pilot's Flight Manual (Third Edition), by William K. Kershner. Iowa State University Press. Thorough guide of maneuvers and skills required of student pilot; includes section on maneuvers required especially for ROTC flight programs.

The following publications are available through:
SUPERINTENDENT OF DOCUMENTS
GOVERNMENT PRINTING OFFICE
WASHINGTON, D.C. 20402

Aviation Weather. AC 00–6. 1969. FAA 5.8/2:W 37

Facts of Flight. FAA 1.8:F 64/2/963. Revised 1963.

Federal Aviation Regulations Written Examination Guide. AC 61–34. 1967. TD 4.8:P 64

Flight Training Handbook. AC 61–21. January 1966. FAA 1.8:F 64/4

Path of Flight. FAA 1.8:F 64/3/963. Revised 1963.

Private Pilot (Airplane) Flight Training Guide. AC 61–2A. 1964. FAA 5.8/2:P 64/4/964

Private Pilot-Airplane, Single-Engine. AC 61–3B. Revised 1968. TD 4.408:P 64/2

Private Pilot's Handbook of Aeronautical Knowledge. AC 61–23. Revised 1965. FAA 5.8/2:P 64/5/965

Private Pilot Written Examination Guide. AC 61–32. 1969. TD 4.408:P 64

Realm of Flight. FAA 1.8:F 64/963. Revised 1963.

Student Pilot Guide. AC 61–12C. Revised 1969. TD 4.8:P 64/3/968

ADVANCED INSTRUCTION

Adanced Commercial Course. Jeppesen & Co. Programmed course for thorough preparation for commercial written exam.

Flying with Floats, by Alan Hoffsommer. Pan American Navigation Service. Transition from land planes to seaplanes; techniques of float plane operation.

Instrument Flight Manual, by William K. Kershner. Iowa State University Press. Guide to the instrument rating.

Instrument Rating. Aero Products Research, Inc. Programmed course for pilots studying for instrument exam.

BIBLIOGRAPHY

Instruments–Procedures and Techniques, by Thomas F. McMahon. Flite Training Aids. Covers necessary knowledge for pilot working on the instrument rating.

Multi-engine Airplane Rating, by T. M. Smith. Pan American Navigation Service. Transition to twin-engine aircraft; includes flight test requirements.

Private Pilot's Flight Manual (Second Edition), by Willian K. Kershner. Iowa State University Press. Guide from the private flight test to the commercial certificate. Includes sections on checking out in advanced models and on commercial flight test maneuvers.

Radio and Instrument Flying. Pan American Navigation Service. Preparation for the instrument written.

Roll Around a Point, by Duane Cole. Ken Cook Co. A top aerobat's explanations of aerobatic maneuvers.

The following publications are available through:
SUPERINTENDENT OF DOCUMENTS
GOVERNMENT PRINTING OFFICE
WASHINGTON, D.C. 20402

Instrument Flying Handbook. AC 61–27A. 1968. TD 4.8:In 7/2

Instrument Pilot Examination Guide. AC 61–8A. Revised 1966. FAA 5.8/2:In 7/966

NOTE: John Roby, 3703 Nassau, San Diego, California 92115, specializes in rare and out-of-print aviation books.

The following publications are available through:
SUPERINTENDENT OF DOCUMENTS
GOVERNMENT PRINTING OFFICE
WASHINGTON, D.C. 20402

BIBLIOGRAPHY

Aviation Weather. AC 00–6. 1969. FAA 5.8/2:W 37

Facts of Flight. FAA 1.8:F 64/2/963. Revised 1963.

Federal Aviation Regulations Written Examination Guide. AC 61–34. 1967. TD 4.8:P 64

Flight Training Handbook. AC 61–21. January 1966. FAA 1.8:F 64/4

Path of Flight. FAA 1.8:F 64/3/963. Revised 1963.

Private Pilot (Airplane) Flight Training Guide. AC 61–2A. 1964. FAA 5.8/2:P 64/4/964

Private Pilot-Airplane, Single-Engine. AC 61–3B. Revised 1968. TD 4.408:P 64/2

Private Pilot's Handbook of Aeronautical Knowledge. AC 61–23. Revised 1965. FAA 5.8/2:P 64/5/965

Private Pilot Written Examination Guide. AC 61–32. 1969. TD 4.408:P 64

Realm of Flight. FAA 1.8:F 64/963. Revised 1963.

Student Pilot Guide. AC 61–12C. Revised 1969. TD 4.8:P 64/3/968

INDEX

INDEX

INDEX

INDEX

INDEX

INDEX

INDEX

INDEX

INDEX